Empathy

Also by David Johnston

The Idea of Canada: Letters to a Nation

*Ingenious: How Canadian Innovators Made the World Smarter,
Smaller, Kinder, Safer, Healthier, Wealthier, Happier*
with Tom Jenkins

Trust: Twenty Ways to Build a Better Country

BOOKS FOR YOUNG READERS

*Innovation Nation: How Canadian Innovators Made the World Smarter,
Smaller, Kinder, Safer, Healthier, Wealthier, Happier*
with Tom Jenkins

Also by Brian Hanington

Every Popish Person: The Story of Roman Catholicism in Nova Scotia

A Hundred Years on a Handshake

The Eight-Legged Urinator: Poems, Songs and Other Stuff

League of Influence

*Operation Medusa: The Furious Battle That Saved
Afghanistan From the Taliban*
with David Fraser

DAVID JOHNSTON WITH
BRIAN HANINGTON

Empathy

TURNING COMPASSION
INTO ACTION

SIGNAL
McCLELLAND
& STEWART

Library and Archives Canada Cataloguing in Publication data is available upon request.

ISBN: 978-0-7710-4906-4
ebook ISBN: 978-0-7710-4908-8

Interior graphics are courtesy of STIFF.

Jacket design by Matthew Flute
Jacket art: (spool) Goroda / Getty Images
Typeset in Adobe Caslon Pro by M&S, Toronto
Printed in Canada

Published by Signal,
an imprint of McClelland & Stewart,
a division of Penguin Random House Canada Limited,
a Penguin Random House Company
www.penguinrandomhouse.ca

1   2   3   4   5   27   26   25   24   23

For my bubble.

Ranging in age from six to seventy-nine, this happy band of teachers has proved to me on countless occasions that compassion is the potent foundation of happiness, progress, and meaning. In gratitude, I salute my astounding wife, Sharon; our daughter Debbie, her husband Doug McConnachie, and their children Emma, Téa, and Ryan; our daughter Alex, her husband David Pickwoad and their children Georgia, Sadie, and Lucas; our daughter Sharon Johnston Jr., her husband Roger Zemek and their children Nicholas and Kate; our daughter Jen Johnston, her husband Eric Sendel and their children Isabella, Joshua, and Jonah; and our daughter Sam, her husband Chris Senna and their children Thomas, Jane, and Christian.

This is the team that has shaped me.

The Johnstons before grandchildren, circa 1994.

(Linda Rutenberg, photographer)

Contents

Foreword

Empathy is not simply the title of David Johnston's book, it's the title of David Johnston's life. I've known David ever since he came to the University of Toronto Law School in the late sixties when I was a student. He came to teach corporate law, and since corporate law and I kept our distance, I never had the benefit of him as a professor, but we all knew about this wunderkind who'd been a hockey star and, more magnetically to some of us, a friend at Harvard of Erich Segal, the uber-famous author of the uber-famous book (and movie) *Love Story*. Not only his friend but also, they say, one of the characters in the book was named after him.

And he was really nice. While law professors at the time were certainly really nice, they were not usually hockey stars or friends of world-famous people. So David Johnston's aura while I was at law school was mythic—a superstar in the real world who was, at the same time, modest, caring, humane, fair, and generous. That means wise and compassionate. And being wise and compassionate means being empathetic.

When I next heard about David Johnston, it was because he had just become the principal of McGill University after serving as a beloved dean in Western University's Faculty of Law. Our older son Jacob was a student there while David was principal, and once again, I heard his reputation described with the same adjectival quintet I'd first heard at the University of Toronto Law School: modest, caring, humane, fair, and generous. That package of empathy, along with his brilliance, led him to an unprecedented three terms as principal. He was a principled principal who gave empathy a good name.

His career unfolded into many spectacular positions and achievements that stretched not only across academic fields but also into the wider territories of public policy such as economics, science, technology, and innovation, to name only some. And through them he tenaciously lived up to the empathetic adjectives that defined him, never once allowing their integrity to be sacrificed on the altar of expedience. His inner engine was the public interest, and the fuel that kept it running was an empathic understanding that, to protect the public interest, you have to protect it from empathy's antonyms: arrogance, indifference, cruelty, injustice, and selfishness.

That's why when David Johnston became governor general, the country cheered. Here was a national symbol who represented Canada's best self, who trumpeted the values that keep us at our best, and who reified those values in everything he did and believed in. He reminded us how proud we should be of our singular commitment to making Canada welcoming and accessible to all, regardless of identity; he encouraged us to look over our shoulders to see who had fallen behind so we could help them up.

The magic ingredient in his selfless and respectful approach to his role was that we all knew he meant it. It was who he was. It was aspirational for sure, but it was also, to him, realistic. That made it irresistibly inspirational. We wanted the country he wanted. And we wanted him to help us figure out how to get there and stay there.

Hence this book. It contains the symbiotic reflections of a powerfully rigorous mind and an unabashedly loving heart. The book's integrated personal, historical, philosophical, and occasionally whimsical observations give us a template that can help guide us in our own lives, the life of our country, and the future of a world currently at profound risk from too little empathy. I was mesmerized by the stories of his family—his enduring and eternal love for his wife, Sharon, their beloved daughters and their partners, and their adored grandchildren—and marvelled at the way he was able to turn those stories into insightful metaphors. He is devoted to his family's happiness and uses the emotional nourishment he gets, relies on, and cherishes from them to teach us why and how empathy starts at home.

Yet he is also a public intellectual and servant, so he finds guiding metaphors in the public sphere too, especially those he has personally seen or experienced, to help us understand how to improve our economy, save the climate, protect refugees and minorities, invest in ideas, stay healthy, listen with an open mind, strive for fairness, and be brave.

It is a timeless book, not only because its values are timeless, but because as individuals, as communities, as governments, and as countries, we need to be wise and compassionate for justice to triumph. And there is no justice without empathy.

That means empathy is our best hope for the future. And this is the book that shows us how to turn that hope into reality, because David Johnston's whole life is a tribute to the triumph of wisdom, compassion, and justice. In other words, the triumph of empathy.

Rosalie Silberman Abella
March 2022

Preface

There are strange things afoot on our planet. As we prepare to send this manuscript to the publisher, we're struck by how different our world is from that in which we began to work on this project two years ago. Among the great events, of course, has been the COVID-19 pandemic, still rampaging worldwide; claiming lives; tearing families apart; bringing health systems to the point of failure; shuttering businesses; emptying schools; halting sports; emptying restaurants, bars, pubs, cinemas, and theatres; fostering public protests; and confounding even the humblest of people's ambitions. Climate change has taken on new urgency, with improved science backed by artificial intelligence painting an even bleaker picture than before of coming floods, habitat loss, and widespread extinction of species. Here at home, occupation of city centres and international crossings in Canada by truckers, joined by the discontented stowaways who chose to hijack their convoys, left communities confused, fearful, and injured. And then a war in Ukraine, whose senseless cruelty passed all understanding, exposed both the inhumanity of authoritarianism and the perils of obedience to it, while at the same time awakening world attention to how carefully we must preserve and defend our democracies. The ensuing rebalancing of world power will shudder on for decades.

The toll of these calamities has been staggering, living deep in our emotional and social lives. For too many, the cost can be tallied in stark rates of death. For others, the reckoning has paid in ragged mental health, with anxiety, sleeplessness, exhaustion, depression, lethargy, and doubt heaped on the usual stresses of daily life. Rates of substance abuse, domestic violence, and even suicide have shot through the proverbial roof. At the community level right here in Canada, the pandemic alone has cast a glaring light on the gross inequities seething in our social systems, with Indigenous, immigrant, and elderly segments of the population blindsided by unbearable levels of disease and death. Even as grateful families applauded the courage of our front-line medical staff from their stoops and windows in the evenings, around the corner, gangs of anti-maskers taunted the timid. Clearly, we weren't ready for this.

Experience is a teacher who routinely hands out the exam before teaching the lesson, and we know it's now up to us to decide whether we're interested enough to take the current lessons to heart. From our experience, which we share with you in this book, we're confident that together we are able to tackle and solve the many problems all of us now hold in such vivid focus. We have long been convinced that the answer lies in the exercise of that most formidable human quality: empathy. As we explore here, empathy is not so much about feeling what someone else feels as it as about entering and understanding that person's experience with such clarity that one can see how to help. Thus, empathy is the deliberate movement from compassion to action. That's why each chapter of this book ends with a list of things we propose that people do.

In our view, the route to a brighter fate requires that we confront the issues that face us with empathy that is both deliberate and practiced. Moving from compassion to action will build trust and inspire innovation, two qualities of such critical importance that we featured them exclusively in two previous books. This book completes the continuum by exploring practical ways to deepen and harness one's empathetic instincts to bring about the changes necessary for a healthier society and a more certain future.

That said, humility demands and experience proves that many perspectives are needed when complex issues are at play. The recommendations made here spring from David's own life, and offer just one way of addressing the issues at hand. At the end of the book, we offer suggestions of other, even wiser books to read and films to view that will broaden your understanding and give you greater insights into the nature of the challenges addressed here and, most important, the best way to meet them with action that is both smart and caring.

Things we can do as individuals

1

Learn from the young.

I had to learn over time how to be a good dad. My own childhood had been happily spent in selfish pursuits and, while I often witnessed and routinely benefited from the kindness of others, I didn't spend much time figuring out how to be kind to anyone. I was more concerned with my performance in football and hockey. My greatest ambition as a teen was to join the National Hockey League, and I was thrilled at the age of fourteen to be visited at home by a coach scouting for Junior A recruits. During his first encounter with my mother, after she had taken his hat but before she had offered tea, the man unwisely let it slip that most kids trying out would not have time to both play at the Junior A level and finish high school. The focus would have to be on sport. The gentleman's hat was quickly returned, and no tea was served. The interview was over. My mother, as always, was looking out for my best interests, beginning with my education. I suspect she sensed that the competitive drive that pushed me out of bed and off to the rink before dawn each Saturday would serve me in academics as it had in athletics. As usual, Mother was right. While I never lost my zest for sports—especially hockey—my deepening interest in my studies led to degrees from Harvard, Cambridge, and Queen's and set me on my life's work in the fields of law and education. Thanks for knowing me so well, Mum.

Mother was a stoic. Besides running the household and raising three kids, she worked as a nurse's aide on night shifts at the local hospital. Never once did she complain. My father played a more remote role in my early life. He ran a hardware store in our hometown of Sault Ste. Marie and had enough cares and concerns of his own to keep him at something of a distance from his kids. This was especially the case after the business failed in one of the cyclical economic downturns that too often afflict northern, resource-based communities. That was hard on Dad, who had difficulty with drink, which contributed to the failure of the business and was intensified by it. We just got on with our own projects, guided when needed by the instincts and insights of our mother.

The opening lines of Tolstoy's *Anna Karenina* remind us that "happy families are all alike; every unhappy family is unhappy in its own way." Our family fit into the second category. My father developed a serious, chronic problem with the bottle and for long periods could not provide adequately for the family. My mother kept our family of three children—my sister two years older, me, and my brother nine years younger—solvent by taking in boarders and working at the hospital, at least until her progressive blindness caused by retinal detachment made that impossible. What our mother injected into the family was the importance of learning (all three of us became teachers), strong religious faith, and awareness of the combined value of resilience and self-reliance.

My sister, who had been most affected by our father's alcoholism, could not accept unreliability. Childhood was tough on her, but she was tenacious and became a high school teacher and later a senior public servant in the Ontario Ministry of Education designing physical education and health curricula until her retirement. My brother, supported by his two older siblings, was an unselfish and good-natured soul and an accomplished athlete who derived much satisfaction from encouraging and enjoying the success of others. He studied and played hockey at Dartmouth College and then completed his master's degree at the University of Michigan, during which time he served as an assistant coach with its splendid hockey team. He worked as an admired primary and middle school principal in Toronto until his retirement; he was renowned for his inimitable ability to move into a dysfunctional school and, over several years, transform it into a vibrant and successful learning space.

For my part, I came to know my father's burden as illness which, mercifully, he overcame later in his life. Today I remember him as two different persons. In his first iteration, he was only minimally involved in our worlds, bragging at the local tavern to anyone who would listen about the athletic accomplishments of his sporting sons, but never actually taking the pleasure of watching us play. In the second iteration, I see him as a grandfather greeting his grandchildren on their occasional visits with deep joy. He became a markedly different person, and that was a joyful change. Each time our family showed up, he offered his granddaughters an immediate challenge. Marching all five over to the fireplace, he pointed to the large glass Mason jar on the mantle. Where once it contained fruit, he said in sombre tones, it now held something far better. Taking the jar down and slowly holding it aloft, he invited them to peer in at the treasure: pennies, pennies, pennies! He then told the little ones it would be impossible to open this jar and take out any pennies unless they had the magical power that comes only from being kind to one's sisters. If they earnestly thought they had been kind and would continue being kind (they swore they had and would), they could then begin the ceremony of shutting their eyes tight, thinking hard about kindness, and attempting to unscrew the lid. If successful, they could then shove in a hand, scoop up all the pennies a fist could hold, tuck them in their pockets, and take them home. The smallest of the granddaughters often had difficulty opening the top; even when one could get that far, her hands were so tiny she wouldn't score much loot. In such cases he gravely declared the first effort to have been null and void, likely because there had been insufficient concentration on kindness at the critical eyes-closed step. The ceremony was then repeated, this time with his large weathered hands over her tiny smooth fingers. Magically, the lid then gave way. In whispered conspiracy, granddaughter and grandfather would then fill each of their fists in turn, with all proceeds going to the amazed little girl.

In retrospect, by experiencing my father's dark side as a boy, I learned independence and self-reliance while evolving a trust-but-always-verify philosophy that protected me from disappointment, even if it made me a little too skeptical sometimes. When I returned home later with Sharon Downey on my arm and in my heart, I re-encountered my father, now sober, and saw him in a different way. This transformation I owe to Sharon. With our children in tow, I learned that Dad too could learn to see things in a fresh way. Those jar-and-pennies years were a great inspiration to me, for I discovered that, even in my depths, I could line up my inner periscope to view a turbulent ocean surface from another person's angle. I began seeking everywhere to tease harmony out of discord, to mediate in times of opposition and confusion. I no longer expected to be disappointed, but rather knew I would eventually be satisfied, even delighted. That growing sense of positive expectation grew with the arrival of each of our five children.

The Thing About Babies

When Sharon and I married in 1964, we both wanted children, but only one of us was ready for the challenge. Never having given a thought to raising a family, I was wholly unqualified for the job of parent, and the subsequent onslaught of five daughters (Deborah in 1968, Alex in 1970, Sharon Jr. in 1972, Jenifer in 1974, and Sam in 1975) would soon make my ineptness obvious to all.

Babies teach you early on what you must focus on. Lodged in such tiny bodies, their gargantuan needs will fill a home of any size. First-time parents determine under fire how to interpret and respond to individual sounds and movements. By listening intently and watching closely, parents soon learn enough to be quite useful. This process of parental domestication takes time, but one thing is certain: through it all the baby stays completely in charge.

Parenting for me was a profoundly humbling process—one in which I gained confidence only once I learned to be present to each child on her own terms. Not having had much of a role model, I had to figure it out myself over time. My first great insight as a dad was this: being able to solve a child's problem is nowhere near as helpful to her as simply being there as she navigates each little storm. Early mechanical solutions (warm bottle, dry diaper, bubbly bath, cuddly teddy, and heaps of Band-Aids) are of time-limited utility. As she grows, each child faces dilemmas whose solutions lie not in which ointments to apply but rather which choices to make. Trained on the job, I learned that children crave insight, not direction. To be able to give insight wisely, I had to spend enough time listening to my children's concerns to understand the full and personal nature of each predicament. Only then could I possibly know which of the lessons from my own experience might be helpful.

As they grew, my daughters taught me the set of skills now broadly referred to as emotional intelligence. After learning to listen, I had to master a number of those disciplines, including focus, empathy, resilience, self-awareness, mindfulness, happiness, self-confidence, conflict resolution, influence, and leadership. Unexpectedly, these skills came easily to me over time. (Sharon may dispute my claim.) My bond with my kids made my interest in their welfare my priority, and just putting time in did the rest. By being with them, I got to see them come at problems differently than I would have. They showed compassion in ways I hadn't considered, sorted sense from nonsense with uncomplicated ease, overcame challenges with courage that I did not possess, and, above all, approached life with an unquenchable enthusiasm that gave rise to my own. So while I was just trying to be a good dad,

I became a student of human relations. My family was my emotional schoolhouse, and the education I got at their hands has been more useful and more precious to me than any of my formal degrees. I'm sure I'm not the only male of my age to admit that, led by my wife, my family saved me. And it gave me great joy.

Watching our daughters as they encountered the world on their own terms, I made mental notes. For example, as I spoke with them, I learned that they were usually not thinking about things as I would. Whenever I said anything like "I know what you mean; that other kid is being mean to you," I'd get a quizzical look and a "No, Dad, that's not it" or, worse, "Dad, aren't you even listening?" I stopped saying the first thing that popped into my head, knowing that the real matter would emerge as my daughters took the time to find their own words. I learned to say less so I could hear more. To this day, I advise young people heading into important meetings to resist saying the first thing that pops into their heads too. Better thoughts will follow.

While we ourselves had more than enough income for food, clothing, and housing, our girls were keenly aware that much of the world, including some of our own neighbours, did not. As they threw themselves into volunteer work with their friends from home, school, church, and community groups, Sharon and I observed that the predominant human response to the hardship and suffering of others is the desire to help. That ran counter to conventional wisdom, which held that in times of crisis people become selfish; they hide, they hoard. Watching my kids and all their friends, I revised my opinion of humanity and began to trust that people are instinctively caring and generous. My conclusion was that I should presume the best of people. That perspective changed everything.

Around age twelve, each daughter became involved in international exchanges. The first was arranged with the help of a family from Lyon, France, who were neighbours on our street in Montreal. Our children spent two or three weeks in the summer with those neighbours and their extended family in France, and their French cousins then came to Canada to live with us. These exchanges extended through their teenage and university years, and further as they attended universities in Canada and beyond both for degree programs and summer courses as well as overseas assignments with volunteer organizations. They met, played, studied with, and taught other young people in France, the United States, England, Czechoslovakia, Russia, China, Hong Kong, Jordan, Portugal, Costa Rica, Colombia, and Mexico.

By doing so our daughters became global citizens. They also developed more pronounced expressions of four important qualities: curiosity, tolerance, judgment, and empathy. First curiosity, the beginning of all learning: beyond asking why—that question so innate and expressive in children—they began to ask how and when and where and if and should and would and could. Their questions became more focused, and the answers they received gave them a deeper understanding of the issues and events around them. Travel and travellers made their world more interesting and more friendly. It was their fast track to learning. Second, tolerance. Most intriguing to me was their exposure through these programs to differing approaches and opinions. They noticed immediately, of course, that people in countries ate different foods and wore different clothes. But they also grew to appreciate that their new friends read, watched, listened to, pursued, debated, enjoyed, and feared different things too. And yet because these young people had quickly become cherished friends, those differences were met with delight, not suspicion. Befriending people from different places, our daughters learned more than just tolerance; they learned pluralism. They grew to welcome divergent opinions, knowing that these were the result of different physical environments and different cultural realities. They embraced inclusivity; their hearts opened and stayed that way. Different approaches are not different and wrong; they are different and valid. My conclusion: travel to learn; welcome others into your home and then visit others in theirs. Third,

their growing curiosity led to analysis, and through analysis they exercised increasingly sound judgment. They wanted to see things whole,
hear the other side of every story, and, like good surveyors, work to get
an accurate measurement of the scene at hand by triangulating from
several vantage points. The truth attracted them; they were quick to spot
pedantry and bigotry, and just as quick to call it out. Fourth, and most
telling and notable to me, they became profoundly empathetic. They
moved from sympathy, in which one feels another's pain, to empathy, in
which one walks in another's shoes and finds new ways to lighten the
steps. Today, all five of our daughters serve in public-service professions.
No coincidence. Empathy leads to action.

The Back Pew at Girton

For six months in 1972, Sharon and I lived with our daughters Debbie
and Alex (with Sharon Jr. on the way) in the village of Girton outside
of Cambridge, England. At the time I was on what would turn out to
be the only six-month sabbatical leave of my career, writing a book on
Canadian Securities Regulation, and we had returned to Cambridge
for additional research. Each Sunday we trooped down to St. Andrew's,
Girton's Anglican church, which has been welcoming the local con-
gregation since the twelfth century. Given that Debbie was only four
years old, we routinely packed pencil and paper to occupy her during
the service. As the four of us sat in our usual pew during one Sunday's
sermon, Debbie stopped drawing, stood up, wheeled about, and stared
at the back entrance to the church. She then silently gathered up her
drawing materials, exited our pew, and moved to the back of the
building. Craning my neck to see where she had gone, I spied an
elderly man of humble means steadying himself with two canes as he
shuffled in. Bent by age and infirmity, he wore clothes as ancient and
ragged as himself. I had seen him before and had been struck that
anyone would have to live in such reduced circumstances. When he

finally took a place in one of the rear pews, Debbie hopped right in beside him, took up her pencil and paper, and finished her drawing. Then she handed it to the man, taking some time to point out the features of the artwork. He looked at it, made a few appreciative comments, and tried to hand it back, but Debbie would not take it. It was a present. The gentleman was clearly delighted and deeply touched. I was struck that a child so young could sense the loneliness of another and would be moved so instantly to make things better. Here was empathy in action. It occurred in a place that had seen almost a millennium of human interaction and was the natural instinct of a child with the courage to show her care in the best way her young mind could conceive. She created something out of nothing and made a present of it. When I asked Debbie about this, she simply said, "I knew I had to." She and I had looked at the same man, yet she had seen him from the heart, not just the eye.

Sharon had been pregnant with our third child when we arrived in Girton, and we had looked for a doctor right away. The National Health, as they call their system in the United Kingdom, helped us find a family practitioner, a gent of sixty or so who could monitor Sharon's progress and assist at the birth, an event that would be undertaken at home as was the local practice. That made me nervous, but Sharon, far more courageous than me, was fine with it. About six weeks before the end of our stay, Sharon went into labour late at night. The doctor appeared, examined her, and just before midnight exited the bedroom to say, "Something's wrong. The baby isn't emerging, and your wife is beginning to bleed. I don't have the instruments to see what's going on, so we have to get her to the hospital." He then called ahead to Adenbrooks, the hospital in Cambridge about six miles from our home, and requested that an ambulance be sent to our house. We got ready and waited. Yet an hour and a half later, long after Sharon had begun to turn white, no ambulance had come. I phoned the doctor again in alarm. Moments later he called back to report that the ambulance had tried to find us, but the drivers had been relying on maps printed fifteen years before our subdivision had been built. Unable to find us, they had returned to the hospital and had neglected to report the problem. With better instructions in hand, they set out again, this time arriving at 3 a.m. Awakened by the commotion across the street, a neighbour came over to offer help. We hardly knew her, but I happily put the care of our two daughters into her hands and then climbed into the ambulance with Sharon. At the hospital, a young resident examined Sharon, misinterpreting her small stature and belly to conclude, "The baby seems quite premature, so I'm going to give your wife some medicine to slow the birth process down. Then she can go home and will probably deliver in another month or so." He was wrong; Sharon was fully at term. At that point, a Swedish nurse on duty touched my arm and whispered emotionally, "I'm stepping out of line here, but you must insist that Mr. Chatterton be called. This woman is ready to deliver, and she's bleeding to death. You must insist." Mr. Chatterton, a highly respected specialist, happened to be the obstetrician on call.[1] I firmly insisted that he be consulted. About twenty minutes later, he appeared, elegantly turned out in a three-piece suit. He then went to examine Sharon with an experimental imaging technology called ultrasound, and soon after emerged to say, "I can see that the baby is lodged in a transverse position, and they're both hemorrhaging. We'll do a Caesarian. I cannot guarantee that I can save both, but I can probably save one." And with that he disappeared back into the room.

Hemingway had described this exact situation as the final, dismal scene of *A Farewell to Arms*. In that story, both mother and child died. With that in mind, I walked the corridors of Adenbrooks with no idea how our own story would resolve, yet I had been warned not to expect a happy ending. My overwhelming feeling, however, was not of fear but rather of the profound love and admiration I had for my wife. Sharon was a spectacular feature of my life. Forthright, clever, selfless, optimistic, and without a shred of artifice, she had been to me a beacon of uncomplicated humanity. While I had many mentors, she had been my first true role model, and was still the only person in my life I had felt safe enough around to express my own fears and confusions, of which I had a boatload. For me, just watching Sharon be herself was a master class in how to be fully alive, fully present. Now, in my lonely vigil, one tiny memory resurfaced. In the early months of our courtship, as Sharon and I had been walking on the grounds of Sharon's school, a woman, who I understood to be Sharon's French teacher, came up to us and presented her pupil with a French textbook saying, "Sharon, I thought you would enjoy this." I was intrigued by how overwhelmed Sharon was at the kindness of this person. Her eyes beamed, her mouth broke into a wide smile, and she thanked the woman with almost giddy excitement. As the teacher observed the degree of Sharon's delight, a wave of joy crossed her own face. It was a look I've always remembered, and an important learning moment for me. I'd been a pretty reserved kid in my youth and had thought of gratitude mostly as a matter of good manners, and never, until now, as the profound and authentic response to the joy of life it most certainly is.

My reverie was interrupted by Sharon's medical team, and I soon heard from Mr Chatterton that both mother and baby were alive and recovering. I wept, and my tears were those of gratitude, of course.

Mother and daughter were later moved to a comfortable facility adjacent to the hospital known as the nursing home. Sharon was too weak to speak much and would be so for days, so when I was informed that they needed the baby's name for the records, it fell to me to make the decision. Easily done. Ladies and gentlemen, let me introduce Sharon Junior. Twenty-one years later, while in Cambridge studying law as her father had before her, Sharon Junior made an appointment at Adenbrooks and presented herself to Mr. Chatterton as living evidence of his professional excellence.

Are humans actually kind?

Contrary to prevailing opinion, humans in times of crisis are outgoing, caring, generous, and supportive of those in need, and our instinct for selflessness and cooperation has been a significant factor in our survival as a species.[2] Of the many powerful images that have stayed with me, the one that touches me most deeply is a photograph of our eldest daughter, Debbie (of picture-drawing fame), weeping uncontrollably as she clutches a five-month-old child. She and her husband were unable to have children. She had endured months of fertility treatments in vain. She had invested countless days of information seeking, interviews, and meetings in the quest to adopt. Finally, after years of effort, she was called to an orphanage in Cali, Colombia, to meet at last the child she had so long yearned for. Housing children of all ages, the orphanage cares for children who have been left for adoption by their mothers, many of whom live on the street. Most of these children simply age out as teenagers without ever knowing the love, comfort, and security of a permanent home, but one little girl fared better. She was about to have a new family of her own. The day she arrived in Cali, Debbie headed directly for the orphanage and into the foyer, where her new baby daughter was placed in her arms and the photograph taken. It was the very moment that our daughter Debbie became a mum. Emma, the five-month-old, became our first grandchild. The photograph still moves me deeply, in part because I know the backstory, having witnessed the long struggle our daughter underwent to have a family. Her face is a study in the end of agony and the transformative welcoming of joy. It's an unusual image and one of the most beautiful pictures I've seen. It epitomizes the eloquence of empathy, experienced here as both a deep sense of relief after overcoming oppressive obstacles, and the unbounded love set free by bringing a child into a loving home, a sublime act of kindness.

Many years later Debbie and I wrote a book called *Cyberlaw*. It explored the complexities at play when rapidly evolving paradigms such as the digital revolution butt up against sober and ponderous institutions like the law. One day as we worked through the clash between legal principles and disruptive technologies, we began considering what is the most necessary human virtue. Debbie declared that the most necessary of all the virtues is empathy. Churchill had once said the same about courage, but I fully agree with my daughter. Having seen her in action in all those years between the church at Girton and the orphanage in Cali, I knew that being able to project oneself with kind attention into the lives of others and find meaningful ways to make a difference in those lives was a gift of incalculable value and an agent of limitless transformative power.

From Regret to Reform

Perhaps the most lasting teaching on empathy comes from living through the sorrows of your children while being unable to do anything for them. In her candid memoir, *Inconceivable*, our second daughter,

Get in there.

Empathy is a recent word for English speakers, appearing only in the early 1900s. A translation of the German *einfühlung*, the term originally described the intense experience of losing oneself in a work of art, such as a painting, statue, poem, symphony, or ballet. The concept proposes that only when you project your personality into an artwork can you understand it fully. In human relations, the term *empathy* now carries a similar meaning. Only when you abandon your own beliefs and biases to enter the world of another without judgment can you understand that person fully. So whereas sympathy suggests feeling the same feelings as another, empathy means appreciating their circumstances accurately enough to be able to help.

Alex, tells the story of the loss of her first child. Unable to conceive, Alex worked with a number of surrogate carriers in a string of unsuccessful attempts to have a baby. On the ninth try, her luck seemed to turn. The surrogate became pregnant with the foetus from Alex and her husband, David. That baby, quickly nicknamed Sam, seemed healthy, reaching full term without incident. Alex and David were alerted when the surrogate was rushed to the hospital. They were over the moon and raced the hundred kilometres to the hospital to meet their first child and take the little baby back to their home and a waiting nursery. But they were met at the door of the obstetric ward with terrible news; the baby had died in the birthing process. Here was a tragedy common in history but beyond any comprehension in one's own experience . . . for the surrogate, for Alex, and for our whole family. Over the next two years I spoke to Alex on the phone almost every day, but never about the loss of baby Sam. Through those same two years, Alex, with seldom a smile, pressed on with efforts at surrogacy. Through the darkest gloom

Empathy—green-eyed monster?

Inherently imaginative, humans can respond as strongly to fiction as to reality. Yet sometimes our empathy—our projection of ourselves into the stories of others—can blur the line between real and pretend. Anyone who has screamed during a horror movie, cried at a death in a novel, or hoped for revenge against a fictional villain knows the power of drama. Shakespeare knew just how to trigger that kind of response. Norrie Epstein, author of *The Friendly Shakespeare (1994)*, cites some choice examples, including that of a cowboy in America's old west who attended a production of *Othello*. The man was so outraged when Iago convinced Othello to murder the innocent Desdemona that he stood up in his seat, aimed his pistol, and shot the actor dead. Empathy in action? Sadly, yes.

she showed her tenacious character, finally realizing success with two daughters born through surrogacy within four months of one another, each with some peril in their journey. Then miraculously Alex became naturally pregnant and gave birth nine months later on Christmas Day to Lucas. While her memoir ends with joy, *Inconceivable* offers Alex's deep analysis of the public policy behind infertility and surrogacies, and how modern science has changed our traditional definitions of both children and families. Her critique was honest and tough. Inspired by her story, a number of people, her dad among them, have since worked on the Ontario provincial committee tasked with reviewing related government programs. Among the committee's recommendations have been important reforms in the areas of fertility monitoring, funding for in-vitro fertilization, and post-adoption subsidies and supports. Almost all these recommendations have been instituted, including the creation of a reformed provincial adoption agency. Once again, empathy leads to action.

Empathetic things to do when you intend to Learn from the young.

Listen patiently to the young.

They're not yet biased. Don't rescue; observe until you identify what you can control, then take action. Don't advise; support. Don't say the first thing that pops into your head. Say less so you can hear more, and loudly applaud the courage of the innocent.

Be relentless in your pursuit of knowledge.

Imitate kids you know and ask why and why not until you get to truly understand something. Only then will you be able to analyze its purpose and optimize its effect.

Presume the best of people.

See from the heart, not just the eye. Humans are instinctively caring and generous. They want to help. Be amazed by the courage, humbled by the caring, and grateful for the generosity of others. Be kind to one another and be gentle on yourself.

Hold back on judgment.

Just as children tend not to disapprove, relate to others with patience. Learn all you can from others, knowing that difference of opinion comes from difference of experience.

Travel to learn.

Welcome others in your home and then visit others in theirs.

2

Stay curious.

We humans have a slew of problems to think our way through, and the clock is ticking. While we may not agree on the causes of all our troubles, most of us have become painfully aware of the nature and degree of the issues we face as a human family. The big environmental questions—how to stop air pollution, how to reverse climate change, how to revitalize our oceans, how to produce clean energy, et cetera—are matched by the need to overcome disturbing, entrenched social ills including racism, violence, gender inequality, wealth hoarding, bullying, suicide, et cetera. Everywhere you look, there's something going on that needs improvement. In many cases, the need is urgent and the perils of inaction arguably catastrophic.

How does the human psyche cope with the scope of such problems? At a time when unbridled creativity is most needed, many of us feel frozen, up against an unscalable mountain of problems that defy solutions. Glancing at the news, it's clear that every demographic is affected. Young people are despondent, justifiably angry at the mess they've been handed by their dopey parents. Middle-aged people are consumed by their herculean struggle just to make a living, keep a job, run their businesses during a pandemic, and find affordable housing in a hostile real estate market. Older citizens are just glad they'll be gone before we all run out of drinking water, seafood, sweet air to breathe, and room to move. For this last group (my own), the settlement of Mars doesn't loom as an exciting option.

Admit it.

Since the Industrial Revolution, when ingenious machinery first made mass production possible, we have relied upon epic and unsustainable amounts of resources to operate. Our successes have been spectacular, but each increase in production has created its own scarcity: we're having trouble finding rare earth metals, we're shy of heavy metals, almost out of phosphorus, and by many credible estimates are dangerously low on trees, fish, soil, whales, undersea coral and beach sand, polar bears, bananas, chocolate, copper, cobalt, lithium . . . and on and on. The stark truth is that we continue to use far more resources than nature can produce. Every year, we overshoot the planet's biocapacity, gobbling up more than 160 per cent of its sustainable resources. If our consumption through each year were to be averaged daily, we'd run out of resources every August 5 or so. Even in 2020, when the pandemic lowered almost all production and consumption across the world, the dryly named Earth Overshoot Day was pushed back only to August 22. After that, we were dipping into next year's supply as we always do, like addictive gamblers betting our next paycheque on today's hand of blackjack, yet in our case we're betting other species' paycheques as well. As we consume the habitats of animals and plants who can't take us to court for trespassing, we rob them of their shelter and food, and they die out because of it. A wide variety of species are being cornered into extinction in the wild. If animals had Academy Awards, these ten creatures (among many others) would have appeared onscreen under the In Memoriam banner in just the past fifteen years.

In Memoriam
2006–2021

Pinta Giant Tortoise (*Chelonoidis abingdonii*)
Splendid Poison Frog (*Oophaga speciosa*)

Spix's Macaw (*Cyanopsitta spixii*)
Pyrenean Ibex (*Capra pyrenaica pyrenaica*)
Bramble Cay Melomys (*Melomys rubicola*)
Moorean Viviparous Tree Snail (*Partula suturalis*)
Po'o-uli (*Melamprosops phaeosoma*)
Yangtze River Dolphin (*Lipotes vexillifer*)
Maui 'akepa Songbird (*Loxops ochraceus*)
Alaotra Grebe (*Tachybaptus rufolavatus*)
Western Black Rhino (*Diceros bicornis ssp. longipes*)

Clearly, where our ecological footprint is concerned, humans are the new locusts. When we descend into any new field, we consume everything in it and leave it empty, dry, dead.

Now imagine.

Is it really all that bleak? Must we relocate to another planet or die here? Absolutely not. The species that wrought so many of these ills has done so not through malice, but rather through ingenuity fuelled by imagination, albeit shortsighted imagination. That same faculty will be our key advantage in overcoming the sticky problems we now face. Humans are among a small percentage of species (as far as we know) with the ability to think of things that have not yet happened, experiencing them merely by pondering them, feeling what it would be like if those very things came to pass. The ability to imagine is a quirk of our evolution—first, to a brain whose right and left hemispheres freely access each other's resources through the corpus callosum and second, as neuroscientists have recently understood, through an unusually complex network of neural pathways. Not only can our brains store massive amounts of memories (although not as raw data as computers do), but they can also get to these memories through an almost infinite combination of pathways and, in doing so, happen upon other adjacent memories. We don't just make a memory by tucking a new fact or experience into an empty drawer; we wander around our heads looking for the best drawer to put it in, first peeking in countless other drawers to see what's there. It's both sightseeing and storage, and we do it while we sleep.[1] That quirky way of sifting through old memories before we store new ones gives us our ability first to think by analogy (*if I do this, it would be much like that other thing I recall*), and then by comparison (*but that won't be as useful in this case, so I'd better refine the idea*). The process of comparing and refining a host of possible outcomes is our imagination in a nutshell. It's a rare talent in the animal world and the key to our continued persistence as a species.

There's never been a better and more important time for us humans to improve our future by being more creative in the daily exercise of thought, and it warms me that we're just the species to pull it off. We got ourselves into the mess; we have the talent to get ourselves out . . . if we have the will. We must now bend our creativity to the tasks at hand. And that all starts, as my kids taught me, with being relentlessly curious.

Make creativity a habit.

Staying curious is an art that must be practised. If you want to innovate (I'm sure that you can and keen that you do), you'll have to build habits that improve your creativity while avoiding habits that kill it. Need inspiration? Here are a few thoughts that may help. First, creative people tend to live longer, in part because, as they get more practised in being creative, they find more creative ways to manage stress, and stress is a killer. Creative people tend to be messy, and the mess doesn't bother them. They know that boredom is not to be feared. While bored, just as while meditating, their minds are not occupied with merely doing and can open to the subtle murmurs rising up from the unconscious imagination. They also know that being positive makes them more creative; despite the overgeneralization that great art springs from personal pain, people can't create well at the moment they are actually in pain themselves. They're also more creative when more empathetic to those around them; opening themselves to the realities others face allows them to see the world from concurrent, varied perspectives, appreciating both problems and solutions more clearly. They've learned that physical exercise improves creativity, just as it does any thought process. And they know that doing something creative every single day keeps the tap turned on as well; a few days of creative sloth and they lose their shape. They know that, while isolation is often important for the quiet that comes with it, being apart too long dulls their talent. So social balance is key. They can't be hermits, but conversely nor can they fritter their time on social media. Such distractions drive channel noise into their creative processes, making it harder to detect any nascent creative idea and turn it into something useful.

Your Human Brain: Installed and Ready!

For animals who want to better their individual lives while ensuring the persistence of the species, the human brain offers an imagination engine featuring smart storage, active analysis, limitless innovation, and steady improvement. Unlike brains of the lower orders, the human brain optimizes the learning experience and allows for early correction and refinement of less-than-ideal plans. If you're ready to experience the result of any action long before you take it, the human brain is ready for you. Yours has already been installed and is now being upgraded nightly. Use yours daily to enhance the likelihood of success, reduce the risk of injury (to you and those you love), and make a lasting contribute to the survival of the species.

Figure out how you learn.

Most of us end up depending on analogy for our understanding of the world. If we cannot immediately understand all the facts of an issue, knowing what that thing is similar to can open a useful shortcut to assessing that thing's relevance to us. Presented in the form of metaphors and similes, an analogy is simply a comparison of two things, typically on the basis of their structure, for the purpose of explanation or clarification. If you want to teach someone about racquetball, you might say, "It's squash with bigger raquets and a bouncier ball." The movement of blood through an artery might be explained to a child as "water flowing through a pipe." The states of an electric signal might be likened to "on and off" or "one and zero" when in fact they are neither, even then we might metaphorically say a light goes "on" when we close a circuit. Analogies teach well, but they are not accurate. They show only a proportional likeness of one thing to another. As you move further into any topic, the analogy that helped you understand it at first will break down and become an impediment to your deeper understanding. So if you want to innovate, you'll have to get past this limitation.

Curious kids learn early on to suspect that analogy is a limited tool. When they demand to know why, and then ask why the answer you give them is the way it is, and why that answer is the way it is, they push themselves away from the generality of analogy toward empirical truth. My kids taught me that over and over. Instinctively, they wanted to get past the rhetoric and down to the facts, just as Aristotle had almost 2,500 years ago.

Aristotle was a born polymath. Never satisfied with people's assumptions about reality, he dedicated his life to figuring out how things work. He wrote comprehensive analytical texts exploring physics and metaphysics, ethics and aesthetics, music and theatre, poetry and logic, politics and psychology, rhetoric and linguistics, biology and zoology, economics and government. Aristotle never stopped questioning what he saw, heard, or believed. Besides driving people crazy at cocktail parties (one supposes), he transformed the way people think. In particular, he devised a rigorous method of questioning, analyzing, thinking, organizing, and communicating ideas that has influenced Western thought ever since. His system was a simple way to ferret out the fundamentals of any idea, which he called first principles.

In the science of nature as elsewhere, we should try first to determine questions about the first principles. The naturally proper direction of our road is from things better known and clear to us to things that are better known to nature.

ARISTOTLE, C. 330 BCE, FROM *PHYSICS* (184A 10–21)

Analyze, optimize, augment, teach.

Helping others takes imagination. Those who practise empathy gain insight into the predicaments of others, but being a spectator, even if insightful, is not enough. To make a lasting difference, empathizers must use their insight to think imaginatively about possible solutions. They must be innovators, and innovators work best from first principles. They gain knowledge through their own experience, and then they use their own reason to sort that knowledge into a logical order. They notice how something is built and then ponder its structure to understand it better.

Imagine someone seeing a piano for the first time. A curious novice would hit the keys with varying pressure, listen to the whole range of notes by running low to high or high to low, then see what effect the pedals have, whereas an innovator would notice that while the keyboard has eighty-eight keys, they fall into patterns (octaves) and colours (white for root notes, black for sharps and flats); thus there are really only twelve notes, repeating at various octaves. So an innovator would immediately think, why don't we just make a keyboard with a single set of twelve notes and find a way to vary the octaves as we need them? A century ago, that seemed impossible, but it became doable once sound could be digitized. Many homes now have small keyboards that can still play the full range of frequencies of a grand piano. Tricky for four-handed duets, but brilliant nonetheless.

Once you find the structure that underpins anything, you can do four useful, powerful things. You can analyze why something is structured that way. (Must a piano really have all its sharps and flats on a different plane?) You can optimize the structure by changing one thing to improve the whole. (Let's make keys that trigger a particular note in any of many octaves.) You can augment by adding a feature that will make the thing more useful. (How about self-tuning strings?) Lastly, you can teach others how to use it, by progressing from the basic to the complex, adding further explanation when you see a student getting confused. All innovators tend to organize their thoughts in this way.

Ask "Why?" and "Why Not?"

In his 1949 collection of plays called *Back to Methuselah*, George Bernard Shaw pondered the process of innovation with the words, "You see things; and you say 'Why?' But I dream things that never were; and I say 'Why not?'" For innovators, hearing that something is impossible is an irresistible invitation to be curious and pose questions as a child might. Asking, "Why not?" is a good start. Several notable space travel innovators in our day come from the private sector breakthrough industries. Like so many great innovators, they are walking proof that empathy comes in many forms, and those who make great contributions to humanity can exhibit uncommon traits, express unsettling political views, and act in unconventional ways. Most, however, think about problems in a similar way. These innovators apply first-principles thinking to peel away the assumptions that inhabit any system that piques his interests. If we stylize his thinking as a set of questions, you can see below how much his own exploration is like that of a child asking, "But why?"

The SpaceX Origin Story	
INNOVATOR	POPULAR ASSUMPTION
Can I build a better space rocket?	Nope. Not with private capital.
Why not?	The cost is too high. Only governments can afford it.
But why is the cost so high?	There are so many middlemen for all the systems, parts, materials, etc.
But what if we brought all those functions into one company?	You still couldn't make it affordable.
Why not?	Because rockets are single-use products. After a single trip, you have to build a new one.
But why is that?	You can't relaunch a rocket.
But why not?	Both NASA and the Russians have tried. They couldn't do it.
But why couldn't they re-use them?	Systems take too much of a beating during launch and re-entry. Technology breaks down.
But their technology is decades old. Is it possible that current technology has finally made this possible?	Um, maybe.
Let's find out.	

The merit of that kind of thinking was affirmed on December 15, 2015, when SpaceX achieved the first successful landing of a multiple-blast, multiple-use rocket booster, which reduced the cost of building a spacecraft by 75 per cent. And they're just getting started. Now they are asking, "If our planet is under threat of environmental collapse, why don't why just all move to another planet?" Are they crazy? No, just endlessly curious. As always, they want to know what current assumptions have led us to believe that such a move is impossible. When they hear the usual answers, they try to move beyond them to first principles, because they know from their achievements that worthy solutions are built on them. Aristotelian thought has become innovation thought: why things are as they are is always the first question.

Be at peace with contradiction.

I worked hard in school. My marks were strong across the board, which I assumed came from my habit of studying any topic until I knew it cold. I had all the correct answers, which made writing papers and exams easy. As with any kid in high school, I was drawn more to some subjects than others. History was one of them. I loved it, not immediately for its broadening effect on one's perspective, but because I could get great marks. I had a knack for digesting a textbook and, during an exam, being able to recall vividly those passages that pertained to any question. My memory was not photographic, which I would have killed for, but one sharpened by long study. I pored over my books until I had the right answers down cold. I memorized all the dates, people, places, terminology, formulae, theorems, poems, verses, citations, and precedents that could be tested later. Math problems? No sweat. I had worked everything out in advance. Biology tests? I could give the Latin species, genus, and family of everything that grew, walked, and swam. History tests? I knew every date of everything that ever happened (or so I fancied). My cramming served me well right through high school. I was never arrogant, but my confidence was so high that when I scored only 97 per cent on my Grade 13 final history exam[2] I was mystified. At that point, my world was full of right and wrong answers. In Grade 13 history, we had only one textbook, and I knew the material backwards. So where could I have gone wrong?

Flash forward to 1960. In my sophomore year at Harvard, I jumped at the chance to study American intellectual history with Donald Harnish Fleming, a bright light who had come to Harvard from Yale just a year before. Not even forty years old at the time, Professor Fleming was a balding, short, jovial enthusiast whose students found his curiosity contagious. Gourmet cook, bon vivant, and something of an expert in gemstones, he taught that the best way to learn anything is to be curious and throw yourself into the subject with everything you have. There were no textbooks in his courses—in fact, few secondary sources at all. We were given lists of original documents to read and only then pushed for context to peruse scholarly interpretations of major historic events. In week two (I recall it vividly), there were three such documents and seven interpretations to digest before we met as a class. I read all of them, of course, summarizing each in my notebook. Intrigued to discover that many of the opinions about a particular document disputed the conclusions of others, I made a meticulous summary of each before heading to class. I was itching to learn which positions were right, which was the truth?

I was disappointed that during class that week the relative merits of the seven interpretations never came up. Many of my peers took the opportunity to voice heated opinions of their own. So many viewpoints, so little agreement; the class was more food fight than lecture, and I stayed quiet. After class, I caught up with Professor Fleming and explained my dilemma. "I don't understand," I said. "Which interpretation is right? What is the truth?" To his credit, instead of asking where on earth I had gone to school, he simply put his arm around my shoulder and whispered, "Maybe none of them." That's when the light went on. I left pondering the question "What is truth?" not recalling at the time that Pontius Pilate had asked the same question of Jesus. Till then, truth and falsity had been black and white elements in my mind, and I had thought of education as a way of distinguishing right from wrong, with higher education making one even better at doing so. But the big lesson I learned in history class that year is that truth itself is a debatable quantity. This was an outstanding lesson in critical thinking and so kindly delivered from the master teacher at work. Different truths can and do co-exist. There is always another viewpoint, another priority, another revelation or nuance that casts a topic in a new light. Empathetic people must be on the lookout for all these variants, for behind any truth on which an assumption is based lies a person or community whose fates depends on a particular interpretation.

"I would fire you."

As societies progress technologically over time, they tend to accelerate the rate at which they adopt new tools. It was two centuries after Gutenberg before the printing of manuscripts made copyists redundant, yet only a hundred or so years before steam power replaced human power in most industries. Digital computing went from miracle to mainstream in just three decades. Ten short years after its introduction, the smartphone was widely considered indispensable and had become ubiquitous. So it took three centuries for the writing press to touch the majority of the population of western Europe, and just a decade for the Internet to rock the majority of the population of the planet.

As is true of the ages of civilization, so is true of stages of life. The older we are, the slower we are to embrace innovation. Knowing that gives us one more reason to be respectful of the instincts of youth. Our daughter Sam once bluntly instructed me on the practical wisdom of this principle during my time as president of the University of Waterloo. As I was basking one evening in the news that *Maclean's* Canadian

University Rankings had named Waterloo as Canada's most innovative university (yet again, as it would for several decades running), Sam said, "Really? If I were chairing the board of your university, I would fire you for running a school that is, in fact, the opposite." That perked me up. Though still in her twenties, Sam had a lifetime of experience behind her, and I figured she must be onto something. Sam, like Jen before her, had entered life as a rebel. Youngest, smallest, and spunkiest of our five daughters, she decided early on that, to be thought of half as well as her sisters, she would have to be twice as nimble and three times as assertive.

Her real name is, in fact, Catherine, but her four older sisters had been hoping for a brother, and, in indignation, saddled her on Day One with a boy's name. So Sam grew up knowing that if you don't stand up for yourself, people will push you around; they'll even take your name. At each stage of life, she set her own course. Her sisters studied Chinese, so Sam picked Russian. Then at McGill, instead of just taking another Russian course for credit, Sam had a better idea. She had noticed that students in the Russian program, as with those in almost every other language program at the university, couldn't actually use the language to converse with native speakers. They could read Tolstoy and Turgenev, spout the third declension of a noun, and even debate whether the so-called past tense in Russian should more properly be called the non-present, but they could scarcely order a plate of stroganoff at a Russian restaurant or ask a Russian speaker for directions, let alone inquire how a family was faring with the break-up of the USSR. This fluency gap struck Sam as inane, so she gathered a group of classmates and headed down to the old-age home in Montreal at which many Russian unilingual speakers reside, just next to the Russian Orthodox Church. There they engaged in conversation, albeit haltingly at first. Residents were delighted; they freely corrected mistakes, taught new words, and helped refine the accents of the students, who, in return, helped the residents with their own fluency in French and English or helped them fill out complicated forms. That session quickly blossomed into a habit. Simply by offering their company two hours a week, Sam and her friends accelerated their learning and became conversationally fluent. After thirty hours of these sessions, Sam, being Sam, outlined the achievement to McGill's senate, arguing that all participating students should be awarded a course credit, which typically rewards thirty hours of class time. This was somewhat disconcerting to her father, who, as university principal, chaired the senate, and this novel proposal on credit for practical experience and application had not gone through the several curricular review committees. The senate resisted. Sam pushed harder, arguing that refusal to acknowledge better ways of learning was wrongheaded. In the end, the senate capitulated and each student received the well-earned credit, and learning by doing became a respected pedagogical tool.

Then upon graduation, instead of continuing her studies as her sisters had, Sam went off to teach English in Kaliningrad, the isolated patch of Russia (the USSR had indeed just collapsed) between Latvia and Poland. In what she would later describe as the roughest year of her life, Sam had to figure out ways to teach a language in a failed, now corrupt, system using methods she devised, deploying only those technologies and resources she could scrounge. Little surprise that Sam eventually landed at Harvard, earning her master's and PhD while studying the relationship between information technology and learning with a professor who was an expert in the field. It was there that she gathered empirical proof of her long-held hunch that attending lectures on their own—no matter how brilliant the professor—is a poor way to learn. With access to varied opportunities to put their theoretical knowledge into practice, students can triple their comprehension and retention. Each student is different, and empathy requires that we give each a wide range of options to apply and deepen what they know. While Waterloo had impressive pockets of innovative genius, many of our professors were still teaching students only by lecturing. That's why Sam said she would fire me. And I agreed with her.

Innovation in Canada

Innovation is one of the primary driving forces behind Canada's prosperity, standard of living, and quality of life. Yet while Canada has produced some of the world's most accomplished innovators, we do a poor job of celebrating what we've done, and how we've improved our own society, let alone how we've bettered the lives of those in other parts of the world. Back in 2016, we launched the Governor General's Innovation Awards to change that. We engaged the Rideau Hall Foundation, which we had created in 2012 initially to raise funds for the Innovation Awards program. The awards celebrate excellence in innovation across all sectors of Canadian society and inspire Canadians, and more recently Canadian youth in particular, to be entrepreneurial innovators. Here is a handful of the recent winners.

- Jeff Dahn worked quietly for twenty years at Dalhousie University to perfect the technology that would eventually make lithium batteries stronger, longer, and cheaper. Until his work, the practicality of lithium-ion batteries was uncertain; afterwards, their ingenious advantage earned the inventors a Nobel Prize. Alas, Dahn was not named among them; given that his own practical research proved the utility for their theoretical discovery, he should have been.
- Canada's Dr. Frank Hayden's work validated the need for the Special Olympics movement fifty years ago. In 1965, Hayden received a call from Eunice Kennedy (JFK's sister), then running summer camps for individuals with intellectual disabilities and interested in Hayden's work. Together they built a whole new institution. On July 20, 1968, athletes from twenty-five states competed in the new Special Olympics modelled on Hayden's work. By the late 1980s, Hayden had helped launch fifty more Special Olympics organizations around the world.

- Maayan Ziv, the founder of AccessNow, created a crowd-sourced mobile app designed to empower people living with disabilities to live more independently.
- SmartICE's specially designed technologies such as the SmartQAMUTIK and SmartBUOY empower communities to monitor their own ice trails.
- Nunavut's Pirurvik Preschool pioneered a transformational early childhood education (ECE) initiative that blends Inuit Qaujimajatuqangit (Inuit Ways) and Inungnuinniq (traditional Inuit child-rearing) with Montessori methods.
- Mary Gordon, founder of the organization Roots of Empathy and author of a book of the same name, has evolved a set of creative techniques that can inspire and encourage empathy in young people.
- Embers Staffing Solutions has provided temporary and transitional jobs to people in Vancouver facing multiple barriers through low-barrier employment opportunities, helping thousands of individuals transform their lives, and in turn improving the health and safety of the communities in which they reside.
- Jad Saliba, founder and chief technology officer, started Magnet Forensics to address the growing challenge police agencies face in the collection, analysis, and reporting of digital evidence when investigating crimes such as human trafficking, child sexual exploitation, and terrorism.
- Chief Dr. Ronald Ignace (Stsmel'cqen) and Dr. Marianne Ignace (Gulkiihlgad) created a model of collaborative approaches to research in and with Indigenous people and communities.

Make it useful, better, and transformative.

If you still don't think you are creative, you may be confusing creativity with genius. Extraordinarily gifted people such as Marie Curie and Albert Einstein are rare, but most life-changing innovations are introduced by people of average intellect fuelled by active curiosity. Typically, improvements to everyday tools and routines are innovations, not inventions, and the path to them is the exercise of one's imagination after first principles are established. What emerges then are pretty obvious improvements to things, systems, and approaches that may seem ingenious in hindsight. Let's take a stroll through history and look at some. In each case, imagine yourself as the person who got the idea that brought this better thing to life.

A few thousand years ago, Cree and Ojibwa knew well that ducks are difficult to hunt one bird at a time. Why is that? Because water fowl are both skittish and fast, which means they avoid danger and can exit rapidly when any danger threatens. But how do they sense where danger is? Given that predators hide, ducks can never be sure they're safe, so they've learned to accept that, wherever they see another duck sitting peacefully on a stretch of water, there is less likelihood of danger in that spot than in others. Some hunters wondered whether those passing ducks could be fooled by a fake duck placed on the water; they fashioned one out of reeds and, from then on, the duck decoy was the hunter's great advantage.

In 1853, Robert Foulis was walking home on a foggy, rainy night in his seaside town of Saint John, New Brunswick. As he approached his own house in the dark, he caught the sound of his daughter playing piano. At first, only the low notes were audible. That intrigued him. Living on the coast, Foulis knew that fog and rain made lighthouse beams invisible and coastal navigation treacherous for mariners. Hearing the piano that night convinced him that, just like piano music, a low-frequency note would travel much farther through fog than a high-frequency sound. His simple idea was to convert a steam whistle to emit only loud, low notes. His foghorn became one of the greatest lifesaving innovations of maritime history, all from an idea that came to him on a walk home.

By 1894, house builder Theodore Witte had been impressed by the way bakers in his town of Chilliwack, British Columbia, squeezed neat rows of icing onto their creations with cake-decorating guns. These guns made the bakers' work quick and tidy. Witte wondered if the devices could handle window putty as well. With a few small design alterations, his new puttying tool (or caulking gun as it soon became

Where is innovation needed most?

In 2015, the United Nations adopted a set of seventeen goals which, when (and if) met, will create a better and more sustainable future for all by 2030. If you want to exercise your curiosity and engage your creativity to make a contribution, these urgent goals will inspire you to think of new ideas in almost every field of human endeavour. Scan the list to find a topic that intrigues you, then dig down for more details by searching for Sustainable Development Goals on Wikipedia.

1. End poverty in all its forms everywhere
2. End hunger, achieve food security and improved nutrition, and promote sustainable agriculture
3. Ensure healthy lives and promote well-being for all at all ages
4. Ensure inclusive and equitable quality education and promote lifelong learning opportunities for all
5. Achieve gender equality and empower all women and girls
6. Ensure availability and sustainable management of water and sanitation for all
7. Ensure access to affordable, reliable, sustainable, and modern energy for all

known) saved many hours of labour. It remains a construction industry standard to this day.

A decade later in 1906, Léo-Ernest Ouimet of Montreal, Quebec, was curious why playgoers got to watch performances in comfortable theatres while those watching motion pictures still had to gather in dingy barns and cold church basements to be entertained. The year prior, a store in Pittsburg had been converted for film use, but it was still just a makeshift solution. To Léo the remedy was obvious: build a dedicated room with comfy seats for the paying guests and a soundproof

8. Promote sustained, inclusive, and sustainable economic growth, full and productive employment, and decent work for all

9. Build resilient infrastructure, promote inclusive and sustainable industrialization, and foster innovation

10. Reduce inequality within and among countries

11. Make cities and human settlements inclusive, safe, resilient, and sustainable

12. Ensure sustainable consumption and production patterns

13. Take urgent action to combat climate change and its impacts

14. Conserve and sustainably use the oceans, seas, and marine resources for sustainable development

15. Protect, restore, and promote sustainable use of terrestrial ecosystems, sustainably manage forests, combat desertification, halt and reverse land degradation, and halt biodiversity loss

16. Promote peaceful and inclusive societies for sustainable development, provide access to justice for all, and build effective, accountable, and inclusive institutions at all levels

17. Strengthen the means of implementation and revitalize the Global Partnership for Sustainable Development

booth for the projector. He did just that, and the purpose-built movie theatre was born.

In 1920, Robert Mawhinney of Saint John, New Brunswick, was growing frustrated by the amount of time it took to shovel earth into and out of his truck. He rigged up a box and attached it with hinges to his truck bed, where he could tip out the contents with a winch and cable: voilà, the dump truck.

While working as assistant curator of McGill Medical Museum in Montreal in the 1930s, medical pathologist Maude Abbott wondered why no one had gathered all the ailments and abnormalities that afflict the human heart into a single list. It seemed obvious to her that such a resource could greatly improve cardiac care. She was right; when her creation appeared in 1936 as *The Atlas of Congenital Cardiac Disease*, the profession (as sexist as it was) applauded her scholarship. Even better, physicians applied the content of her bestselling book to their practices, making immediate, sweeping improvements to cardiac medicine.

In Montreal in 1948, Professor John Humphrey of the McGill Law Faculty concluded that human rights could never be guaranteed until a

Bonnie Henry: Leading with Empathy

When COVID-19 reached North America in early 2020, it spread like wildfire from coast to coast to coast. In those early weeks, statements from politicians and public health officials often ranged from pure denial ("We have this under control") to toothless solidarity ("We're all in this together"). In the ensuing flood of messaging, spin, and crisis communications, too little rang sincere. One voice stood out for its earnestness. Dr. Bonnie Henry, provincial health officer for British Columbia, made headlines for her March 7, 2020, press conference that year. Dr. Henry took a twenty-second pause between questions as tears welled in her eyes. Finally, she said,

THINGS WE CAN DO AS INDIVIDUALS | 39

formal list of rights was created and endorsed around the world. The United Nations agreed; the young organization took Humphrey's list and shaped it into the UN's Universal Declaration of Human Rights.

By 1980, garbage man Nyle Ludolph of Kitchener, Ontario, was sick of the vast amounts of plastic and paper being tossed each day into the local landfills. Many ideas had been proposed for separating these recyclable products from the other garbage at the dump, but no system for doing that messy work had been devised. Nyle's innovation—obvious to him—was curb-side recycling, in which the citizens could do the sorting themselves. His "blue box" is now ubiquitous.

In Vancouver, British Columbia, around 2000, Janet Werker's long study of the ways in which children learn to speak inspired her to feed the wealth of data she had collected into the high-tech, analytical tools that researchers were already using in other fields. The resulting revelations sparked a whole new science: Very Early Language Learning. Janet didn't invent anything but, by being both curious and creative, she brought a whole new discipline into being and made it possible to help children with speech difficulties at much earlier ages than before.

"I'm feeling for the families and the people that are dealing with this right now." Her emotion was plain, her composure was failing. British Columbia Health Minister Adrian Dix summed it up several days later in a comment to the CBC: "She feels it. She doesn't just think it." The response from the public was immediate and overwhelming. Almost overnight, a Dr. Bonnie Henry Fan Club account went viral on Twitter. Dr. Henry ended each of her broadcasts with the invocation "Be kind. Be calm. Be safe." The face of Bonnie in her youth even became the poster child for a Science World fundraising campaign. The slogan? "The world needs more nerds." The copy would have been just as effective if it followed Dr. Henry's lead: "The world needs more empathy."

By 2008, nutritionist Toni Desrosiers of Calgary, Alberta, had long questioned whether beeswax and tree resin, two of nature's best preservatives, could be used in food storage. That year she created wrappings of hemp and cotton saturated with these two ingredients, and her abeego wrap has since become a popular, commercial alternative to plastic wrap. Good for the environment, great for home cooks.

And in 2014, a group of concerned citizens in Saskatchewan wrestled with a painful social dilemma. Given that the first six months of mother–child relationships are pivotal in any child's mental and physical well-being, how could that critical period be protected? Not easy in poorer families where young mothers have to get back to work quickly just to afford groceries. The answer was found in a social investment bond, a newish-but-proven mechanism for raising money specifically for humanitarian purposes. The innovation lay in applying a known mechanism (social investment bonds) to a new situation (infant care). In the case of Sweet Dreams, as the group called its project in Regina, the new idea was to earmark such funds specifically to give young mums a worry-free six months to bond with their infants. Life changing.

You may have noticed that these innovations share several characteristics. They all sprang from empathetic understanding of the pressing needs of a wider group. All the innovators were experts in their own fields, which means they knew enough to exercise their own curiosity and harness simple logic to devise a new approach that might help. And each had a huge impact. In this way, every innovation here had (and, frankly, must have) three qualities: it is useful, it makes things better, and ultimately, it transforms the lives of those who need it most.[3] Those three outcomes are why, in my opinion, innovation is the most helpful application of empathy.

Empathetic things to do when you intend to Stay curious.

. . . as an individual

Be relentless in your pursuit of knowledge.
Ask why and why not until you get down to first principles. When you truly understand something, you'll be able to analyze its purpose, optimize its effect, augment its capability, and teach others about what you've done.

Master something.
You have to know enough about a topic to see the holes. As you grow in curiosity, delve deep enough into at least one area to become an expert. Then you can use your deep understanding with your inherent empathy to find ways to help improve situations for others.

Practise holding two contradictory ideas in your mind.
Seeing things in black and white is a self-limiting habit. Nothing is simple; if it seems so, there's probably more you need to know. No matter the topic, try to be a non-judgmental observer. A great way to get better at that is to recognize inherent contradictions without having to choose one side over the other.

. . . as a community

Cherish our teachers.

Whenever you struggle to find a helpful and appropriate answer to a child's direct question, give thanks for all the teachers who dedicate their lives to doing just that all day every day. In our Internet age when kids can mistakenly assume they can "find it all online," teachers shoulder the crucial role of teaching kids to think critically and distinguish sense from nonsense.

Celebrate innovation.

It's great to be acknowledged for doing something creative, and even better when you get a prize for it. Take joy in publicly recognizing those who innovate in ways that make other people's lives better. The joy of the recipients will be quickly exceeded by the contagious effect on those around them.

. . . as a nation

Recruit the best teachers and students from around the world.

In a world that changes daily, we must prepare our kids to adapt, innovate, and prosper, and that will require a series of teachers at the top of their game. Yet policies dictating who can be hired are often restrictive and counterproductive. Any region or nation seeking to improve its performance on the world stage should take action to make sure the *best* teachers are engaged at every level, even if it means making deep changes to hiring policies, collective-bargaining agreements, and immigration rules. Well worth the effort. Then go further and ensure that Canada stands out as a country that welcomes students from all parts of the world to embark on a Canadian educational experience.

Collaborate nationally and internationally.

As much as creativity is an individual quality, innovation is a collaborative art. All innovations must be useful, make things better, and be transformative for large groups of people. That will require teams of people working together. Nations have a unique responsibility to foster international cooperation in ways that get the best ideas moving in all directions. Programs supporting youth exchanges, trade development, academic postings abroad, open research, and international conferences should be accelerated.

3

Be charitable.

And though I have the gift of prophecy, and understand all mysteries,
and all knowledge; and though I have all faith, so that I could remove
mountains, and have not charity, I am nothing.

1 CORINTHIANS 13:2

About four thousand years ago, likely during the ninth or tenth
dynasty of Egypt's Middle Kingdom, a tale appeared about a peasant
named Khun-Anup who travels to a market to buy supplies for his
family. On the way, he takes a narrow road between the river and the
farmland of a greedy landowner named Nemtynakht. Aware of
Nemtynakht's reputation for trickery, Khun-Anup sticks to the road,
careful not to set even a single foot on the farmer's property. Safely in
town, Khun-Anup then makes his purchases, loads the goods onto his
donkeys, and sets off on his return journey.

Having spied the humble caravan heading to market that morning,
Nemtynakht had since hatched a plan to trick the unwitting peasant
out of his possessions. At the narrowest part of the road, he lays a length
of exquisite cloth on the ground, filling almost the whole space between
his own field and the steep riverbank, leaving a path wide enough only
for travellers to pass in single file. Then he hides and waits.

When Khun-Anup reaches the trap, he sees the ornate cloth on the ground and senses his predicament. If he steps on or even touches the garment, he will have defiled one of the owner's possessions. If he veers too hard toward the river, his animals might stumble down the steep embankment. Yet if he puts a single foot into the farmer's field, he will be trespassing. Aware of the setup, Khun-Anup positions his animals in single file and cautiously urges them forward.

Everything goes well until the last donkey takes its final step past the cloth. Closer now than ever to the field, the donkey leans over and plucks a single flower from the stem of a single plant to munch on. In rehearsed outrage, Nemtynakht then springs up from his hiding place and arrests the perpetrator for trespass and theft. As punishment, he insists that the hapless peasant forfeit all his livestock and goods.

Khun-Anup, however, is no fool. Instead of going home empty handed, the determined victim makes a forceful and, as the story goes, articulate case to Nemtynakht's master Rensi, high steward to the Pharaoh himself. After consulting with the Pharaoh, Rensi sides with Khun-Anup and repairs the injustice by returning the peasant's possessions and granting him all of Nemtynakht's lands, titles, and possessions as well. For his knavery, Nemtynakht is forced to change places with Khun-Anup forever.

The moral of the story? Treat others as you would be treated yourself or pay the price. It's a familiar instruction, and its variants have existed in every culture, society, and religion and philosophy since the ancient Egyptian epoch. The Eloquent Peasant, as this version has become known, is just the first example on record of the ethic of reciprocity. You may know it as the Golden Rule or the Golden Law, or perhaps the Do Unto Others rule. Whatever you call it, you have certainly been taught it, for it has been upheld as a tenet of virtually every religion, code of ethics, and school curriculum in human history. The iteration we cite at the opening of this chapter happens to be from the Old Testament.[1] It's the version I grew up with, but it's only one version of many thousands to be found in sacred texts, literature, and rules of conduct.

Why is the Golden Rule so widely and enduringly popular? In a Darwinian sense, being thoughtful and kind to others has likely been key to the survival of our species and, we are now learning, the persistence of many other species as well. Kindness to and tolerance of others is one of the central definitions of charity, and being charitable makes good karmic sense. We all have ups and down. What goes around comes around, so it's smart to be kind to others for we will certainly need their kindness in turn. We are all charity cases.

The Golden Rule is a fundamental determinant of all healthy relationships. The force that gives that rule its effect is empathy, the habit of considering your neighbour as yourself and acting accordingly. In doing so, you needn't think of your neighbours as identical to you, but rather as having lives at least as complex as your own and deserving the same access to opportunity as you. Their mere existence makes them worthy of understanding, appreciation, and assistance. Your situations are not identical, so conditions needn't be equal, but they should always be fair.

Living the Golden Rule is one of the most direct ways to exercise your social humanity, less as strict adherence to any moral imperative and more as a potent contribution to the well-being of the species. When you act on this millennia-old axiom, you build trust with other people. When whole communities embrace the rule, collective trust grows and these communities thrive. Big claim, I know, but read on.

Charity begins at home, then strolls around.

The maxim "charity begins at home" is often taken as a reminder that one's first obligation is to one's family. I see it differently. In my experience, charity did indeed begin at home—with my wife, Sharon—but because that's where I was first pummelled with relentless, indelible proof that kindness makes everything possible and most of it enjoyable. Having started out as a self-absorbed youngster myself, I was astonished to be treated with selfless, open-hearted, non-judgmental love by my wife and then my kids, no matter how half-baked my ideas and goofy my actions. I had not anticipated the consistent, patient appreciation my entire family would give me unasked. Even the youngest seemed to know instinctively that, because life is complex, one should not rush to judge anyone's motivation for doing what they do.

Children don't come into the world suspicious or cynical; they just show up expecting the best of everybody. As my kids entered the picture (five daughters boom boom boom boom boom), I learned that human nature is inherently good nature, and that good-natured people are a delight to be around. This conviction was routinely validated as each of our fourteen grandchildren made their subsequent entrances. So when I wrote a book about trust in 2018, my dedication read "To children, who offer their trust instinctively and with full expectation of fairness." I think we should all keep doing that. Swedish American physiologist Anton Julius Carlson, who contended further that everyone expects and deserves fairness, gave his own suggestion: "Let us keep our mouths shut and our pens dry until we know the facts."

Feeling the effects of generous spirit within my household, it became instinctive for me to try to carry that same spirit with me. I didn't make any big decision to be more outgoing but, as I grew calmer in my own life, I seemed at last to have the emotional bandwidth to be less concerned about my own situation and more interested in that of others.

Neighbours were an easy first target for my experiments. Whenever and wherever I walked, I tried to reach out. I started by smiling. Among strangers, the mere act of tightening cheek muscles to pull up the edges of one's lips takes courage. What if they think I'm a psychopath? I'm exaggerating (somewhat), but you're probably already aware of how often in public you have to decide whether to smile at someone once you've made eye contact. I stuck to it, and somewhere in my academic brain I conceived a list of management decisions. Eye contact while passing a stranger? Affirmative. Utter "good morning" to fellow shopper in a grocery aisle? Roger that. Wave at a passing bicyclist? Yup.

As I put my new greeting regime into practice, I observed that my cheery overtures were almost always reciprocated. Most people responded immediately, as though they too had been wondering if any exchange were going to take place. Even those whose minds had been miles away when we passed managed to raise an eyebrow, grunt something, or at least lift a few fingers off the handlebar once they came back to Earth. Almost never did people refuse to acknowledge my gesture or, worse, look miffed. So without going full Forrest Gump, I became more overtly genial in public. By doing so I grew certain that most people are friendly; they're just not sure going in that you are too. Human willingness to connect is proportional only to the confidence both parties have that a greeting is genuine and not, God forbid, precursor to a hostile look or even physical attack. As I gradually internalized that truth, I was able to quiet my inner voice from reciting what urban dwellers assume is the eleventh commandment: don't talk to strangers.

Everyone needs something.

Waves of acknowledgement, friendly-but-noncommittal greetings, and short conversations led then to longer discussions with neigh-bours about topics of mutual interest. Walking in our community became more social but never more intrusive or tiring. Being friendly never robbed me of my privacy, and even better, never intruded on my (almost nonstop) private thoughts. Connecting with other humans in our vicinity became an easy pleasure.

Easy, of course, for a man. The situation is far more complex for women, many of whom after wretched experience choose to hurry eyes-down through public spaces. Catcalls from men who are either unaware of or, alas, unconcerned about the frequency with which women suffer abuse (not to mention attack) in public are a pathetic low end of the unwelcome spectrum of behaviours women routinely endure. Thus at times, women are compelled to dampen any inclination to friendliness they might have. That said, anywhere you look you will see women being outgoing and warm. We men have much to learn here.

When Sharon and I had kids in tow, there was always plenty to gab about when we met others who lived nearby. Conversing, even briefly, led to familiarity, familiarity to understanding, understanding to empathy. When I was open to hearing people speak about their situations, it didn't take long to hear about something they needed, be it better health, a less busy schedule, a ride to the clinic, help carrying furniture, or just a plate of sandwiches for an upcoming wake.

Soon, I began to listen with my eyes too. When I did, it became easy to respond. The sandwich board outside that deli had blown over, so I righted it. Ten seconds. Garbage cans were still at the end of some guy's driveway, so I rolled them up to the house. Ninety seconds. That other neighbour was on crutches one day, so I asked if she needed anything at the grocery store. An extra two minutes max on my next outing. These miniature acts may seem inconsequential or even trite, but they formed in me both a sensibility and a habit. Once I got onto the notion that I could help anyone, ways to do so presented themselves in endless succession, and by helping I met more people over time. It didn't distract me: I could still be an introvert, a daydreamer, a quiet guy with an unsatisfiable appetite for alone time, but, by helping other people for a few minutes as a habit, my world seemed to make better sense. Anything else just wouldn't be fair to those I met, and all that came just from strolling around the neighbourhood.[2]

I say it didn't change me, but I did notice a gradual shift in my perspective: I moved from helping those I bumped into to actively considering where else need might be. Once I put that question out there, the answer came roaring back: everywhere.

What do people need?

Any city, no matter how small, is in fact divided into two,
one the city of the poor, the other of the rich;
these are at war with one another.

PLATO, C. 738 BCE

In any community, the range of need is vast. Some of the needs are absolutes in that they relate to survival. In every community some or many may be suffering from want of these necessities. Clean water, breathable air, enough food, safe housing, warm clothing, medicines, decent jobs, affordable child care, and transportation to work come to mind. Other needs spring from the specific context in which any community exists. As Canadians, we are keenly aware that geography and climate play a central role here. In remote communities the doctor–patient ratio may be small, and basic things such as prescription eyeglasses, dental care, fresh vegetables, and gasoline maybe unobtainable or unaffordable to many. (It's no mystery why people flock to gas stations when the price per litre dips even by a dime.) In a country such as ours, where annual temperatures in some towns can swing from −40°C in winter to +40°C (even higher lately) in summer, heating and air conditioning both become seasonal necessities of life, and expensive necessities at that. In the suburbs of large cities, cheap and frequent public transport to and from work might be the single factor that determines if low-income families can survive at all.

Some needs, like those I heard about on my walks, are peculiar to the local inhabitants and will vary street by street, family by family, and person by person. Perhaps commuters are endangering children at play by zipping too fast through a neighbourhood to get to a feeder road. Maybe a swath of street lights has gone dark. Shoplifters and vandals could be targeting specific stores or homes in the area. Perhaps young school kids need more crossing guards or better after-school care. Or it could be that a family with a severely disabled member just needs some regular relief. The tricky thing is that only some of these needs will be spoken aloud. Many people are shy or nervous about voicing their distress or discontent, and the reasons for their not coming forward can be as diverse as the needs themselves. Some people may be too ill, old, or timid to ask for help. Newcomers from other countries may not yet have enough command of the local language to express themselves or might find it humiliating to reveal the true state of their affairs. I have known new Canadians who, despite desperately needing the help of the police, have refused to approach them. If you've just arrived from a regime in which police demand payoffs and know how to coerce people to make them pay, you may just shut up instead of applying for assistance.

So many needs and so many reasons, and too many that go unheard. My mother's advice to me as a child still rings in my ears: "Be considerate to everyone, for you never know what battles they're fighting."

Address common needs with shared resources.

Whether openly expressed or privately suffered, needs common to many in a community can be met only with the coordinated efforts of others. The spontaneous gift on a frigid day of a warm coat to a homeless person is a beautiful gesture, but before long more sweeping interventions are required. Volunteering (on which I'll offer a few thoughts in the next chapter) is critical and effective, but long-term solutions to systemic problems require not individual but institutional intervention. That's where charities come in.

Charities handle a myriad of activities that governments simply cannot. Here's why. Governments at all levels have a broad duty to address the shared concerns of all their citizens. They often do that well; it's one of the reasons we refer to them as representative. With the big picture always in mind, however, governments are pretty clunky at the small stuff. They move slowly, and they're not adept at focusing their programming on small groups of citizens with particular needs. Governments can't act out of love; as a result, small groups of vulnerable citizens often slip though the cracks. Charities, by name and by nature, are motivated by love.

Charitable Canada

As Europeans appeared, then poured into North America from the sixteenth century onward, they came upon a myriad of Indigenous civilizations with long established, smooth-running systems of government, food security, spirituality, arts, justice, transport, and trade. These nations also had deep traditions of charity that surprised and impressed the would-be settlers. Leading the first successful effort to establish a permanent French presence in Canada, Samuel de Champlain wrote openly of his admiration for the Indigenous inhabitants who, when judging of the sophistication of any neighbouring tribe, would cite the degree to which that community took care of its orphans and widows. Like his king and patron Henri IV, Champlain

Love, Actually

Our word *charity* is a modern variant of the Latin *caritas*, which itself springs (though not obviously) from the Greek ἀγάπη (agapē). The word refers to love founded on esteem, the instinctive regard for a person's inherent worth. A spirit of charity implies the voluntary giving of help to those who need it, as exemplified in parables such as "The Eloquent Peasant" and "The Good Samaritan."

was intent on building a trans-Atlantic society based on respect, tolerance, and kindness to all citizens in equal measure.[3] He was impressed by the sophistication of the social fabric he found in place, which in many ways outshone that of France.

Governors general aren't supposed to pick favourites from among their predecessors, but mine is definitely Champlain, who, as governor of New France, was the first to hold our evolving office. When my appointment was announced at a press conference in the foyer of the Senate chamber, I was holding a copy of *Champlain's Dream*, the biography by Pulitzer Prize winner David Hackett Fischer published in 2008. On the cover, Champlain is described as a remarkable leader who "dreamed of humanity and peace in a world riven by violence, built the first European settlement in Canada, founded on a dream of humanity and respect, and played a role in starting the growth of three populations—Québécois, Acadian and Métis in the place we call Quebec. His legacy is with us today and it helps define Canada." Carrying that book on the day my appointment was announced was a reinforcement of my journey of constant learning. Until I read

Pick something that means something to you.

The range of charitable activities in Canada has grown pretty much every year for the last five hundred years. If you're ready to help in a sustained way, make a routine contribution, no matter how small, to a charity with a mission, programming, and impact that resonate with you personally. There are many resources to help you make a meaningful choice. Sites such as charityintelligence.ca and canadahelps.org will guide you through a process of categories of priority to you and offer a rating system so you can quickly assess an organization's track record. You can link directly to a charity's website and set up a donation schedule in a minute or two.

Fischer's work, I had pictured Champlain as a kind of French conquistador come to plant a flag bearing the fleur de lis, Christianize the locals, and then ship fish and fur back to France at a profit. I had much to unlearn.

Inspired by Champlain's philosophy, the early settlers soon acknowledged that, if they were going to survive (let alone thrive), if they were going to build better lives for themselves and their neighbours, and if they were going to be able to build brighter futures for their children, they must give freely to others of their time, toil, and talents. They must see others as themselves and act on that understanding. Like the Indigenous peoples of this land, they understood that our country is too vast, climate too harsh, challenges of starting anew too daunting for anyone—even the strongest and most resourceful—to make it on their own. Only by being charitable to others, by seeing their neighbours as themselves, in short being empathetic, could they survive.

This spirit of empathy and action then ran like a vivid thread through the fabric of our country's history, at least from settler to settler. In 1688, the citizens of New France set up the first voluntary agency in Canada, the Bureaux des Pauvres (Office of the Needy). The Bureaux gave food, money, and shelter to the sick, the elderly, and the incapacitated; found work for the unemployed; and gave tools to labourers so they could ply their trades.

Other organizations soon followed. Local parishes, religious orders, and lay groups founded charities such as the Hall of God, the House of Providence, and the Society of Saint Vincent de Paul, expert organizations focused on caring for the sick and the elderly, supporting the destitute, and educating children—both boys and girls—from poor families. Centuries later, a sad chapter in a long story of service would see appalling neglect and abuse of Indigenous children under the care of some religious orders, especially those administering government-funded residential schools, raising loud questions in Canada about why the Church had been given such sweeping authority in the first place.

In the decades following Confederation, charitable groups sprang up across Canada to help settle European immigrants and keep their traditional cultures alive. Immigrants from Iceland set up a network of libraries and reading clubs. Canadians of German descent in Halifax established the country's first funeral and burial society. Canadians from Poland in Kitchener founded Canada's first mutual-aid society, which later evolved into a thriving network of mutual, life, property, and casualty insurance companies. Homesteaders from Hungary and Ukraine became unofficial settling agents, helping newcomers from all lands start lives in the Prairies.

As our country grew, advocates such as the St. John Ambulance Association, the Canadian Red Cross Society, and the Young Women's Christian Association provided services for vulnerable people such as children and young women and spearheaded social reform to help ensure all Canadians had access to decent homes, adequate health care, and free education. Dozens of community groups such as the United Way, Habitat for Humanity, and the Community Foundations of Canada were formed to respond to community needs, economic hardship, natural disasters, and war. National charitable organizations such as the Canadian Lung Association, Canadian Cystic Fibrosis Foundation, Muscular Dystrophy Canada, Alzheimer Society of Canada, and many others have raised hundreds of millions of dollars to help find cures for diseases and help treat and comfort those afflicted with them.

Lastly, modern not-for-profit and charitable organizations were augmented in North America, many of them operating in Canada, with the development of some of the great personal foundations of the late ninetieth and early twentieth centuries, bearing illustrious American names such as Rockefeller, Carnegie, Pew, and Ford, as well as Canada's own Massey and McConnell foundations—well-funded, albeit on a smaller scale.

Today, with some 170,000 charities and non-profit associations working 'round the clock, the charitable sector is an essential component of Canadian society.

Modern Samaritans

I was lucky as governor general to learn a great deal about these organizations even though I already knew of the atypically central role played by charities and non-profits in Canada. For starters, as a percentage of gross domestic product, Canada's non-profit sector is the world's second largest, representing more than 8 per cent of our annual economic activity, making it larger than our automotive sector and almost on par with oil, gas, and mining lumped together. One of the benefits of that activity is employment, with almost 2.5 million Canadians taking their annual salaries directly from organizations with a charitable focus. Our charities and non-profit organizations generate about $200 billion in income and harness the talents of more than 13 million volunteers over the course of any given year. That means that half of all Canadians over fifteen years of age routinely devote their time to helping others with the guidance of these institutions. The economic value of the combined effort is incalculable.

In my role as GG, I served as the patron of more than 150 charities. I took a keen interest in how those institutions contribute to the well-being of Canadians and to the lives of vulnerable populations overseas as well. Having served on a variety of corporate boards of directors in my career, I also wanted to know exactly how they operate. What makes some agencies average and others great? How can a few keep their administrative costs to 10 per cent or lower while others need 30? Why are a handful of charities able to maintain their legendary reputations for integrity while others raise suspicious eyebrows among potential donors? And what leads people to believe fervently in the missions of some outfits while they shrug off the interests of others? My curiosity wasn't academic: I wanted to know because the outlook for charities in Canada is not good. You would think, looking at the economic data alone, that the sector is booming. Paradoxically, it is not.

The problem isn't entirely a want of government funding. Far from it; three levels of government happily contribute more than 20 per cent of charities' annual budgets, with provinces typically kicking in about seven times more than the feds and about twenty times as much as municipal governments each year. Government backing makes sense, because charities offer the kind of supports that allow people to maintain their health and make their own contributions to society, thus reducing the strain on government programs such as health care and employment insurance. Neither does the problem stem from lack of generated revenues, as institutional sales of merchandise and services impressively account for almost half of charities' annual budgets. The difficulty comes instead from fluctuating levels of donations from individuals, corporations, and foundations, sources of revenue that have been wobbly for the past decade. Before 2007, the figures had risen steadily each year, from $4 billion in 1985 to almost $9.6 billion in 2007, just before the big crash of 2008. Then things went wonky. Now the amount of total donations fluctuates every year, sometimes down, sometimes up but never steady. Imagine if your employer said, "Your income will fluctuate year to year, sometimes up, sometimes down, and I'm afraid you'll never know by how much till the year is over. You okay with that?" That's what Canadian charities face, and plenty of people are trying to figure out why. Why, when the sector produces so much employment, inspires so much volunteer activity, is so productive and improves the lives of so many, should people be less committed in some years than others to chipping in? The answer comes down to one word: trust.

We trust other humans when we judge them to be interested in our welfare, willing to cooperate, open in their dealings, and capable of delivering what they promise. We think of charities the same way; we trust them when we judge them to be doing things we care about, cooperating sensibly with other groups, and able to make measurable changes in the lives of their intended beneficiaries. With these conditions met, we feel we know them enough to trust them. But when we do not know them well enough or, worse, have a poor image of their behaviour, we do not trust them and will not give them money.

Sustained giving requires that trust, and trust is rooted in knowledge that leads to favourable judgment. The necessary knowledge is possible only when the dealings of an organization are visible. Too many have slipped into the shadows.

Who's giving and who's not?

When I became governor general, we at Rideau Hall believed that the non-partisan Office of the Governor General was an ideal place from which to reinforce the shared Canadian value of charity. In 2012 we created the Rideau Hall Foundation to focus our efforts and make them permanent. The foundation made it possible for us—with our partners across Canada—to launch campaigns to promote giving and other shared Canadian values. Going in we wanted to understand what motivates people to give today, what stops them from doing so, and what strategies we could best pursue to help them give more. As one leg of our journey, we created the Giving Behaviour Project, whose first job was partnering with Imagine Canada to analyze data from the past thirty years so we could understand how giving has changed. Here are some of the findings:

Our country relies on an aging cohort of donors who are giving more and more. People fifty and over now account for three-quarters of all donations, while those seventy and older make up 30 per cent of that group.

For young people, the fact that tax-receipted donations are deductible is not a compelling advantage as it was to their parents.

Forty-one per cent of donors worldwide have given to one-off
crowdfunding campaigns that benefit individuals, with 44 per
cent of these donations used to cover direct expenses related to
medical treatments and family emergencies.

Once they have supported these crowdfunding campaigns, 16 per
cent of donors then choose to give less money to non-govern-
mental, non-profit, and charitable organizations.

Some 18 per cent of donors worldwide have given through
Facebook fundraising tools; of those, 88 per cent say they are
likely to give through these tools in the future.

These figures point to the fact that an increasing number of givers are
not only making their contributions online, but are also guided in
their choices by online culture and its visible options. Less concerned
about the tax implications of their contributions, they are more
inspired by the authenticity of the connection between themselves
and the recipients of their gifts. They donate out of empathy and no
longer see meaningful distinction between giving directly and giving
through charities. All giving is on par. That being true, nothing less
than a rapid digital transformation is required if Canada's charitable
organizations hope to remain relevant.

Going Digital

The status quo is a death knell for Canada's charities. Even slow
and steady evolution is a non-starter. Charitable organizations
must take advantage of digital technologies and their impact on
prospective donors in a strategic and intentional way and not a
reactive way. Charities should approach their digital transformation from four strategic perspectives.

Channel strategy means being at the same places as
prospective donors.

Most people running non-profits are baby boomers or those trained by them. These people gained their expertise in fundraising in the age of telephone campaigns, live donor events, television and radio promotion, and the distribution of annual reports and direct-mail solicitations. The digital age is now fully underway; all younger donors get their information, impressions, and feedback online. Why give to long-established charities when you can donate to a crowdfunded campaign helping a needy individual cause whose photos, stories, and even video testimonials are all right on your desktop? These campaigns—through instruments such as GoFundMe—have eclipsed the efforts of legacy organizations who haven't yet found the funding to create a mature and appealing digital presence.

Further, I suspect online donors assume that the full amount they give through these platforms ends up in the hands of the needy, but of course there's a cost. Even when known, typical platform fees of 3 to 5 per cent will seem low, but these sites usually charge an additional processing fee of about 2 to 3 per cent (to run your credit card), and then a per-transaction hard cost of about $0.30 (to move that money to its destination). So for any $5 donation, the platform might extract in the vicinity of $0.70. That's a total administrative fee of 14 per cent, really no better than that of most charities. Yet

Data strategy asks and answers why and how charities collect, store, clean, and use information.

Social business strategy covers social media and how charities use these networks to engage and sell.

Content strategy requires charities to determine their individual story and then where and how to tell it.

Successful change is sustainable and must deliver increasing value both to contributors and beneficiaries, including those who do not directly receive the money given, but rather essential services that only an expert organization can provide.

these online campaigns are far more attractive, easier, and in many ways more satisfying to contribute to. The great advantage of digital, after all, is instant gratification. I'm not disputing the value of those donations. I know people whose prospects have been quickly improved by crowdsourced campaigns. It's just that they really are just one more iteration of the warm-coat-on-a-frigid-day model. They offer a much-needed but one-off solution. The root problem is always deeper.

As with so many new things, a word of caution is in order. There is less transparency and less opportunity for due-diligence in the online transactions that make these instant donations possible. Better procedures must be developed to ensure both the identification of donors and the use of funds collected. Many abuses can be prevented when we're able to follow the money.

Be virtual to be visible.

Charities exemplify empathy. They see the needs of Canadians clearly. They strive to give support and ensure that vulnerable citizens can access the opportunities and protections enjoyed by others. Canadian charities and non-profits have shown a penchant for bringing new approaches to giving. That spirit for giving is needed now more than ever.

With 170,000 charities to choose from, no Canadian is likely to stick with one they don't know much about. It's not true that people are reluctant to change, just that the rate at which they change is usually proportional to the degree of effort required to make the move. So whereas people might complain for years about the rotten service and sky-high service charges at their banks before undertaking the long and painful process of switching to another financial institution, they will dump a charity in seconds if they cannot be certain their donation is having an impact.

Any hint of bad behaviour will drive donors away. Woe betide the medical-research fund, food bank, disaster-relief agency, child-sponsorship program, animal shelter, family-support group, wildlife-conservation trust, or art gallery that raises funds for one purpose and then spends them on another, overpays it staff, lies about its administrative costs, fudges statistics, throws lavish parties, or, God forbid, cooks the books. As we've seen recently in Canada, the mere suspicion of cronyism can send donors running, even if the players are later vindicated by interventions such as ethics audits. Shenanigans, however, are rare in Canada's charitable and non-profit sector. Despite a few recent PR controversies, which spring, in my opinion, more from poor judgement than ill intent, our charities behave with consistent integrity and measurable impact. So why again are donations wobbly? I think it's related simply to awareness. Donors acting online can make quick decisions to be generous, perhaps not aware as donors once were of the benefits of making their donations to institutions with more sophisticated, integrated systems for meeting real needs with focus and consistent effect. Our charities are losing touch with donors because donors are going digital quickly and charities aren't keeping pace.

Empathetic things to do when you intend to Be charitable.

. . . as an individual

Do unto others . . .

Be charitable. Life is an inexplicable miracle, a grand mystery to be savoured with a few tantalizing puzzles thrown in to ponder along the route. When you're grateful to be part of it, it's natural to reach out and share what you have with others, just as countless others have shared their good fortunes with you. Keep your eyes open and be aware of opportunities in which you can make a difference—in your family, in your neighbourhood, in your nation, and in your world. By giving to others, you express your thanks for what you have, acknowledge our interdependence as members of the human family, and change the lives of others.

Make a regular contribution to charity.

When a need is suffered by many, the best response is an institutional response. Charities are expert at finding those in need and helping them more efficiently than you can on your own, but they need stable funding to do that well. In these days of one-off, crowdfunded campaigns, it's easy to forget that regular donations to established charities are the best way to make a long-term difference. A regular donation to any charity whose mission you find meaningful will be an important and rewarding addition to your own spectrum of generosity. Be sure to consider the merits of planned giving, sometimes dubbed legacy giving, by which you can make commitments in your will to support charities after you die.

Teach your kids to give.

Children are instinctively generous. Show them early on that kindness is valuable. Celebrate their selfless acts, from helping their friends and neighbours to chipping in part of their earnings and allowances to a worthy cause. Encourage them to build lifelong philanthropic habits early on by teaching them how to pick a favourite charity and donate regularly. They will feel invested in a greater cause and rightly proud of their part in it.

. . . as a community

Include charities in decision-making.

Philanthropic organizations are one of the sturdy pillars of social organization. They offer focused programming that meets the particular needs of the most vulnerable members of society at impressively low cost, allowing governments to funnel public funds into services that meet more widely shared priorities. Invite representatives of the non-profit sector to be involved in community planning from the get-go.

Celebrate philanthropy in your community.

Many people do not give to charity simply because they are unaware of what those charities do. Find opportunities to publicize the great work being undertaken by charities in your neighbourhood and make sure citizens know how they can donate. Inspire your elected officials to do their part by endorsing fundraising campaigns, including donorship forms in their mail-outs, including website links to charitable agencies during specific campaigns, and being vocal about their own donations. Open your community facilities—from church basements and recreation spaces to auditoriums and city halls—to charitable events, then make those events known to the public.

Help charities work better together.

Isolation is the enemy of social progress. Your community will function better when charitable organizations coordinate their efforts, just as it will when government branches coordinate theirs. Use your community leadership to help charities punch collaboratively by pooling their resources, sharing their expertise, uniting their fundraising efforts, and celebrating their joint successes. Avoid overlap of government and charitable programming through routine communication and collaboration between offices in both the public and non-profit sectors.

. . . as a nation

Demand integrity

Because charities rely on voluntary donations from members of the public, their reputations must be spotless. Hold the directors and staff of non-profit agencies to the same high standards as professional societies or doctors, lawyers, and engineers. Insist on full transparency in accounting, and monitor activity to confirm competency in operations and programming. At the same time, do not allow any public official to subvert the established protocols for funding or contracting of government support of charitable organizations.

Respect the independence of non-profit organizations.

With almost half the annual budgets of Canadian charities coming from government grants, it is tempting but perilous for elected officials and public servants to tell service organizations how to do their jobs. Government funders should greenlight only those proposals they deem fit and then leave charities alone. Those organizations need the liberty to do their best work on their own terms.

Refuse to politicize success.

While it is fitting and helpful for those in public office to celebrate the contribution of the public good made by non-profits, it is risky for those officials to associate themselves overtly with that success. There is a line that cannot be crossed, so let sound judgment prevail and resist the temptation to grandstand even when a charity has performed beyond all expectations.

4

Donate your talent.

The best way to find yourself is to
lose yourself in the service of others.

MOHANDAS KARAMCHAND GANDHI, 1932

If you fetch up in the heart of almost any bustling Italian city late at
night, you may happen upon a winged angel garbed in white. If you
look distressed, confused, or even downcast, that feathered apparition
might drift over to you, ask what language you speak, and then inquire
in your language how she might help you. She could direct you to a
landmark, hail you a cab, find you a police officer, drive you to a hospital, or just slip you a cigarette, train fare, or money for a meal. Your
wish is her command. As you converse, that ministering angel will
likely be joined by others of her species, some winged, some wingless,
yet all equally interested in your welfare. These ethereal creatures have
three things in common: they were all born outside Italy, they all dress
in white, and they are all volunteers.

These urban angels are in fact Romanian immigrants to Italy. As
volunteers they are eager to show you and everyone in Italy that
Romanian newcomers are grateful, kindhearted, and active contributors to Italian society. Theirs is a lofty goal, for not all Italians think

kindly of Romanians, who have been part of the fastest, largest, most controversial influx of immigrants to Italy since the Vandals sacked Rome in 455 CE. In the past twenty years, migrating Romanians have favoured Italy over all other nations as their new home, growing as an immigrant population from fewer than seventy-five thousand in 1999 to well over a million in 2020. About 10 per cent of these are known as zingari, a pejorative term for the Roma[1] people, about whom a majority of Italians hold unfavourable views. So the volunteer work of the angels has a pressing goal—to make Italian nationals more appreciative and therefore welcoming to the Roma and Romanian people alike. That goal is dauntingly ambitious. The mountain they have to climb to overcome prejudice is steep and high. So how do these angels find the energy and willpower to keep going?

Whenever I wrestle with this question, I take heart in the insights of David Brooks, author and *New York Times* columnist, expressed in his latest book, *The Second Mountain*. In Brooks's view, contemporary Western society urges each of us to indulge our self-interest, pouring all our sweat into the great business of achieving our professional ambitions. Unbridled individualism is his so-called first mountain, an ascending series of career wins, external recognition, professional promotion, and amassing of personal wealth that together lure us ever upward. Yet as enticing as such achievements may be, their promise is hollow. Those who devote themselves to conquering the summit of that first mountain must sacrifice their precious time, relationships, and often their health to succeed. Then at the top, where they imagined they would plant flags of triumphant self-satisfaction, they find themselves strangely unfulfilled. The solution, Brooks tells us, lies in setting one's sights on a second mountain. Easily visible as one is climbing the first, this second mountain is built of awareness of and devotion to family and community, kindness and caring, social responsibility and sharing. That second mountain should be tackled with the same energy as the first.

Ultimately, it is a mountain scaled only by helping others in response to one's empathetic appreciation of the needs, concerns, joys, and ambitions of everyone in one's neighbourhood, city, nation, and world. While labouring on the first mountain is critical, deciding to look across the valley and then climb this second mountain too is the true path to enlightenment and fulfillment, for it is the move from self-satisfaction to joy. It is the path of empathy along which one freely gives one's time, talent, and treasure with no expectation of personal gain. It is the path of the volunteer. In my opinion, all volunteers are angels, whether or not they sport wings.

It's in our Canadian blood.

As a child I came to understand the value of such intervention as a receiver myself of many small kindnesses. Two indelible incidents stand out. They occurred some seventy years ago. At age seven, I was excited one weeknight to be driven by my father to the parish hall of our church where I was to join the Cub Scouts. Being a Cub was the coolest thing I could possibly do at my age and in my town, so, given that one had to be eight to join, I went in fully prepared to lie about my age. I had high expectations of endless adventure in the wild and was chomping at the bit to learn everything I could about camping, boating, and crafts of all kinds. Best part? When I proved myself in any of these areas, I would get to wear a badge.

My father dropped me off, promising to pick me up at the time scheduled for the event to be finished. I can't remember anything about that first meeting save that, when it ended, my father was nowhere to be found. As other boys exited the hall one by one, I began to worry, then panic. Darkness was falling, and I didn't know my way home. The hall had almost emptied out when, sensing my anxiety, a fellow Cub slid over and asked about my dilemma. He was just two years older than me, but at my age the interest of a nine-year-old was as good as that of any adult. He told me not to worry—that he would stay with me and that we would both get home safely. He calmly waited, and we just got to know each other. My father pulled in about half an hour later, and my new friend just skipped away saying, "See you next week." That was my first insight into the true object of the scouting movement: readying kids to help others through preparedness and good deeds. In his selflessness and gentle confidence, a nine-year-old had taught me that simply offering to wait with someone qualified as empathy in action. His contribution was the precious gift of presence.

Small gestures speak volumes. I was an avid hockey player as a youngster, as were all my friends. We played with second-hand equipment, of course, and there was no stigma in leaping over the boards wearing someone's older brother's best friend's discarded skates, gloves, pads, and a well-worn stick. Knowing that new equipment would never be in my family's reach, I contented myself with wearing what I could scrounge and over time gained the power and agility to be quite an asset to my team despite the state of my gear. The winter I turned fourteen, word went out that a scout from the Toronto Maple Leafs was coming to town. Rumours circulated that he might even be attending our team's upcoming playoff game. Dan Taylor, a local sporting-goods storeowner caught wind of that rumour, phoned me, and asked me to come to his store before game time. When I arrived, Mr. Taylor handed me a new pair of skates in my size. There was no fuss or fanfare. He simply handed me a shiny black pair of CCM Specials, wished me luck, and disappeared.

I felt like Hans Brinker. Those new skates gave energy and jump to my stride, power to my legs. More important, that retailer's kind gesture filled my heart and lifted my spirit. Wanting to reward the man's kindness with my best performance, that evening I played with the ferocious determination of an NHL player (in my humble opinion). I scored three goals that night. Give the skates all the credit. It seemed as if they had flown over the ice without ever touching down. The next day, I resolved to be as generous to others as he had been to me.

Ten years later, I moved my appreciation into action in a deliberate choice to donate blood. I was seventeen. Back then, blood-donor clinics were routinely staged all across Canada in larger workplaces such as government buildings, military armouries, and manufacturing plants. Working during the summers at Algoma Steel in Sault Ste. Marie, I soon learned how enthusiastic the labour union could be in support of all community activities. Each month, as the day for our on-site blood-donor clinic approached, shop stewards in each department would race around whipping up our competitive spirit, urging us to trounce some other department's record in numbers of donations. We were keen, and not just because we wanted to snag the trophy (which we most certainly did). Blood donation seemed to be a quintessentially Canadian thing. Blood transfusion as a viable, portable service had been innovated by the legendary trauma surgeon from Montreal, Henry Norman Bethune,[2] in the course of the Spanish Civil War. A decade later, during the Second World War, the Canadian Red Cross had led the effort to collect and bank civilian blood, sending it for the care of wounded soldiers, sailors, and aviators in Europe. At war's end, that campaign continued; within a decade Canada could boast a national blood bank serving every hospital and clinic in the country. It was an outstanding example of brilliant organization and cutting-edge medical technology, all propelled by ambitious volunteer programming. Just as in the war, donors in my day were given lapel pins bearing distinctive deep-red drops of blood to show they had each given their pint. We all felt proud wearing those pins on blood-clinic day, as proud I thought as the Irish with their shamrocks on Saint Paddy's Day, Catholics and others with their smudges on Ash Wednesday, and everyone with their poppies on Remembrance Day. We were all doing our bit, comforted by the knowledge that as citizens we would get all the blood we needed in any subsequent medical emergency, and at no charge. As Dr. William Stuart, the colourful national commissioner of the Canadian Red Cross, loudly insisted at every opportunity, in Canada there would be no price tag on blood, meaning that no Canadian would ever bleed out for want of funds.

When I left for Harvard a couple of years later, I fully intended to continue giving blood, but soon learned that the system is different stateside. There were no blood-donor clinics at Harvard, not even in Cambridge proper. Determined to keep up my habit, I had to hike into a particularly seedy corner of Boston that, I was told, was the spot where the local blood-collection service operated. When I walked into that clinic, I was taken aback. Far from the festive mood of the clinics I was used to, I was now in a dismal little waiting room in the company of a group of homeless men whose reduced circumstances forced them to sell their own blood for cash. Cash? That was the first I'd heard of such a thing. We were selling our blood to a system that would then sell it for a profit to patients who needed it, but only, I guessed, if they had insurance or enough cash to afford it. Whereas in the Soo I'd been proud and eager to give away my blood in the company of my caring friends, in Boston I was just another guy pocketing money for parting with something my own body had automatically produced. The experience was gloomy and unpleasant, not because I was in the company of unfortunates who needed the money, but because the commercialization of human blood fell a mile wide of my own values.[4] I wanted to volunteer, to donate my blood as the gift of life that as Canadians we know it to be.

I once shared this story with Edgar Shantz, a Mennonite neighbour and dear and indispensable friend of ours at our farm in Waterloo. Edgar countered with his own tale of the value of our Canadian reliance on volunteer blood donation. As a Mennonite, Edgar valued the old ways. He shunned modern conveniences such as electricity to the home and automobiles, preferring wood fires for cooking and horse-and-buggy rigs for transport. We hugely enjoyed and admired his family and their community, particularly for their Christian pacifism, a dedication to peaceful ways that made perfect sense to us. Living a simple life, Edgar's family seldom went to local doctors or hospitals, and they did not ordinarily donate blood. But when their son fell gravely ill, he soon found himself in The Hospital for Sick Children in Toronto, in part because he required transfusion of substantial quantities of blood just to stay alive. He got that blood, and at no charge of course. In gratitude, Edgar began giving blood himself. Some years later, a routine check of his donated sample revealed a low hemoglobin count indicating anemia. He was advised to see a doctor. Further blood work soon uncovered colon cancer in its early stages. He was treated and over time recovered fully. From then on, he told the story widely, ending with the declaration, "Donating blood saved my life." What goes around comes around indeed.

In 1979, while back in Bethune's stomping ground of Montreal where I had been principal and vice-chancellor of McGill University, I was delighted to learn that there was a regular blood donation clinic open for several days each quarter. So on the appointed day I walked over to the student-centre clinic "for a pint." As I waltzed in, I was approached by a reporter from the *McGill Daily*, our popular student newspaper founded in 1911. On hand to do a piece on the clinic for the next edition, he asked if he could take a picture of me in the act. I declined, advising him instead to choose a student for the shot. "That would be more appropriate," I said without thinking. Then I reconsidered. Who knows, my own appearance might inspire other members of the faculty or students to join in. The next after-noon, my assistant dropped a copy of the paper on my desk. Smack on the front page was a photo of me flat on a cot looking ghastly grey with a needle in my arm. Above it, a 24-point headline announced, "See! You Can Get Blood From A Stone." My first thought was that if that is the worst that the students can say about their principal, we're bound to be all right together.

Voluntary blood donation is a singular index of empathy and a measure of social solidarity in Canada. I felt that when I began giving at seventeen, which I did regularly until I turned sixty-five, the donor's upper age limit at the time. All in all, they took more than one hundred pints out of my arm, and I'm honoured to have been able to give

Highway of Heroes

When philanthropy and volunteerism intersect, miracles happen. A stirring example can be found along the stretch of Highway 401 between the Canadian Forces base in Trenton, Ontario, and the coroner's office at the Centre for Forensic Sciences in Toronto. This is the roadway along which the bodies of fallen Canadian soldiers, sailors, and aviators are carried when repatriated from overseas.[3] In 2002, Ron Flindall of Cobourg, Ontario, first rallied a group of volunteers to show their respect by standing motionless on an overpass of that roadway as the fallen passed beneath. The practice of honouring the brave in this way appealed to thousands, and soon each grim convoy was met by large groups of grateful citizens standing in silent vigil on all the overpasses along the route. Covering the story, *Toronto Sun* columnist Joe Warmington used the term "highway of heroes phenomena" to describe that remarkable outpouring of public gratitude. Soon after, 20,000 people signed a petition to rename the road, and in 2007 the route was formally dubbed Highway of Heroes. That gave three of Canada's greenest thumbs an idea. Tony Di Giovanni (executive director of Landscape Ontario), Mark Cullen (gardener, author, and broadcaster), and Michael de Pencier (creator of Toronto's Green Living Show and founder of *Toronto Life* magazine) then proposed that 117,000 trees be planted by volunteers along the roadway, one tree for every Canadian who has in this simple and critically important way. It's who we are, what we believe to be kind, and what we all do to make sure everyone in need can access the same blood services that we do. Just as in the matter of charity, our volunteerism is a matter of fairness.

fallen in action since Confederation. Mark formed a volunteer board to propel the project and in 2018 asked Sharon and me to serve as patrons, a role to which we enthusiastically agreed. Board volunteers then urged other Canadians to come forward to plant the trees. The response was overwhelming. Thousands of volunteers signed on, many of whom were serving Canadian military personnel. At the same time, the board appealed to philanthropists to donate the funds required to buy the trees. More than 4,500 Canadians donated more than half the required $10 million, which in turn inspired federal, provincial, and municipal governments to pledge the rest. With the enthusiastic support of member of Parliament and minister of veterans' affairs Seamus O'Regan, public planting events became ceremonies of their own, attracting wide media coverage and producing even greater interest. A schedule was then determined that set Remembrance Day, November 11, 2022, as the date the final tree would be planted in a public ceremony. And it didn't stop there. The project further inspired a national movement to plant 2 billion trees across Canada as part of a citizen-led effort to help reduce 78 megatons of carbon emissions by 2030, supporting the nation's plan to reach a carbon target of net-zero by 2050. In this way, volunteers and philanthropists proved that one simple idea can inspire an entire nation to action with deep meaning and practical benefit. Sharon and I are honoured to continue as patrons in the next phase of Tony, Mark, and Michael's marvellous project.

How much do we volunteer?

All of us remember the first time we volunteered and why. Lately, I've wanted to find out if young people these days see their role as volunteers differently than the generations before them. From official records kept by Statistics Canada, we know that the degree to which Canadians give their time for free to others is so huge that most people don't immediately believe the facts when they hear them. Here they are: in addition to their donations to charity, about 44 per cent of Canadians give an average of 154 hours of volunteer activity each year, and year after year that figure consistently edges upward. This is a massive contribution; however, much like the work of parents in the home (mostly mothers, of course), volunteer work is not officially tallied for its economic value. If it were, it would have added more than $50 billion to Canada's economic activity each year from 2010 to 2020. That means that Canadian volunteers are chipping in services equivalent to 6.5 per cent of all paid employment in the country, which is as much as does the entire education sector.

We volunteer for a variety of reasons, most often to help address social issues and needs in our own communities with necessary improvements. We also give our time freely knowing that we can build skills and knowledge that make us better able to do our paying jobs. When we're starting out, many of us volunteer to build our resumés and expand our networks. Whatever our reasons, when we volunteer we're all developing ourselves professionally and socially while making a valuable contribution to economic activity in Canada. I've learned that if you wish to judge the overall health of a community, look to changes over time in its ratio of volunteers to total citizens. If that ratio is going up, it's a healthy community. If it's not, it's not.

Kids These Days

Under the auspices of the Rideau Hall Foundation, in 2021 we launched a study to learn how many young people give their time in volunteer activity. Specifically, we wanted to examine their understanding of the intersection between community life and personal responsibility, probing both the reasons they volunteer when they do and the reasons they don't when they don't. The biggest eye-opener for me, although it makes perfect sense on reflection, is that today's young people think of community not in terms of location but rather connection. Given how Internet savvy they are, how often they text, and how fast their thumbs move compared to my own, they are busy demolishing geographic boundaries everywhere. Little surprise that 79 per cent of those 16- to 24-year-olds surveyed declared that the people they meet online are as much part of their community as are those they meet physically, with many of whom they communicate online anyway. It's a bit like their tendency to give quickly and meaningfully to online fundraising campaigns; they feel just as connected with their neighbours online as they do with their neighbours on the street.

I was heartened to read that 84 per cent of young people say they can think of at least one community to which they belong (although I immediately worry about the 16 per cent who declare they can't make that claim). The most impressive statistic we gathered was that 86 per cent of youth believe it is important to give back to the community to which they belong. How have they managed to do that during the pandemic? For sure, the pandemic has had an impact on the communities of young people in Canada, for better and for worse. Just over 27 per cent said they've found it easier to connect with their community, with the pandemic being a spark to solidify and strengthen relationships of those around them. That sounds encouraging, but these respondents are the exception. At least 55 per cent of young people in Canada say it's been more difficult to connect with their community since the start of the pandemic, so, clearly, those who volunteer have had to overcome considerable obstacles.

When we asked specifically why they volunteer when they do, 40 per cent said they make the effort because it gets them involved with a cause about which they are passionate. And 42 per cent said it gives them the opportunity to make decisions with a real impact. I love that.

Just as intriguing are the reasons that some young people do not volunteer. Fewer than a third of those say it has to do in part with their families not being supportive, half say they're busy with other activities, and three-quarters cite schoolwork as the priority. But here's the kicker: 67 per cent say that they do not volunteer because the cost of volunteering is prohibitive. They're not referring to needing pay; it's rather that they simply can't afford things such as transportation, background checks, suitable clothing, Internet access, and food they might need when they're out doing their volunteer work. What would convince them to volunteer? No mystery. Ninety-one per cent say they would happily do so if their out-of-pocket costs were covered. That floors me. Think of the rich resources of talent and energy waiting to be harnessed for a pittance. Other motivators cited were the possibility of training, the opportunity to work in groups, and the offer of some kind of stipend, really just an honorarium to cover out-of-pocket costs. It doesn't seem like much to ask, and I suspect that most groups that depend on volunteers aren't aware that such small amounts are insurmountable barriers to entry for talented young people. Everyone at the Rideau Hall Foundation is now working hard to make sure that the awareness gap is closed.

Volunteering in Canada

This compact overview comes from arrivein.ca (a play on Arrive In Canada), an online resource designed to help immigrants to Canada find meaningful ways to give back. Because I find the information as valid for those of us born in Canada as those who choose to come here, I include it here.

What is volunteering?

Volunteering is the time you give to strengthen your community and improve others' quality of life as well as your own. There are so many ways to be involved in the community that:

- Speak to your passion
- Suit your personality
- Meet your interests
- Build on your experiences
- Fit into your lifestyle
- Contribute to your health and well-being

How can volunteering fit into my lifestyle?

You may be at a point in your life when you do not want to take on any more responsibility or you may be in a position to take charge. There is a wide spectrum of volunteer opportunities available to suit a range of interests and circumstances. You can volunteer:

- From home
- In an office
- In a garden
- Overseas
- With family and friends
- On your own
- Just in the summer

- Once a year
- Every day
- Now or later
- Short-term, longer-term, ongoing, or occasionally

And you can combine volunteering with other things that are important in your life such as:

- Time with family (volunteer with your family or in your grandchildren's school)
- Travelling (join an international development project overseas)
- Spending time with friends (get a group together to plan a special event)
- Hobbies (teach puppet-making in a community centre)
- Recreation (be a swimming buddy for someone with a disability)

What kind of volunteering can I do?
The possibilities are endless.

Leadership
- Facilitate a strategic planning session
- Serve on a board or committee
- Chair a fundraising campaign
- Help start a tenants' rights association

Management and administration
- Review a human resources manual
- Organize a volunteer schedule for an event
- Enter data at a resource centre
- Provide general office help

Technology and social media
- Design a website for an elder-care co-op

- Write a blog on affordable housing
- Customize a donor database for a food bank
- Teach computer skills in a community centre

Building and handicrafts
- Build a book shelf for a reading room
- Sew costumes for a play
- Teach card-making in a rehabilitation centre
- Build a stage for marathon ceremonies
- Volunteer with Habitat for Humanity

Nature and environment
- Walk a dog for a local animal shelter
- Research pesticide bylaws in different cities
- Plant vegetables in a community garden
- Help build out the Trans Canada Trail

One-to-one support
- Tutor children
- Comfort a victim of violence
- Be a mentor to a teen
- Coach an executive director

Direct service
- Answer the phones for a helpline
- Prepare lunch in a soup kitchen
- Coach a team
- Drive people to medical appointments

Entertainment
- Play piano for a sing-a-long at a retirement residence
- MC at a volunteer service awards night
- Do a stand-up comedy act at a fundraiser
- Join a choir that entertains at community events

Heavy Medals

Although Canada is a wealthy country with generous social programs, millions of Canadians rely on critical services provided by selfless volunteers. As one of the central duties of every governor general of Canada is to encourage excellence in all corners of the country, it was fitting that in 1996 Governor General Roméo LeBlanc instituted the Caring Canadian Award. The intent was to honour volunteers who have made a significant and continual contribution to their communities, making a difference in fields such as the arts, organized sports, youth and community organizations, and on social issues. The hope was that by saluting our unsung heroes, we could encourage others to become such heroes themselves.

Each year the activities of dozens of notable volunteers were celebrated through the program. While the award was both welcome and inspiring, its continuation depended on budget stability, which didn't materialize every year. In fact, when I arrived at Rideau Hall it had been discontinued due to budget cuts. To solve the problem, one of the first priorities when we set up the Rideau Hall Foundation was to raise an endowment fund to bulletproof this excellent honours program. Once we had ensured that it could be permanent, we set out to expand the initiative, increasing the annual number of recipients into the hundreds. Whenever we travelled across the country, we included in our official agenda a ceremony to present the Caring Canadian Award to worthy recipients. For Sharon and me, these were deeply touching experiences, and we were humbled to meet such a broad range of selfless heroes dedicated to helping their communities in endlessly creative ways. We really did come away from each event astounded at the sheer goodness of Canada. After several years, we saw the merit of giving the award even greater gravitas by seeking royal patronage. We asked Her Majesty Queen Elizabeth if she would allow us to name the award the Queen's Medal for Volunteers in her honour. With her usual insight, Her Majesty suggested instead that we title the honour the Sovereign's Medal for Volunteers, no doubt to ensure the award's continuance through the reigns of her successors.

In 2015, the Sovereign's Medal for Volunteers became the highest honour for volunteer service any individual can receive within the Canadian honours system, presented at a wide variety of ceremonies at Rideau Hall and across Canada to those who have demonstrated passion, dedication, and commitment to their communities through significant, sustained, and unpaid voluntary contributions. By 2017, about a thousand of these medals were awarded across the country each year. High time.

Empathetic things to do when you intend to Donate your talent.

. . . as an individual

Climb the second mountain.
Even as you advance your work career, remember that true fulfillment will come only when you have augmented your professional development with community service. Finding ways to share your talents at no charge with those in need will shape both your world view and your professional reputation. Your participation and, ultimately, leadership in volunteer work will also give you powerful insights into the remarkable changes you can bring about when you enlist the will and energy of kindhearted members of the community. They will join you in your mission.

Find your cause.
The most satisfying way to volunteer is to join a team contributing to a cause in which you already fervently believe. With more than 300,000 expert organizations in Canada already tackling a vast variety of concerns, and with a helpful range of online resources to guide your decision, it won't take you long to find a group to which you can donate your time and talent. The following Internet resources will help, and there are more appearing every month.

Volunteer.ca
Smartgiving.ca
Charityvillage.com

While at first glance some of these may seem like tools for donors only, they all offer resources that will walk you through key factors to consider before you get involved as a volunteer and then help you find the cause the appeals to you most.

Be dependable.

No matter how small your contribution of time and talent, it will be more deeply appreciated if it can be relied upon. Find a small, useful thing you can do as a volunteer and commit to it on a regular basis. It might be donating blood once a quarter, staffing a welcome desk at a hospital on Saturday mornings, collecting for diabetes research every September, writing thank-you letters for a food bank every other week, or playing music at a seniors' residence on statutory holidays. With even a modest routine, your contribution will become a vital part of the work an agency does to bring useful services to a vulnerable population.

. . . as a community

Remove the barriers.

There is a powerful army of would-be volunteers ready to go to work in your community, but who cannot because of small, easily fixable impediments. Community leaders must rally coordinated support and funding to give volunteers the training and guidance they need and then ensure that these volunteers don't have to dip into their own pockets for bus fare, uniforms, background-check fees, coffee, stamps, stationery, and the like as they work for free. Having an almost limitless supply of young, energetic volunteers will quickly overcome the modest expense of providing what they need to be able to contribute.

Give volunteers real power.

Never give someone responsibility without also giving them the authority to make decisions. Volunteers are as smart, logical, judicious, and trustworthy as any paid employees, but they too need authority to act in the service of your mission. The satisfaction of making an impact is all they ask. Do not deny it.

Honour traditions.

Canada has flourished precisely because it welcomes diverse opinions, approaches, traditions, beliefs, habits, and preferences. Allow and encourage volunteers to act in ways faithful to their own ideals, values, and priorities. Find ways to create a consistent culture of professional expertise among your volunteers without restricting the diversity of their approaches. That very variety will more authentically reflect the complexity of the population you are trying to serve together.

. . . as a nation

Celebrate noisily.

Sound your trumpets. Light fires on the Internet. Let the world know how much Canada values its volunteers in energetic programs of recognition for their efforts. In particular, take advantage of formal programs by nominating volunteers for honours such as the Sovereign's Medal for Volunteers and the Order of Canada.

Harness the savvy of youth.

A seventeen-year-old with an Internet connection can often accomplish more in five minutes than an office-bound boomer can in an hour. Young people are eager to be involved as volunteers, and their expertise often shines in managing relationships online. Agencies and charities wishing to use volunteers effectively must work creatively to ensure that any service that can be effectively delivered online is redesigned so that can happen.

Reinforce the culture of caring.

While self-righteousness and intolerance are getting more airtime in our age than in previous years, humans are inherently disposed to cooperation and generosity. Thus provincial and national governments have the opportunity and duty to promote the benefits of caring while stressing the reality of interdependence among all citizens. As we now face the toughest challenges of our era, all of us must be frequently reminded to exercise our openness to new ideas, creativity, genuine empathy for each other, and caring stewardship of the world's resources.

5

Build a team.

George Lucas learned early in his career that life is a team sport. He had established a reputation in the more technical aspects of film, first as a camera operator and then as an editor, and he knew that blockbuster films owed most of their success to the teamwork of hundreds of professionals working together to high standards and brutal deadlines. Yet despite his training and experience, he yearned to break out of the technical department and be a writer-director. That twin role was discouraged in Hollywood, where expertise in specialized aspects of production was the norm; many spent entire careers in rarified functions such as focus puller and dolly operator. But Lucas had seen what could be achieved when filmmakers were fully in charge of their own creations, able to craft original stories with the liberating mix of freedom and control that only writer-directors enjoy. His ambitions had been fed by digesting the work of a long list of innovators at the National Film Board of Canada, with rebel Norman McLaren at the top. In categories as disparate as animation, comedy, drama, and documentary, these Canadians had repeatedly proved to Lucas that to be brilliant and authentic, one had to write and then direct a story oneself. He determined to do precisely that.

In 1973, Lucas released *American Graffiti*, a coming-of-age comedy about the cruising culture of early 1960s California. Based on his own teenage years, and told with humorous nostalgia, the film struck a

chord; made for less than $800,000, *American Graffiti* took in more than
$200 million at the box office and earned Academy Award nominations
for Lucas in both writing and directing. It also launched the careers of
aspiring young actors, including Harrison Ford, Richard Dreyfuss, and
Suzanne Somers. As writer and director of that film, Lucas had become,
as they say, a bankable quantity, with the freedom and control to make
stories about aspects of life that mattered most to him.

When he began crafting the galactic saga he dubbed Star Wars, his
instinct was to create a story that would speak broadly to audiences as
compellingly as any story could. Here he had an advantage, for Lucas
carried deep memories of the Greek and Roman myths he had heard
as a child, the Bible stories that had inspired him during services in
the Methodist Church, and the tales of ordinary humans, visionary
prophets, and capricious deities he had lapped up in university. His
suspicion that these tales had universal meaning found affirmation in
the writings of mythologist Joseph Campbell, a professor of literature
and religion at Sarah Lawrence College with a focus on comparative
mythology. Lucas was drawn to Campbell's work, becoming an enthusiastic disciple of the academic's teachings.[1] He knew that Campbell,
after decades of analysis, had concluded that all myths are closely
related and function identically. They help people to have their own
hero's journey, find their individuality, find their place in the world,
and remind them that they're part of a whole, and that they must also
be part of the community, thinking of the welfare of the community
above the welfare of themselves.

Yuval Noah Harari tells us in *Sapiens* that myths began evolving as
a human creation about seventy thousand years ago, concurrent with
the early migrations of our species to new homelands. Shared myths
gave us a way to sustain kinship among like-minded people even
when they could no longer be together in the same tribal community.
They felt connection and trust with others who told and believed the
stories they themselves told and believed.[2] Campbell's fascination

with myths as a kind of social glue led him to study the broad range of these tales as they appear in the oral and written traditions of all cultures and periods of history.

In his 1949 book *The Hero with a Thousand Faces*, Campbell shared his discovery that there really is only one common story, one that all humans tell each other repeatedly, no matter their race, creed, nation, or epoch, a story so authentic to the human experience and so dependably appealing, engaging, relevant, and instructive that, whenever anyone hears it, they fall silent, pay attention, and allow themselves to enter wholeheartedly into the narrative, letting their intellects, imaginations, and emotions run free. Campbell dubbed that story the monomyth, a fictional framework so common you'll find it in books, movies, television shows, poems, dance performances, sculptures, biographies, business-school case studies, self-help books, nursery rhymes, photographs, paintings, and on and on. Here it is as Joseph Campbell laid it out, and you might think of George Lucas and his fictional creation Luke Skywalker as you read. You might also think of your own life's journey, which is probably a lot like this.

The story is about an unlikely hero—be it man, woman, god, or beast—whom we first encounter in that character's familiar, ordinary, and comfortable world. Almost immediately, something unexpected happens that tempts our hero to leave that comfortable world on an adventure into the unknown. The invitation to begin a quest can come from anywhere, often styled as a series of dramatic events to which our character feels compelled to respond. All kinds of circumstances, events, and people then conspire to dissuade our would-be adventurer from setting out. All advice says, "Don't do it." The risks are too high and success all but impossible. Then a wise, usually older, mentor enters the scene and over time gives our hero the knowledge and tools necessary to survive the perils of the journey. This is when the real action begins. Our hero heads off to a strange world in which the landscape, inhabitants, customs, and rules are unfamiliar and confusing. Even though disoriented, and despite the dangers, our hero must press on. As the journey unfolds, a supreme threat looms in the form of an unseen foe who appears to control this world and who now senses the intrusion of our hero. Clearly, things are about to get ugly. The hero cannot succeed against this force without support and is therefore compelled to recruit a group of like-minded allies to join the mission. In a series of lesser trials, these allies share their knowledge, talents, and perspectives, in time making their team strong and agile. But wait; within that team are undeclared rivals who stand to benefit if the hero fails. Over time, these rivals are flushed out and dealt with, and the band gets down to business. Led by our nervous but now resolute hero, the allies learn how to overcome their many individual weaknesses, rehearsing their performance until ready at last to face the ultimate enemy, who now threatens them all equally. A final confrontation takes place in the very lair of that enemy, a kind of inner cave in which the hero must battle the foe with life itself in the balance. During the struggle, the hero is forced to learn something fundamental about his or her own identity. Ironically, even as the enemy is vanquished, we see that foe and hero have much in common. They have not been confronting each other as much as they have their own inner selves. Both emerge with deep new insight, even if the foe's acknowledgement of the truth comes only moments before death. Once the battle has ended, our hero may at last return to the ordinary world, armed now with new powers of knowledge and wisdom. As the story closes, we know that our hero has undergone deep personal growth, and the world will be better for it. End of story.

So there we have *Star Wars*, a deliberate and faithful imitation of the Hero's Journey that immediately captivated the imagination of people around the world.[3] There too we have *Oliver Twist* and *The Lion King* and David and Goliath and the *Ramayana* and Noah's Ark and *Old Yeller* and *Exodus* and *Romeo and Juliet* and *Tess of the D'Urbervilles* and *Don Quixote* and Jesus in the Desert and Knights of the Round Table and *Aida* and *Tosca* and *Carmen* and *The Upanishads* and *The Odyssey* and *Who Has Seen the Wind* and *Madame Bovary* and the *Bhagavad Gita* and the Garden of Eden and Izanagi and Izanami and *Frankenstein*.

Stories Matter

The Hero's Journey is really the story of each of our lives. We come into the world naked, fragile, and vulnerable. In our infancy and childhood, we learn to make our way in the ordinary world. If we're fortunate, we're protected in our family and community long enough to begin learning who we are, what we care about, and what we might do with our lives. Then in adolescence, things from outside our comfortable world begin to call to us. We sense there is something more out there—adventure, romance, and fortune on one hand and danger, even death, on the other. The choice is ours: we can stay safe at home or head out into uncertainty. In time, the call of adventure becomes irresistible, and we begin the perilous, rewarding journey of discovery out in the strange new worlds of work, art, study, travel, business, politics, warfare, or wherever. In these new worlds, all the rules are different. We're excited, but we don't really know what we're doing. We try a few things that work, a few that don't. We bumble, we stumble, and before long we acknowledge that we can't go it alone. Who can we trust to help us? Which person, team, company, agency, community? We think that through and, eventually, we form alliances. These may be romantic, political, entrepreneurial, or creative, yet no matter the nature of our affiliations, all of us yearn for the same outcome. We want to become more whole, more authentic, more mature, more ourselves. That's what all humans wish no matter how grumpy or despairing we may appear to be on any given day. In time we learn that we will have to confront our enemies and, as the Hero's Journey repeatedly reminds us, we will ultimately face off with no one but ourselves. Those of us who manage to survive emerge more confident, calm, and compassionate. Maturity is the gift we bring back to the ordinary world, and in self-knowledge we find wisdom, peace, redemption, and even joy. That's what all our journeying is for.

Because we all aspire to wholeness, even if our ambitions are dampened at times by circumstance and choice, we find constant fascination in the stories of others, whose exploits populate our journals and airwaves, arts, entertainment, and education. Fiction helps us work out our own stuff, but even fiction has an ally in this adventure. Deep in my own experience and dear to my heart, there is another field in which we can explore the endless variations of our Hero's Journey in ways that force us to learn more about ourselves. That field is sports.

Sport: The Other Hero's Journey

Reading Campbell's monomyth now, I can see how the chapters of my own life track with the stages of the classic, mythic human journey. In my case, many of my formative moments came about either in pursuit of sport or as a result of it. I've already mentioned my early days of hockey and my fleeting brush with fame when a Junior A scout sat in my living room for a nanosecond. That was my first hint of an invitation to leave my ordinary world and head to an extraordinary world whose rules I knew nothing of, yet by which I was wildly excited.

Almost everyone my age had the same dream, a hockey-kid phenomenon that our brilliant Canadian folksinger Stan Rogers captured so perfectly in his song "Flying" in 1984.[4] In the reality that Stan had tapped into, all the kids in my town played hockey. In our case, that made sense; Sault Ste. Marie was one of the oldest French settlements in North America, positioned strategically at the crossroads of a fur-trading route that moved pelts from the wilderness above Lake Superior downstream to Montreal, the very birthplace of hockey. Our founders knew hockey as well as they knew lacrosse.

Until the war of 1812, there had been just one Sault Ste. Marie, but a post-war pact in 1817 drove a new U.S.–Canada border right up the Saint Mary's River, splitting the town between two nations. Yet in 1954, the summer I turned thirteen, the border was still fluid—a great advantage to us. My friends and I would whiz east down Queen Street on our bikes, park at the Queen Elizabeth Baseball Field, and spend the last two weeks of the summer at Marty Pavelich's baseball camp. Born and raised in the Soo, Marty was a left winger with the Detroit Red Wings, for whom he would play more than six hundred games in a brilliant career. Like so many elite athletes, however, he excelled at many different sports. Each year, before the Red Wings arrived on the Michigan side for their late-summer training camp, Marty ran a baseball training camp for the kids of his own hometown. The last day of our camp was also registration day for the Red Wings, so Marty would register early, then head back across the bridge to us for our final day of training, bringing with him Mr. Hockey himself, Gordie Howe. He was the finest player of his time, but as he proved to us on a dusty field near home, with ball and bat and glove in hand, he could easily have been a professional baseball all-star. Howe spoke to us of the power of attitude, focus, and drive, inspiring us all to improve our psychological as well as our physical game.

So many mentors. In Joseph Campbell's monomyth is a mentor who comes into one's life at just the right time, giving the hero of the story the necessary tools to survive all upcoming trials. One of my mentors was an angel, both by name and by nature. He was the Soo-born general manager of the Algoma Contractors, the minor hockey team I aspired to and eventually joined, and even though I went on to play on provincial championship teams in hockey, football, and baseball, it was Angelo Bumbacco who prepared me to be a grown-up in the real world of sport. Angelo ran his teams of teenagers like an NHL franchise. Although gentle in speech, he was tough as nails, and we all learned quickly that when Angelo suggested something, it was to be taken seriously. His twin focus on professionalism and obedience was amplified by his equally demanding coach, Abbie Naccarato. Like Angelo, Abbie said little and demanded plenty, and our ragtag group of city kids soon became a smooth-functioning organization that knew how to win games consistently.

We were on fire with ambition and I learned a lot. The lessons I took into my adulthood from those years, however, were not as much about winning as about working in teams. Sault Ste. Marie offered me an early and profound example of how sport can connect people across cultural divides. Our town was a steel town, with Algoma Steel being the principal employer. Many of the employees were Italian steel workers forced to leave their homeland just before or after the Second World War. In the decades following, their energy combined with the vitality of many other immigrant ethnic groupings and helped to mold Sault Ste. Marie into one of the nation's most productive manufacturers of raw materials. As business boomed, other industries such as forestry, energy, and Great Lakes transportation flourished too, which in turn gave rise to professional opportunities in law, medicine, and business management. These newcomers were a key part of our economy and, as I could see, the strength of our sports teams.

Other than me, almost all of the kids on the hockey league team on which I last played at home were children of these immigrants.[5] They were tough, tenacious, smart, and ambitious. Their drive to show Angelo and Abbie how good they were turned the Algoma Contractors into one of the best teams in the province. (Correction: *The* best team in the province. In 1959, we won the seventeen-and-under Ontario provincial hockey championships.) Looking back, we had quite a lineup. My teammates included Lou Nanne, who went on to play, coach, and manage in the NHL; Phil and Tony Esposito were inducted into the Hockey Hall of Fame; and Angelo's team featured future NHL stars Gene Ubriaco and Chico and Wayne Maki.

All of us played other sports as well. The Sault Collegiate Wildcats high school team, which I captained, won the Red Feather Ontario High School Football Championship in 1958 with players with names such as Barich, Bartolo, Bertuzzi, Butkovich, Dazovich, De Laval, DiPietro, Monaco, and Spino aboard. The Soo Van and Storage baseball team (happily called The Movers), on which I played as catcher when we won a provincial championship, had its own ethnic mix again with Lou Nanne, John Sanko, Mike Zuke, and Norm Bolitho. And Ted Nolan from the Garden River Reserve on the Soo's eastern border coached the Sault Junior A team and then became the first Indigenous person to coach in the NHL. So from sport I learned a great lesson: the allies in your life's journey will spring from diverse backgrounds and will surprise and challenge you with their extraordinary talent; be ever on the lookout for such allies as you move forward and look for diversity by insisting on inclusivity. Angelo Bumbacco passed away in 2020, widely remembered and sorely missed by all of us scrappy kids who had learned to reach for the stars, to find our potential, build our self-esteem, and discover our mutual respect under his mentorship. As the years unfolded, we all looked back and gained greater respect for Angelo's teaching. I suspect Angelo broke the Canadian record for the number of occasions on which he served as best man at a wedding or godfather at a baptism. We all thought of him as a member of our family.

Play the team, not the stars.

Harvard did not provide athletic scholarships, so when I arrived at Harvard on an academic scholarship that covered about three-quarters of the cost (wouldn't have happened otherwise), I determined to prove myself both in academics and athletics. I flung myself full-bore into my studies and my play. My habit of going all out earned me the nickname Fullbore; when I was sixteen and seventeen years old, my style of playing football and hockey had earned me three concussions.[6] Our family doctor then advised my mother that I must not go on the ice without a helmet. I resisted, noting that only one NHL player wore a helmet, and only then because he had had a steel plate put in his head after a car accident. My argument changed nothing. I knew I would be laughed at, but logic prevailed; I could play with a helmet and ignore the laughter or not play and not be laughed at. A little chortling was a small price to pay for the rewards of staying in the game, so the helmet went on. When I arrived at Harvard, Ivy League rules required that all players wear helmets and teeth guards, and our coach was strict about it and we had a few concussions. In my four years playing Harvard sports, not one player suffered a concussion nor lost a tooth. The Ivy League was ahead of its time.

Our coach was Ralph "Cooney" Weiland,[7] a long-time Ontario player who had come to fame first as a member of the Boston Bruins Dynamite Line of forwards in 1928, and subsequently as a player and coach taking his teams to several Stanley Cup titles. At Harvard he brought front-line professional experience to university hockey, and he really knew how to get us all going. Cooney schooled us on doing (not merely saying) and to focus on things we could control. He taught us to have no regrets about previous decisions made, to never look back, and, above all, to get on with the task at hand. As with any great mentor (I'm thinking of Yoda now), his wisdom applied to life as a whole and not to any single endeavour on its own. Under Cooney I began to refine skills that would improve my performance in my career and my behaviour in my personal life. Counterintuitively to me as a teenager, much of his counsel was about recognizing and harnessing the strength of a community, rather than depending on oneself. That required enlisting the strengths of others while minimizing the possible impacts of their weaknesses, all with no judgment about the character of the person in question. Success, as Cooney drilled into us, is seldom about individual heroics, and most often about a group's figuring out how to lessen the effect of the mistakes made by its individual members.

That concept was perhaps the most enduring lesson of my life. Authentic achievement will never be due to my isolated talent and effort, but always about our coordinated talents and efforts as we work together as a team. So for leaders, the surest route to success will always be found by making a group of individuals feel and act like a coherent unit on a worthy mission.[8] As Cooney drummed into us all, "We win together; but I fall short when I choose to go it alone." The corollary, of course, is "If I'm not thinking about developing my team as a whole, I am jeopardizing our chances of our success." I understood that thought on an intellectual level but had to learn from a number of monumental mistakes that confirmed its irrefutable truth.

Competitive by nature, I got right down to business at Harvard. A no-nonsense approach made sense to me at the time, and only with hindsight did I understand later that my laser focus was narrow. First, my two roommates and I chose a quieter residence away from the athletic quarter so we could concentrate on our studies. Then I signed up for a Friday-evening gig at the Harvard Library where I could earn seventy-five cents an hour sticking returned books into stacks, which I did so efficiently that I spent most of my shifts studying quietly in a corner. I withdrew from a fraternity[9] and contentedly kept to a restrained social calendar as I was then in a long-distance relationship with Sharon and I followed a strict training regime. I had also taken necessary courses to become a lay reader at the local Episcopal church, so my Sundays were busy there. Not the life of a hermit, but certainly a life unlike those of most of my fellows. Thus there was nothing impeding me from doing my best in everything I did put my mind to. I threw myself into my academics, bent as I was on graduating magna cum laude, and in athletics I was relentless. Besides hockey, I joined in other sports as my tight schedule permitted, the easiest of which to find time for was running. To stay motivated, we often ran in pairs, and one of my partners was Erich Segal, a young tutor of classics. After a canoeing accident, Erich had been advised by a doctor to take up jogging to speed his rehabilitation. He took to running with a vengeance, making the Harvard track team as a long-distance runner. In my last year we often ran together.[10]

While I earnestly believed I was doing everything I should, my achievements were dampened by some sobering disappointments, all of my own making. My tactical isolation from my peers, which seemed so sensible to me at the time, had led my teammates to believe that I was different, leaving perhaps an impression that I was a bit of a hermit. I had alienated some people without knowing it. I had not bothered to make very close friends on my own hockey team. That became crystal clear at the end of the junior season when the team voted for the player they wanted to lead them as team captain the following year. I had been named to the U.S. All American Team that

Canada: Serious About Sport

As Heritage Canada rightly declares on its website, "Canada is proud to be a leading sport nation—both at home and abroad—where all Canadians can enjoy, value, and celebrate the benefits of active participation and excellence in sport. As it should, the Government of Canada, through Sport Canada, is the single largest investor in Canada's amateur sport system.

Through the Athlete Assistance Program, every year $33 million in funding goes directly to approximately 1,900 athletes, giving them financial assistance to pursue world-class results while achieving their academic and career goals.

The Sport Support Program provides about $178.8 million to Canadian sport organizations to strengthen our national sport system and benefit our athletes and coaches.

The Hosting Program provides about $21.6 million annually

year, and I presumed it would be me. Yet I had not been a so-called regular guy on the team, and a majority of my teammates quietly voted for someone else.

Humbled, I became determined to be the best team player I could be, collaborating more actively even as I worked to improve my own game. I did end up setting the Harvard team's career-assist record, and as a defenseman (that's how they spell it) I was selected as a first-team All American in my junior and senior years. Later I was named as one of the top fifty hockey players in the last half-century in the U.S. Eastern Collegiate Athletic Conference and was inducted into the Harvard Athletic Hall of Fame. I had come to the conclusion that playing on a hockey team is as much about forging camaraderie as it is about performing well on the ice.

There would soon be another important lesson about the need to see things differently, one I would learn at Cambridge University. I received

to assist Canadian communities in hosting world-class international sport events and the Canada Games. In addition, funding is provided to support travel costs related to the participation of athletes in the Canada Games.

Each year, about $64 million of the Sport Support Program's total amount is provided as enhanced excellence funding for targeted sports and athletes with medal potential at the Olympic and Paralympic Games, based on recommendations made by Own The Podium, the now-permanent program originally designed to prepare Canadian athletes for the 2010 Olympic Winter Games in Vancouver.

In addition, $5 million of the Sport Support Program's total amount is provided to support the next generation of Olympic and Paralympic athletes who have demonstrated medal potential for the subsequent Olympic or Paralympic Games."

We all play for Canada!

a scholarship by graduating Harvard magna cum laude. But just before leaving Cambridge, Mass., Cooney proposed a tryout with his old team, the Boston Bruins, suggesting I attend a training camp in August 1963 with the prospect of joining the team. This was before the six team NHL expanded to thirty teams and before the player draft was introduced. That appealed but, aiding my decision, Boston was in the proverbial basement at the time, and there was no guarantee that I would ever be put on the ice in an NHL game, especially as I had injured a tendon in my hand and arm that made it difficult to maintain control of my stick. Moreover, I had just spent ten days in hospital recovering from mono-nucleosis, which was brought on by exhaustion. I truly was exhausted. Surviving on only four or five hours of sleep a night, I had been writing an honours thesis, which had to be coupled with a magna cum laude grade just to graduate with the magna honour. My tank was empty. So once again I declined the invitation to make hockey my life and headed instead to Trinity Hall, Cambridge, England, to earn my first law degree. I'm sure Mum approved.

Cambridge had a hockey team, and I was honoured to be named captain of that team going in. I have many happy memories of those days, but the one that has sat heavily in my thoughts since then related to the end-of-season varsity[11] game between our hockey team and the opposing squad from Oxford. To understand my gaffe, you have to know that when university athletes play in a varsity match, they are then permitted to add something to their school wardrobe that signals their achievement to others. In the United States and Canada, this is often a letter (H for Harvard, Y for Yale) worn on a so-called letter-man sweater, while in the United Kingdom it has traditionally been a blazer or scarf of a particular colour (light blue for Cambridge, dark blue for Oxford, et cetera). But there's a snag. You don't get to wear the varsity symbol just because you are on the team during a varsity game; to earn the honour you have to actually play. Waiting patiently on the bench doesn't qualify. At the time I did not know of this distinction, but I should have. As team captain, I was to choose who would go on the ice. The stakes were high, as they always were in contests between our schools, and that day it was up to me to ensure that the right match of players was on the ice at all times. As the game progressed, it was clear that we were out-skated, out-shot, and struggling. I was leery about putting our weakest player on, knowing that keeping our strongest on was our best chance of success. Even at that, we lost by two goals.

Our one benched player was devastated. I sympathized. So was I. He was right; I should have found a way to put him on a line with our four strongest players for a shift or two. Because I hadn't, he would not be authorized to wear the blazer or the scarf. Had I learned nothing from the lesson at Harvard? Unconsciously, I had played to win and not to embrace the talent around me, and by being inflexible I had hurt someone deeply. It was as though the allies in Campbell's monomyth had all showed up to help me in my journey, and yet I had not treated them as allies. I was ashamed. Since then, I have never again forgotten that lesson learned in sport. Take care of those on your team; you are on the journey together, and no one should ever be abandoned.

Let seasoned players build your team.

The world is in crisis. To get us out of the trouble we've created, we now need hard-working, motivated people to collaborate in innovative, productive teams. With the onset and persistence of the COVID-19 pandemic, which accelerated the retirement of many baby boomers who otherwise would have stayed in the workforce, a labour shortage has been felt around the world. There is now intense focus on what companies must do to find, retain, and reward top talent to achieve their missions and prosper. Governments are looking for the best public servants to help them make critical, time-sensitive decisions about public policy. Non-government organizations need brilliant, effective people to deliver programming to an increasing number of marginalized, vulnerable populations. In response, business schools around the world are publishing case studies in papers and books that offer new models for employee acquisition, as recruitment activity is called.[12] Among their favoured techniques are new ways to spot the signs of flexibility, loyalty, and professional maturity that are leading indicators of high employee engagement. I know from my own experience, and a lifetime of watching people being hired for public institutions, private corporations, and non-profits, that one superb indicator of those qualities is athleticism and team play. Simple questions such as "Do you play any sports?" and "Did you play team sports in school?" will spark a lively conversation about a person's record of performance and achievement outside the workplace, one that can help clarify if a candidate has truly learned to

Better to Bowl Together

In *Making Democracy Work: Civic Traditions in Modern Italy* (1993), Robert Putnam writes that northern Italy's history of community, guilds, clubs, and choral societies led to greater civic involvement and greater economic prosperity. The agrarian society of Southern Italy, on the other hand, is less prosperous economically and democratically because of less social capital. Social capital is a form of capital that produces public goods for common purposes. These goods include a shared sense of identity and understanding, trust, cooperation, and reciprocity. These purposes include peace, cohesion, resilience, and prosperity. In his 2000 book *Bowling Alone*, Putnam continued his work on social capital. He describes the reduction of all forms of in-person social intercourse that Americans used to found, educate, and enrich the fabric of their social lives. Putnam argues that this reduction in social interaction, much of which occurs through activities such as team sports, undermines the active civic engagement that strong democracies derive from play on a team. I find consistent correlation between performance in sports and performance at work, and I must assume character development is the reason.

Theodore Roosevelt had come to the same conclusion by 1898 when asked by his commanding officer, Colonel Leonard Wood, to help raise the first volunteer cavalry regiment in U.S. history.[13] The stakes were high; the regiment would have to be trained quickly in Texas, then deployed to Cuba as part of the U.S. strategy in the Spanish-American war.

Roosevelt knew that recruits who had played competitive sports would be ideal candidates for membership in a crack military team on a mission for which failure was not an option. He called the

their citizens. Weaker civic engagement leads to lower voter turnout and decreasing numbers of people attending public meetings, serving on committees, and working with political parties. Above all, weaker civic engagement translates into growing distrust in governments. Putnam uses bowling as a metaphor to drive home his point: although the number of people who bowl has increased in the last twenty years, the number of people who bowl on teams in leagues has decreased. If people bowl alone, they do not interact socially and civically. Is Putnam's theory old news? After all, the Middletown studies[14] of 1929 and 1937 also revealed a disturbing weakening of social capital. The culprit was not television, video games, and smartphones; instead, it was the technological marvel of that time—radio. Sports in Canada have long been a way for us to strengthen social cohesion, to enable people from different backgrounds to share something in common, to understand each other because of their interaction as teammates, and then to build richer relationships and overall awareness of others from there.

regiment the Rough Riders, and it's no surprise that at least twenty teams playing soccer, baseball, softball, volleyball, ice hockey, field hockey, indoor football, basketball, track and field, and football (both indoor and outdoor) in North America today still take Rough Riders as their team name. Why was Roosevelt so confident that great players would be fast learners, competent workers, and great soldiers? Consider these qualities, which I have learned to expect from athletes with team experience.

Athletes are resilient. They don't give up. They have been down often and know that being down is a temporary state, not a life sentence. Game after game they prove to themselves that they can muster strength and courage even when the chips are down, when others have given up, and when they are themselves exhausted. On countless occasions they have risen to the challenge and pull a surprise move out of the depths of their experience. They chase success relentlessly, and they know the work it takes to achieve it. When they win, they celebrate, but only long enough to get ready for the next game. It has been proven in repeated studies that they bring this resilience and perseverance to their workplaces, instinctively applying their values of hard work and creative flexibility to any goal they set for themselves and to any duty they shoulder on behalf of their team.

Athletes manage their time well. Any kid who's had to get up before dawn to make it to a 6 a.m. practice or coaching session can tell you a thing or two about time management. When we care deeply about something, we figure out ways to get it done. This is especially true for young athletes learning to balance the demands of their joint academic and athletic pursuits. In most schools, athletes aren't even allowed to play on their chosen teams unless they keep their marks up. So these players get their homework done, get their assignments in on time, and make their grades. They also show up in class and on the field not just on time, but usually early. They don't fritter away their hours on activities that could distract them from their twin priorities, and that quest for balance persists. Later in life, most athletes continue with athletic pursuits long after they've left school, so they get their work done in their place of employment just as they used to in their place of learning. Eager to get back out on the field, the court or the tee a scheduled time, they are efficient and reliable workers.

Athletes see failure as learning. There are few better ways to teach kids to improve than in a competitive environment in which their failures can cause no harm. Kids who have been in sports from early ages seldom equate failure in doing with failure in being. They decouple their performance from their emotions and learn to look clinically at their relative achievements. When they fumble, foul, or fall, instead of saying, "Why do I bother?" they ask, "How can I be better?" They listen to their coaches, adopting new approaches with the positive attitude it takes to do anything well. That kind of steely toughness in the face of adversity makes them ideal in the world of work.

Athletes invite criticism as insight. Similarly, thin-skinned athletes don't get far. Seasoned players know that improvement requires being open and attentive to the focused criticism of those around them, first their parents and siblings, then friends and teammates and, ultimately, coaches. In the workplace, when an athlete is offered a suggestion for improvement, that worker already has an instinctive trust in the process of criticism and will listen to it with a view to refinement. This makes them quick learners and productive contributors.

Athletes acknowledge talents and flaws equally. Team sport has the benefit of forcing individual players to refine their own performance with discernment; they learn when to rush in and when to back off, when to go for the basket and when to let someone else dribble the ball or take the shot. When employers look for team players, they hope to find this combination of individual drive and team awareness. There are countless books and films about the healthy tension between personal performance and team success, with such notables as *Chariots of Fire* and *Hoosiers* reminding us that the key to team performance is collaboration, which in turn requires humility on the part of every player. Workers who come from sports backgrounds know when to shut up and let someone else take the stage. That makes them outstanding members of project teams where success will require different approaches every time out.

Athletes look out for their teammates. Knowing that the success of the team is more important than the ego of any individual, athletes get to know that the care of every individual on that team is also a critical aspect of improvement. Having even one unskilled or uncertain player on a team can lose a game, and it's a whole-of-team responsibility to make sure that possibility is minimized. Every player can be a coach to any other player of lesser skill, but they must first learn to spot where and when a small suggestion might spark a major improvement. Athletes know how to do that, because they've had precisely that kind of support in their own development. In the workplace, they can do the same by showing empathetic care for others and taking active participation in their improvement. That quality is not easy to teach, especially if an employee has never played on a team, but it's impossible to avoid when you hire someone with a sports background.

Right to Play

Games are instinctive ways for children to grow physically, cognitively, and emotionally. They also can be used to teach kids in developing countries specific lessons they can use to improve their lives. Right to Play is based on this understanding. It's an international-development organization founded in 2000 in Toronto by Johann Olav Koss. Koss is a former speed skater from Norway. He won four Olympic gold medals, including three at the 1994 games in Lillehammer, Norway. He immigrated to Canada and lives in Toronto.

Athletes are bent on improving. One further characteristic I see in folks with team-sport experience is a recognition that today's performance will often not be good enough to win tomorrow's game. Thus athletes are deeply, inherently dissatisfied with things as they are, knowing that the winners of the next competition are going to be better than anyone or any team they've met to date. With their eye on the prize, they know they have to get better to win.[15] The only recipe for sustained success is continuous improvement.

I was just ten years old when I learned that lesson by listening to the news. Until then, no one had ever run a mile in under four minutes. Given decades, even centuries of failed attempts, almost everyone assumed that the evolution of the human species had somehow set a specific limit on self-propelled speed. But then along came Roger Bannister, a junior doctor in England with a fondness for long-distance running. With little coaching, Bannister challenged the mile at a track in Oxford, England, on May 6, 1954. Before a cheering crowd, he was officially clocked at the finish line with a time of 3 minutes, 59.4 seconds. The world was astounded. How could such an achievement be possible? Of course, we look back now and ask only, "How could the four-minute mile ever have been thought impossible?"

Right to Play's teaching method takes the childhood instinct to play and channels it so youngsters reflect on the experience of the game they just finished enjoying, connect what they experienced during it to a similar experience from their own lives, and explore how they can apply what they've learned to an area of their lives. Right to Play's curriculum teaches children life skills that can help them overcome the effects of poverty, conflict, and disease. The organization's method is now at work in developing countries around the world, enabling more than one million kids to experience life-affirming lessons, joy and right to play.

When Roger Bannister broke that speed barrier in 1954, other runners then knew for certain that it was possible to be faster than four minutes. Bannister's record was broken handily only 46 days later by John Landy in Finland with a time of 3 minutes 57.9 seconds, and that record has since been broken just about every year. It now stands at 3 minutes 43.13 seconds.

Athletes know the perceived barriers to performance are often breakable through better technique. They love hearing that something just can't be done. On September 8, 1954, a few short months after Bannister did the impossible, the sixteen-year-old Marilyn Bell of Toronto swam Lake Ontario in a record twenty-one hours in waves topping five metres, all while being bitten on the arms and legs by lamprey eels.[16] Having conquered Lake Ontario, she went on to become the youngest athlete ever to swim the English Channel just two years later.

In 1981, a highly competitive and notoriously stubborn twenty-two-year-old named Terry Fox set out on a run across Canada on one leg, having lost the other to cancer. His goal was to raise money for cancer research, which he knew from personal experience was woefully underfunded. In what has become perhaps the most celebrated achievement in sport by a Canadian, Terry ran almost a full marathon every day for 143 consecutive days, raising attention and money before his disease took him down.

In 2003, a right-handed Sarnia man who preferred to play golf left-handed became the first Canadian and first southpaw ever to win the prestigious Masters Tournament when he hit seven under par in Augusta, Georgia. Mike Weir will be long remembered as someone who just knew he could do better than everyone else.

These are athletes—the kind of people who learn to be humble, open-minded, team-oriented, and wickedly competitive. Worth hiring.

Empathetic things to do when
you intend to Build a team.

. . . as an individual

Join a sport.

The benefits are endless, it's never too late to begin, it doesn't have to be hockey! Every Canadian city, town, and village has a sports organization standing by to help you get into the game. You will be welcomed by amateur teams in sports as diverse as football, lacrosse, rugby, curling, soccer, basketball, skating, skiing, snowboarding, golf, volleyball, tennis, boxing, swimming, wrestling, track and field, rowing, dragon-boat racing, routing climbing, hiking, cycling, lawn bowling, lane bowling, field hockey, badminton, volleyball, and pickle ball for starters. And when you join, remember always to engage within your capacity or just slightly beyond it to improve. Whenever you play, put your team ahead of yourself. As you up your own game, work on supporting, celebrating, and emulating the performance of others.

Get your kids into team sports.

Children want and need to be active. As they play sports, they build their bodies, their confidence, and their friendships. They learn to realize their potential while recognizing and overcoming their weaknesses. Help get them involved, knowing that from time to time you might have to get up early too. After any game, discuss with your children what they've learned and what they've enjoyed. You may hear more about the progress than you typically would on the progress they made in the classroom.

Hire, vote for, and hook up with people who have team experience, whether in sports or the arts.
Being on teams, either as athletes or as members of arts troupes, builds character, deepening a person's sense of self, orientation to success, and empathy toward others. Knowing that, make sure you ask candidates for work positions and elected posts alike if they play or have played sports or joined artistic teams of dancers, actors, et cetera, and, if so, what that meant to them.

. . . as a community

Keep the standard high.
Insist that sports leaders meet the highest standards of trustworthiness and professionalism.

Make it safe.
Make it possible for young athletes to engage in sport safely, affordably, and without fear of discrimination or abuse.

Celebrate athletic achievement.
Herald your community's athletic achievement publicly and loudly, knowing that sport builds social capital with endless community benefits.

. . . as a nation

Promote sport to promote health.
The national benefits are immense.

Go for the gold.

Promote national pride by supporting involvement and competition at all levels.

Include everyone.

Encourage sporting clubs led by inclusion-minded volunteers who provide opportunity for youngsters at all levels of ability—not just those destined for elite performance—to play. Maintain strong support for inclusive opportunities such as the Canadian-invented Special Olympics.

Things we can do as communities

6

Make it smart and keep it fair.

At this point in the human journey, it has become clear that overcoming the range and depth of the problems we face will require our combined resolve and ingenuity. The needed resolve is growing, hastened in part by our recent awakening to the rapidly compounding effects of climate change and the pandemic. But with that resolve, we need to figure out quickly where the needed ingenuity will come from.

So far, we just don't know where that will be. We can't be sure which groups or which lone thinkers within those groups will get the host of ideas that, once implemented, will help us make changes that allow us to survive. While we know that all humans can be creative when they choose to be, we cannot anticipate from which corners of human experience the winning insights will come. Logic demands, therefore, that we get everyone involved.

The principle of inclusion has long been cherished by thoughtful people. Excluding any one group from resources, services, opportunities, and choices strikes us as immoral. Philosophic and religious traditions all uphold kindness and fairness, often not just as high values but as fundamental tenets of dogma as well. They remind us, lest we forget, that we must be both generous to those who need our help and merciful to those who need our forgiveness. Even in our selfish moments, we sense the karmic wisdom of giving everyone a fair shake. What goes around comes around.

Where ingenuity and innovation are concerned, though, are we really giving everyone a fair shake? Do we invite everyone to join in and contribute? We should. When a ship hits rough seas, all hands are required on deck—no exemptions or exclusions—and foul weather isn't just an analogy for our current situation, it's the very definition. Why then do we have a tendency to follow our all-hands order with unspoken presumptions such as "except people who didn't go to my school, don't have my credentials, don't share my physical abilities, don't speak my language, aren't of my gender, don't appear to be of my race, didn't vote for my party, don't go to my temple, aren't in my age group, or don't process information the way I choose to"?

In these times, any arbitrary exclusion is perilous. All perspectives are needed, and if a moral imperative for inclusion isn't convincing enough, let's admit the mathematical reality that every time we cut one person out of our problem-solving process we reduce the possibility of finding a solution by one. Cut out a whole sector of society and we reduce our chances of success by a substantial and stupidly unwise margin.

We have to remember that our individual creativity comes from our individual consciousness. That consciousness can be thought of as our unique, cumulative awareness of our place in time, in space, and in relationships. Because at conception we each begin a different journey through time, space, and relationships, each of our perspectives arising from that consciousness will always be unique too. Absolutely no one else will ever think the same thoughts as I do or see the world the way that I do. That peculiar separateness is a characteristic of all sentient beings and a tactical advantage we cannot afford to waste.

The Downside of Meritocracy

Who could have imagined beforehand that the idea for propagating pecan trees as a food would have come from a slave (Antoine), that a treatment for Down syndrome would come from a toymaker and a children's story writer (Stanley Wade and Roald Dahl), that the best torpedo-guidance system of the Second World War would be devised by a Hollywood beauty queen (Hedy Lamarr), or that the great awakening to the dangers of climate change would come from a fifteen-year-old girl with Asperger's syndrome (Greta Thunberg)? The history of innovation is full of such stories of people who were not invited to contribute and yet changed everything. But here's something to ponder. Can humans strive for excellence in any particular endeavour while at the same time giving people equal opportunity to tackle a problem and contribute to the solution? Put bluntly, can a society be both smart and fair? I've spent my life wrestling with this question.

Let me set out a common opinion about the answer. Humans are animals who applaud achievement. In our age, from the earliest days in school, children learn a system of reward. Gold stars for high marks. Extra credit for additional effort. Better schools for high achievers. Better jobs for grads of better schools. Better opportunities for those in better jobs. And on and on. On the surface, this pattern of reward for excellence seems logical, even obvious. Why wouldn't we teach our kids that achievement pays off? After all, the pursuit of excellence shapes our world for the better. Individuals who excel in their fields—engineering, medicine, technology, law, arts, or whatever—are the acknowledged drivers of progress. Smart people think better. Hard workers move the needle. They both merit reward. Don't they?

They do. But within every meritocracy lurks an assumption that those with exceptional talent will somehow be able to find their way onto teams working on problems worthy of them. If they're any good, their achievements will get noticed. Opportunities will appear. If they work hard, and stay focused, good things will happen. But a dangerous corollary lurks here too. The flip side of assuming that talent and hard work beget opportunity is presuming that those who haven't had opportunity are neither talented nor hardworking. People who haven't risen to the top likely don't deserve to be there, and their lack of advancement is proof of either their mediocrity or lack of character. But that's just not true.

How equal is equal? (Not very.)

Twenty years before her appointment to the Supreme Court of Canada, Rosalie Abella was the commissioner of a groundbreaking federal Royal Commission on Equality in Employment. The commission explored how systemic discrimination prevents women, visible minorities, people with disabilities, and Indigenous peoples from enjoying equal opportunity in the workplace. The watershed report confirmed that discrimination against these groups was widespread. The report's recommendations set out a principle of accommodation by which a process other than raw competition be used to ensure that candidates from these groups be fairly considered for any post. Abella's findings made a difference. In 1989 her key recommendations were enshrined in the first decision of the Supreme Court of Canada regarding equality rights under the Canadian Charter of Rights and Freedoms and have subsequently been adopted by other countries including Northern Ireland, South Africa, and New Zealand.

As Rosalie Abella made clear, systemic discrimination can either deliberately or inadvertently hide the talents of those seeking acceptance from people deciding their futures. Lack of recognition is no indicator of lack of talent. Even in contexts where discrimination is minimal, choices made about who should be given any particular opportunity are frequently subjective and often wrong. J.K. Rowling was told by twelve publishers in turn that her stories weren't commercially viable before one decided to give Harry Potter a chance. None of those twelve thought Rowling deserved to be on their book list. Her novels have since generated $450 million in sales. Mediocre? Arguably not. Agatha Christie went through five straight years of rejection. Her books have now sold some two billion copies, with only

William Shakespeare's works generating more income in English-language publication. Mediocre? Um, no.

In the sciences, such stories are legion. Everyone in 1616 thought Copernicus was daft for saying that our Earth orbits the sun and not the other way around. Yet he was right. Everyone in 1916 thought that Alfred Wegener was nuts for suggesting that the world's continents are not static but rather drifting slowly across the surface of the planet. Yet he was right.

What I've come to realize is that we need not pursue learning over excellence, or excellence over empathy. These qualities do not compete. They are mutually dependent. I believe that excellence itself arises from the universality of opportunity, especially the opportunity to innovate. Innovation is a word that gets used often, in every industry and to serve nearly any purpose. As I put it before, I see innovation as the constant quest to do things better, to bring a curious mind to every task. When we collectively afford one another the chance to begin that quest, we instil the drive for excellence in every heart and mind. That's when the ideas start flowing. We can (must) have equality of opportunity and excellence too.

Fairness Online

It was a privilege for me to serve as chair for the Government of Canada's Information Highway Advisory Council back in 1994. It was the federal government's first attempt to wrap its head around the emerging digital world we live in today. The council's mandate was to decide how best to develop and use the World Wide Web for the economic, cultural, and social advantage of all Canadians. Not an easy task even then—well before the emergence of social media, deep fakes, shadow banning, account hacking, and the many insidious sides of today's tech.

As we considered the use and effect of the Internet on Canadians, we examined fifteen policy questions. The most important centred on how to ensure universal access to essential services at a reasonable cost and how to achieve an appropriate balance between competition and regulation. These were thorny issues, and they remain so today. In the end, we advised the government not to regulate the World Wide Web, and I stand by that recommendation. We all face ethical quandaries. On an individual scale, they allow us to ensure that our moral compass is reading true. On a large scale, they produce a cascade of lasting economic, social, and technological side effects. In all cases, it is the process of wrestling to make things both smart and fair that teaches us most about ourselves. (Sometimes our choices call for a leap of faith.) If I could characterize our deliberations as a direct-message chat, it might go like this:

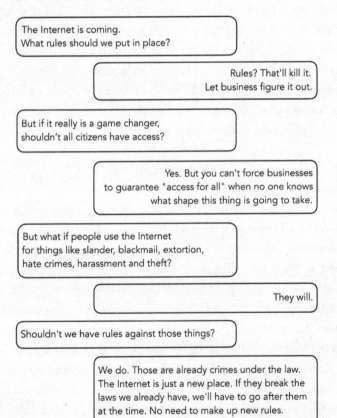

The Internet is coming.
What rules should we put in place?

Rules? That'll kill it.
Let business figure it out.

But if it really is a game changer,
shouldn't all citizens have access?

Yes. But you can't force businesses
to guarantee "access for all" when no one knows
what shape this thing is going to take.

But what if people use the Internet
for things like slander, blackmail, extortion,
hate crimes, harassment and theft?

They will.

Shouldn't we have rules against those things?

We do. Those are already crimes under the law.
The Internet is just a new place. If they break the
laws we already have, we'll have to go after them
at the time. No need to make up new rules.

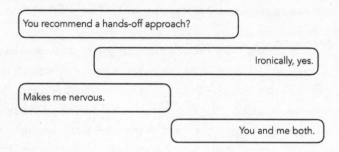

If I could redo the recommendations in our 1994 report, I would add some guiding principles for the unfolding Internet. With the benefit of hindsight twenty-five years later, I gave a speech in Waterloo called "The Tech for Good Declaration." Here's a snapshot.

Tech for Good
A Declaration by the Canadian Tech Community
Build trust and respect your data.
Be transparent and give choice.
Reskill the future of work.
Leave no one behind.
Think inclusively at every stage.
Actively participate in collaborative governance.
SIGN UP NOW AT
canadianinnovationspace.ca/tech-for-good/

The Internet Today: Smart but Still Not Fair

Flash forward thirty years. In the three decades since its inception, the Internet—and in particular the World Wide Web—has proved to be far more than an information super-highway, a moniker that seems quaintly narrow in hindsight. In one of the fastest uptakes of technology in history, the web has transformed business, government, entertainment, community, advertising, journalism, political advocacy, and shopping.

Yet, as the World Wide Web Foundation observes in its introduction to the new Contract for the Web, "half of the world's population still can't get online. For the other half, the web's benefits seem to come with far too many unacceptable risks: to our privacy, our democracy, our health, and our security." Sadly, as predicted, the web has also given bad actors infinite opportunity to steal, coerce, extort, blackmail, and slander. Worse, it has given nation states and rogue groups a whole new way to wage war.

Like Canada's Tech for Good declaration, but now international and multi-disciplinary, the Contract for the Web offers a global plan of action "to make sure our online world is safe, empowering and genuinely for everyone." The authors of the contract—eminent experts in technology, governance, social behavior, and business—"invite governments, companies, civil society organizations and individuals to back the Contract and uphold its principles and clauses."

In its first few months, the Contract for the Web earned support from more than 1,100 organizations in 50 countries. Signatories include leading tech companies such as Google, Microsoft, Twitter, Facebook, and Reddit. The government of Ghana has signed on. So have human rights groups: Reporters Without Borders, Electronic Frontier Foundation, Paradigm Initiative, and Public Knowledge. Another nine-thousand contract backers are leaders and influencers from numerous fields. The founders report that entrepreneur Sir Richard Branson, former U.K. prime minister Gordon Brown, U.S. congressman Ro Khanna, and actor and writer Stephen Fry have all pledged their support, along with many others. Here's the contract in a nutshell:

GOVERNMENTS WILL . . .
1. Ensure everyone can connect to the Internet
   So that anyone, no matter who they are or where they live, can participate actively online

2. Keep all of the Internet available, all of the time
   So that no one is denied their right to full Internet access
3. Respect and protect people's fundamental online privacy and
   data rights
   So everyone can use the internet freely, safely, and without fear

COMPANIES WILL . . .
4. Make the Internet affordable and accessible to everyone
   So that no one is excluded from using and shaping the web
5. Respect and protect people's privacy and personal data to build
   online trust
   So people are in control of their lives online, empowered with
   clear and meaningful choices around their data and privacy
6. Develop technologies that support the best in humanity and
   challenge the worst
   So the web really is a public good that puts people first

CITIZENS WILL . . .
7. Be creators and collaborators on the web
   So the web has rich and relevant content for everyone
8. Build strong communities that respect civil discourse and
   human dignity
   So that everyone feels safe and welcome online
9. Fight for the web
   So the web remains open and a global public resource for
   people everywhere, now and in the future

Apply the innovation formula.

As members of progressive societies, we think of learning, excellence, and empathy as worthy values. Yet sometimes our decisions promote just one or two of these to the exclusion of the third. In my experience, holding certain values above others produces outcomes such as those in the following diagram. The juxtaposition of activities here show how innovation depends expressly on the deliberate and sustained combination of education, excellence, and empathy. Any two will produce benefits, but, without the third, those benefits will not solve the challenges we now face.

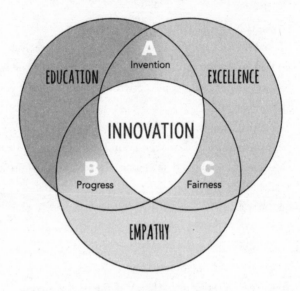

As you can see, if we give greater priority to education and excellence (A), we get inventions that may change whole industries but might not benefit large segments of our population. I believe we can put many of the offerings from the high-tech sector into this category.

Similarly, if we give priority only to education and empathy (B), we'll get steady progress for the general population but may miss out on ingenious advances of critical importance to the long-term survival of society.

Lastly, should we give priority to empathy and excellence only (C), we'll build a society that is fair, but those we advance might not have the critical components of education they would need to focus their talent productively.

Ideally, we should attend to all three in equal measure. Only then do we make innovation the norm, ensuring a society that is inventive, progressive, and fair. And the best way to ensure empathy is to be inclusive in the process. We need not pursue learning over excellence, or excellence over empathy. These qualities do not compete. They are mutually dependent. I believe that excellence itself arises from the universality of opportunity, especially the opportunity to innovate.

Here's the formula to remember:

$$E_d + E_x + E_m = I$$
Education + Excellence + Empathy = Innovation

Advocating for Inclusion Abroad

As governor general, I had numerous opportunities to witness first-hand how Canada's leadership is welcomed and respected overseas. Two memories strike me now as proof that the combination of learning, innovation, and excellence does produce innovation that makes meaningful improvements in people's lives.

Most Canadians are well aware that our country's relationship with China was sorely strained by our detention of Meng Wanzhou, CFO of Huawei, in Vancouver for extradition to the United States on fraud charges, and the reciprocal arrest by Chinese authorities of Michael Kovrig and Michael Spavor on trumped-up charges of espionage. As startling and mutually infuriating as these events were, our two nations have long enjoyed close relations in many endeavours of mutual interest. This was evident on our 2017 trip to China, the second of two state visits we made to that country during my time at Rideau Hall.

Among the members of our twenty-strong delegation was Carla Qualtrough. Carla is an amazing woman. Visually impaired since birth, she has only 10 per cent of normal vision and only then with glasses on. Determined and devoid of self-pity, Carla is also athletic and brilliant. She competed for Canada in swimming at the 1988 and

1992 Summer Paralympics, bringing home three bronze medals. She then earned a law degree, joined the Americas Paralympic Committee, and chaired the Sport Dispute Resolution Centre of Canada, among other activities. Little surprise that Carla was named as one of Canada's Most Influential Women in Sport in 2007. In 2015, she became the first Paralympic athlete to be elected to the Canadian Parliament and was immediately named Minister of Sport and of Persons with Disabilities.

During our China visit, we talked a lot about sport. Building on China's success staging the 2016 Summer Games, President Xi and the members of his government were looking toward the 2022 Winter Olympics and Paralympics, keenly interested in how domestic attention on the Games might encourage greater interest in athletics in all provinces of China. Their ambitious goal was to have 300 million Chinese actively engaged in winter sports by 2022. He then acknowledged that that China was lagging behind in ten sports categories and would welcome Canada's expert help. We were delighted. I had visions of Kissinger and Nixon's breakthrough with China more than four decades earlier through ping-pong. (Alas, subsequent hostilities around the two Michaels dashed these hopes.) Minister Qualtrough soon signed agreements on sport, cooperation, and assistance with the Games preparation and stayed deeply engaged with her Chinese counterparts. I was impressed by how eloquently Carla spoke about persons with disabilities generally and in sport in particular. I wasn't alone in my admiration. On one of our visits we were joined by representatives from One Plus One, a local NGO providing services to disabled people and promoting social acceptance of the disabled. The organization had made great strides in athletics, forming China's first blind-staffed sports broadcasting team, registering the first-ever disabled media for the Chinese Olympics and the Asia Games, and even making the first online broadcast in China by disabled persons. As the One Plus One reps looked on, our Canadian delegates loudly signalled Canada's strong support for inclusion, equality, and diversity, and we pointed out that we had already put our money where our mouth is. Two years earlier, the Canadian Embassy had given seed funding to translate all Chinese university entrance exams into Braille. Because of Canada, blind Chinese students could now attend university for the first time ever.

When Minister Qualtrough mentioned this initiative, we could feel a surge of emotion in the room. As it turned out, all the One Plus One reps were themselves blind Chinese students. They came forward and said that they were humbled and grateful (if nervous) to meet with our ambassador and Minister Qualtrough, but felt honour bound to attend and offer public thanks as it had been our embassy that empowered them to train Chinese instructors to adapt the exams. Without Canada's support, Chinese students with disabilities would still have been hidden in the closet, as they put it, making it impossible for any blind Chinese student to attend an institute of higher learning. Through twenty centuries of China's administering entrance exams throughout the country to qualify citizens for entrance to the Mandarin class of civil servants, and lately to the country's most elite universities, blind people were never allowed to participate. Now all that had changed.

But as they were speaking, they stopped abruptly, confused all of a sudden by our reaction, which they had not expected. They believed they must have offended us in some way, because tears were streaming down both my face and Carla's. I then explained that my mother had lost her sight when detached retinas had progressively made her legally blind. Forced to quit her job as a nurse's aide, she had then enrolled in our local university, the oldest student ever to take correspondence courses adjusted for her disability. I further explained that Carla, our own minister of sport, was legally blind herself and yet had earned her law degrees with distinction, become a Pan American Games medallist, and had been elected to Canada's federal government to represent her constituents and all disabled people in our country. She was now a minister of the Crown. Our Chinese friends joined us in tears of joy and laughter at the uncharacteristic display of emotion from the Canadians.

My second memory is of a visit to Israel, Jordan, and the Palestinian Authority in 2016. It was busy; we met one king, one prime minister, and two presidents in under four days. While visiting this region of historic hostility and current conflict, I keenly remember stopping in at a makeshift school in a broken outbuilding behind a warehouse in Beit Jala in the Palestinian Authority Territory near Ramallah. Now a school for blind Palestinian boys and girls, the humble institution had been founded by a Palestinian serving in the Palestinian security force who was himself a Canadian citizen. He had obtained a grant from the Canadian Mission to the Palestinian Authority to build and equip the school and to train teachers to use Braille so they could

The Human Library: Unjudge Someone

Ever wish you could ask someone directly to explain why they think as they do? Perhaps you've wondered why anyone in the twenty-first century would believe the world is flat, refuse to support transgender rights, resist vaccination against COVID, join the Communist Party, log old-growth forests, live by choice on the streets, wear the hijab, stick with an abusive partner, or insist that aliens live among us. At the Human Library, you can meet these people one on one to find out how they think.

The Human Library is, in the true sense of the word, a library of people. The organization hosts events where readers can borrow human beings serving as open books and have conversations they would not otherwise have. Ronni Abergel, who founded the Human Library in Denmark in 2000, put it this way: "Every human book from our bookshelf represents educate about two dozen young children who could not see. Without this school, they would have been outcast—marooned in their homes, uneducated. They all knew how lucky they were—these chosen ones from among hundreds of others in the territory. I was called over to the desk of a beautiful little girl, perhaps six years old, eyelids closed over sightless eyes, who asked me if I could read the letter she had just typed for me. I did. It read: "General Governor from Canada will you be my friend?" I embraced her with tears flowing down from my wide-open eyes and said, "I will be your friend forever, and so will my granddaughter Téa, who is about your age and was adopted from a shelter in Cali, Colombia."

I will long remember that small, indispensable school in Ramallah, hoping that it might by now have expanded to serve other blind children in that tragic territory. Of all the experiences on the fifty-six

a group in our society that is often subjected to prejudice, stigmatization or discrimination because of their lifestyle, diagnosis, belief, disability, social status, ethnic origin etc. I had a theory that it could work because the library is one of the few places in our community where everyone is welcome, whether you're rich or poor, homeless or living in a castle, professor or illiterate. It's truly the most inclusive institution in our time."

Abergel's idea was to boost inclusion by making it possible for people to experience diversity of opinion and circumstance without judgment. With its apt tagline "Don't judge a book by its cover," the Human Library has hosted events in eighty-fve countries on six continents, most often in libraries but also in museums and schools and at corporate campuses and festivals. The library has been operating in Canada since 2008, with fifteen Canadian cities involved so far, all with the support of the CBC, the national media partner for the initiative and the first broadcaster in the world to take on the role.

international visits I made on behalf of the people of Canada, these two stories stand out as extraordinary illustrations of the power of empathy and the positive action to do something about the challenging circumstances of others, particularly in regions that are so far away from our own.

Empathetic things to do when you intend to Make it smart and keep it fair.

. . . as an individual

Talk to people whose choices you can't understand.
Wisdom and creative insight will come from every corner of society, and we need to look for it in all the right places. Once we appreciate the perspectives and trust the potential of those we haven't understood before, we will be able to find the best ways to be inclusive.

Make new friends.
Seek to bring different people into your circle of friends. Listen to their music. Watch their films. Try their recipes. Read the books they read. Learn their languages. Have their kids over. At gatherings, seek out the people in the corners who don't seem to fit in. (They're bound to be interesting.) Sponsor refugees. Make friends with someone physically or mentally handicapped. Get your kids involved in family-to-family international exchanges.

Thank those who reach out.
Find a volunteer activity about which you can be compassionate. Give generously of your time and leadership. Make a habit of sending short notes to those who have made the effort to reach out to others.

. . . as a community

Invite everyone.
Just as diversity is a fact, inclusion is an act. When we neglect being inclusive, we design things for a fabricated world. At any meeting, ask who isn't there but should be, and make sure they're invited next time. That may require having interpreters working at community meetings.

Encourage local businesses to be inclusive.
Publicly acknowledge their efforts to emphasize diversity in both recruitment and staff development.

Twin your town and city.
By doing so you will give citizens a positive opportunity to learn about different cultures and habits.

. . . as a province or nation

Make innovation part of every school curriculum.
Given that school attendance is mandatory and therefore universal, young people from every background, of every ability, and in every circumstance will learn that they have an essential and welcome role to play in making the changes that will improve our world.

Recruit the best talent from around the world.
We're all in this together, and cross-pollination of ideas from and to other parts of the world is critical. National isolationism is a mistake. Open the doors (with appropriate visas) to bright professionals who want to work and students who want to study in Canada; by doing so, they will bring their solutions to us, and we will gain the knowledge to help find solutions for them too.

Help Canadians study and travel abroad.

Just as we need to invite others, we need our own citizens to bring Canada's insights and experience to the rest of the world. Travel teaches both those who journey and those who meet them at their destinations. In the same vein, encourage international sports and arts competition so we can all learn from each other.

7

Build a healthy neighbourhood.

Barn raising became a powerful metaphor in my life after our family moved to Waterloo, Ontario, in 1999. Rallying the community to erect a barn on the farm of a new neighbour was a time-honoured tradition in Britain, and then in North America, and had, unsurprisingly, become a universal symbol of community spirit and collective action. For our family it was also, quite literally, an insurance policy.

While I busied myself with academic management as president of the University of Waterloo, Sharon ran a thirty-six-horse boarding and instructing stable on our hundred-acre farm. Our land was nestled among the adjacent farms of our Mennonite neighbours, descendants of the seven families who had first migrated to the region and cleared land on the banks of Laurel Creek around 1820. The welcome end of the Napoleonic Wars just five years earlier at the Waterloo field in Belgium was fresh in their minds and became the name for their community.

Before insuring our property against damage by fire or flood, Sharon asked one of those neighbours to suggest a reasonable replacement value for our barns. He shook his head and said, "You don't need insurance, Sharon. If it burns down, we'll remove the debris one weekend and rebuild it the next weekend or two. We'll produce the lumber and door hinges on our own farms. All the neighbours will come over to do the work." Then he paused: "But we don't make roofing sheets;

you might insure your roof for a couple of thousand bucks so we can buy some tin."With that, we knew our neighbours had our back. Even though we had been there only a few weeks, we were no longer alone, but rather among people who cared for us and would assist us when we needed them. We could do anything.

Healthy neighbourhoods are like that. When you are surrounded by those who know you, who care for you, who look out for you, and who will come to your side when you're down, life is good and anything is possible.[1]

Neighbourhoods are where change takes shape.

I wrote earlier that the experience of consciousness might be described as awareness of one's place in time, space, and relationships. Ours is a dynamic existence, our movements through the peculiar features of time, space, and relationships charting our life's journey. At times when we feel safe, in spots we find familiar, and with people we find welcoming, we think of ourselves as having found a safe haven on that journey, a neighbourhood. Those who share coordinates, moments, and kindness with us are our neighbours.

Historically, neighbourhoods have been known by their geographic boundaries. The word itself is ancient, springing from roots meaning nearby (as in nigh) and place (as in borough). But for most people, neighbourhoods are more attractive for their character than their coordinates. They may be home for people of the same ethnicity, religion, language, culture, work life, architecture, cuisine, or artistic bent. These days, they can even be digital. Whatever the glue that holds it together, every neighbourhood strengthens the sense of community of those in it. In my neighbourhood, I understand and can relate to everyone living around me, and I am known in the same way. When we moved to Waterloo, Sharon and I and all our kids felt that immediately and deeply, I suppose because we were moving into a smoothly functioning social dynamic that had been refined over centuries, a dynamic of which we were now part.

Wherever one feels known and part of something, one also feels the freedom to change, and that creates an exciting sense of power, of potential. When a whole neighbourhood feels that way, miracles can happen.

Ultimately, the strength of a nation is directly proportional to the health of its neighbourhoods, villages, and towns. In their communities, citizens have a right to expect safety and peace at home and on the street and to rely on the active support and friendship of their neighbours. The proof that empathy in action can transform lives and change fortunes is often most visible in one's own community.

On countless occasions it has been demonstrated that, in any neighbourhood, worthy individuals are ready to propel community action that changes lives for the better. To do so, they require the full commitment of educated, visionary, and effective leaders. When they enjoy such leadership, they will eagerly engage with others to improve the quality of life for all.

Examples of this kind of improvement can be found everywhere, and it's worth considering a few. Until the Beatles came along, for instance, Liverpool, England, was known almost exclusively for the misery of its large, underpaid working class. That all changed when Liverpudlians banded together in the 1980s to unite their many neighbourhoods as a sparkling cultural hub for England's art and architecture scene and a recreational haven for nature lovers. Their improvements paid off; the city's seemingly endless stretch of Victorian parks and gardens was acknowledged as the "most important in the country" by England's Register of Historic Parks and Gardens of Special Historic Interest.

Detroit, Michigan, is now often cited as the poster child of comeback cities. Teetering many times on bankruptcy and breakdown, the city has at last been reimagined entirely through the grassroots movement of its citizens, who took neighbourhood action when their government on its own could not. Among their initiatives was the Heidelberg Project, an ambitious set of programs to shift attitudes, habits, and outcomes among the residents of the once-troubled East Side, all through street art. Close to my heart is the construction of a modern and welcoming new hockey arena, the new home for the Detroit Red Wings. And with extensive new bike path networks linking an almost endless choice of architectural landmarks worth visiting, Detroit has at last decided to reclaim its spot among the great cities of America . . . and this time stay there.

Once notorious for pollution and crime, Marseilles was the one metropolis in France that everyone tried to avoid. The nation's second-largest city was noisy and crowded, but those who lived there knew it could be a jewel. Its history, dating back to 600 BCE was rich, and the Vieux Port was ripe for rebirth. With focused efforts by the public and substantial budgetary support from the city itself, the former haunt of car thieves and pickpockets is now a historic marvel, with music, cafés, Michelin-starred restaurants, museums, galleries, and markets operating peacefully and safely under the watchful of eye of volunteer citizens working closely with local police.

Twenty years ago, Seoul, South Korea, opted to become a leading centre of high tech in Asia. By doing so, citizens turned their city from an ignored world capital into a magnet for foreign investment, which in turn made infrastructure modernization possible. Businesses then flooded in, convention centres became busy year-round, and once-dingy neighbourhoods such as Gangnam (of dance fame) became tourist centres on their own. Seoul is now an economic powerhouse and one of the world's great capitals.

Melbourne, Australia, was generally thought to be Sydney's awkward, ugly cousin until citizens decided to redesign their downtown at the neighbourhood level. Their first and toughest challenge was to drain a smelly swampland and erect a sparkling centre for culture and business. Within five years, the city was almost unrecognizable, and the changes earned Melbourne its title as of one of the world's most liveable cities.

And here in Canada, countless communities have improved their quality of life, their fortunes, and their reputations through the deliberate and dogged efforts of the people who live and work there. When the recession of the 1980s forced a deep drop in the prices of B.C. forest products, the logging town of Chemainus on the southeast coast of Vancouver Island seemed doomed. With little notice, the mill was closed after 120 years of steady operation, and 700 residents were laid off work in a town whose population had been only 4,000. Then one resident got an innovative idea: What if artists from around the world were commissioned to paint huge murals depicting local logging history on downtown buildings? This eye-catching solution to a threatening economic disaster turned a moribund industry town into a tourist centre that draws several hundred thousand visitors each year.

Once a fishing outport, the Quebec town of Bonne-Espérance faced extinction when cod stocks collapsed. But locals had no intention of deserting their beloved neighbourhoods for jobs elsewhere, so they invented a whole industry from an unlikely agricultural resource—berries. Using the deep knowledge of local elders, they launched a cooperative to develop novel products from indigenous plants, including marshberries, cloudberries, and Labrador tea. These plants are natural producers of vitamins and antioxidants, which when extracted can be processed into healing skin creams, rejuvenating face masks, and luxury shampoos for the world's multi-billion-dollar beauty industry.

Home to some four thousand people, the beautiful village of Atholville, New Brunswick, suffered high unemployment and a steadily declining population when CN Rail shut down operations in nearby Campbellton and laid off a thousand people in one go. Secondary industries in the town were devastated too, and the local business park was forced to close for want of business. But locals were loyal to their town and stubborn to the core. They banded together and began a search for a new industry that could benefit from an available, skilled workforce with a reputation for hard work. That was enough to attract a Canadian cannabis operation specializing in medical marijuana, whose management team was quick to take advantage of Atholville's culture of enthusiasm and welcome. The immediate result was a manufacturing facility. Residents who had been forced to head to Fredericton, Saint John, and Halifax for jobs are now able to return, and grandparents wanting still to be near their grandchildren are following in their wake. So once again, Atholville has an industry and secondary industries at the beginning of a promising growth cycle.

What's in the water in Waterloo?

Clearly, neighbourhoods are dynamic centres that, when healthy, become havens for happy, safe, and productive lives. But more than that, healthy neighbourhoods can themselves be both the echoes and the agents of change in nations all over the world.

Two examples in my lifetime illustrate the sweep of empathetic transformation that can be launched in any community bent on building a healthy neighbourhood. The first began in 1957, during the eighteen-month period the United Nations proclaimed to be International Geophysical Year. This was a watershed event in the progress of science, as some seventy nations agreed to share their research openly in the interests of mutual advancement. Universities around the world collaborated in exploration and data collection, taking strides such as establishing a permanent research station in Antarctica and mapping the floor of the Arctic Ocean for the first time. Navigational error was improved with better understanding of geomagnetism, and longitude and latitude could finally be charted with pinpoint accuracy. Prediction of earthquakes became possible with leaps in seismology, electricity was generated with nothing but solar power, computers got memory disks, and sporty folks jumped around in track suits made of spandex, the first fully synthetic fibre.

I was just sixteen at the time, and I vividly remember the wave of excitement and optimism that rolled over us that year. We were all dreaming about the marvels that would soon come thanks to the sharing of scientific research and its application through advanced engineering. Newspapers and magazines were full of predictions of imagined wonders, from high-speed undersea trains that hurtled through trans-Atlantic tunnels to space stations that welcomed wide-eyed visitors to zero-gravity hotel rooms, each with an unobstructed view of Planet Earth.

Yet behind the international collaboration there was fierce competition. We were just ten years into the Cold War, with both the USSR and the United States racing to prove to their own citizens that they were the more technologically advanced society. Both nations had vowed to put communication satellites into orbit, knowing that whoever controlled outer space would truly gain the upper hand. In May 1957, Americans launched the rocket Vanguard 1 from Cape Canaveral in Florida, a kind of dress rehearsal in Eisenhower's plan to put an American satellite into geostationary orbit first. But to the president's chagrin and, I suspect, horror, on October 4 the Russians beat him to it. Sputnik 1 became the first artificial Earth satellite, orbiting the planet every ninety-six minutes while transmitting signals from space that any amateur radio buff could pick up, and which all of them did. As Sputnik's first orbit was completed, the Soviet news agency TASS transmitted its own proclamation, declaring, "As result of great, intense work of scientific institutes and design bureaus, the first artificial Earth satellite has been built." While interpreted by some as an acknowledgement of international achievement, that message was a slap in the face to Russia's rival superpowers, and the Space Race was now on.

Not unlike the race to develop the atom bomb in the 1940s, the space race of the late fifties and sixties sparked a wave of innovation that promised to transform almost every industry. But as we all looked up in 1957 to spot Sputnik glinting in the night sky, a sober realization took hold: we might not be well enough educated to take advantage of the coming changes. Just as the citizens of Chemainus and Atholville and Bonne-Espérance would experience later, communities across Canada in the late fifties began to suspect the legacy industries upon which they depended for their employment were about to die out.

In the twin-cities region of Kitchener-Waterloo, that suspicion was especially keen. Not a hundred kilometres from Toronto, the cities and surrounding towns were still primarily agricultural, boosted by industrial activity *inter alia* focused on booze and tires. Joseph Seagram joined partners of the local distillery in 1869, making a fortune during the 1920s by distilling liquor there, rebottling it in Montreal, and moving it downriver to St. Pierre and Miquelon to be loaded into the hulls of smugglers who would then sail it covertly to the prohibition-bound United States.

Over time, Kitchener-Waterloo attracted a broad variety of other industries, including leather, furniture, meat packing, baking, rubber and insurance, with names like Lang, Krug, Dare, Westons, Electrohome, Mutual, and Sun Life intimately associated with the area. That diversity was a great asset, allowing Kitchener-Waterloo to survive many economic downturns that hit other regions hard.

B.F. Goodrich had set up there in 1923. The company had been making tires for cars since 1870, enjoying some celebrity in 1927 when their bespoke tires safely landed Charles Lindberg's Spirit of Saint Louis after the world's first trans-Atlantic flight. In 1947, the company had pioneered the first tubeless car tire and then set up a plant in Kitchener-Waterloo specifically to engineer and produce a bigger class of tire for the Chevrolet models appearing in ever greater numbers in the mid-1950s. But new technologies were fast arriving, and it would be imperative to keep innovating to stay competitive. One man knew that well, and he intended to rally the whole Kitchener-Waterloo community to make it happen.

The man was Gerry Hagey, a public relations and advertising whiz who, until recently, had headed up Goodrich's PR department, his final position after having joined the company upon graduation from Waterloo College. Hagey was a savvy ad man with a keen interest in science and an unquenchable love of education. As much as he loved communications, in 1953 he retired from the tire business to take an opportunity even closer to his heart, as the president of his alma mater.

By the time of the International Geophysical Year and the launch of Sputnik in 1957, Hagey needed no convincing that the end of the old industrial era was nigh: that was the challenge. A few months back he had noted an article in the *Globe and Mail* that echoed his feelings and underlined this passage: "In the next ten years, one engineer will be required for every 100 persons in the nation's labour force. In other words, we will need 150,000 engineers. At the present time, our universities are graduating only approximately 1,700 to 1,800 engineers a year." That was the opportunity. Hagey then called Ira Needles, his former boss at Goodrich who also served as chair of the Canadian Chamber of Commerce. Hagey suggested that they lead the community in a makeover of higher education. It was a bold idea, and Needles jumped aboard. A networker and motivator with a reputation for convincing people to follow his lead and then be delighted to pester them until they got stuff done, he was just the man to make it happen. The word *Needles*, they said, was more than just his last name; it was the method he used to keep people moving forward.

Days later, Needles made a speech to the local Rotary Club. To a rapt audience, he set down the so-called Waterloo Plan for educating engineers and technicians on the co-op principle for the first time. Anyone enrolled would be required and supported to work in their chosen profession or trade even as they studied. The notion was novel and practical; urgency demanded that book learning be applied in the real world, then adapted and improved. Theory and practice would go hand in hand.

The speech kindled a fire, and the community burst into flame. Hagey became the first president of the newly founded University of Waterloo in 1957, welcoming the first cohort of freshman to the new model. There were only 75 souls in two portable classrooms that year, but by the time Hagey retired only 12 years later, the university was an $80 million operation with 9,000 students enrolled. Buildings were erected. Farmland was acquired for later expansion. Professors were recruited from around the world, and every local industry invited (perhaps needled) to invite students into their workforces. The Government of Ontario, at first sluggish in response, eventually made large grants to the initiative. Under the Waterloo Plan, industry had better-educated and practiced talent to drive innovation, the community of Kitchener-Waterloo prospered, and the university continued to innovate and grow, so much so that is now routinely named in *Maclean's* university rankings as the most innovative university in the country. Today, the University of Waterloo is the largest co-op university in the English-speaking world. Notably, the university also reinforced its belief in technology transfer by adopting a creator-owns intellectual property policy. This reversed the traditional practice whereby the university owns the patents and intellectual property created by professors and students in its labs. Instead of monetizing the innovations of its people, it chose rather to foster trust between its professors and students on the one hand and business interests on the other. The businesses themselves could then produce the applications and take them to market, while the creators—professors and their students—received the royalties from the innovation.

As president of that same university forty years later, I was the happy inheritor of those founding principles. I spoke proudly to audiences around the country with a speech I called simply "What's in the

Water in Waterloo?" The answer was also simple; there was nothing different in the water; the transformative magic that made so many enduring benefits had come directly from the power of a healthy neighbourhood. I illustrated this answer with three slides: the first showed an overview of the Grand River running through the area. The second showed a hundred or so Mennonite neighbours raising a barn for one of them. The third simply superimposed the second image over the first. Point made.

Empathetic things to do when you intend to Build a healthy neighbourhood.

. . . as an individual

Be gracious to all you meet.
It's wise to be polite and patient when you speak with people. For you never know what battles they're facing. As a gracious neighbour, you will have great success both in welcoming others to your community and helping them make their best contribution, which will ultimately benefit all.

Reach out.
No need to wait to be encountered. Be bold and reach out with hospitality, with encouragement, and with help. No one minds being approached in kindness.

When conflict arises, slow down.
The mark of a healthy neighbourhood is not the absence of difference, but rather the will to navigate difference when it arises. Take the time to talk things through; there is always common ground.

. . . as a community

Ask citizens what they want.
Never assume that a community's priorities or objectives will be static for long. Engage all citizens in the complex, rewarding process of

deciding what kind of community, then ask them to suggest how they think that could be brought into being. You will be astounded at the range of innovative yet pragmatic ideas that come forward. That said, edit judiciously.

Get citizens involved.

Encourage community members' participation in community programs, from Welcome Wagon and Neighbourhood Watch through the whole range of volunteer and philanthropic activities that drive your community forward.

Keep institutions focused on service.

Citizens depend on (and pay for) the expert services that local governments provide and oversee. Ensure that local authorities, such as police, firefighters, friendship centres, bylaw officers, social services, athletic programs, parent–teacher associations, and sports teams act as servants of the community.

. . . as a nation

Support municipalities that practise holistic planning.

Enact legislation that encourages healthy environments, workplaces, communities, and habits, then celebrate those communities that innovate new models of planning that drive progress.

Dig down.

Create mechanisms by which individual citizens can offer ways to improve the state of the nation.

Spread the word.

Broadly communicate your successful innovations in collaboration and governance to civic associations such as community foundations, service clubs, and municipal governments, thereby helping communities in other regions across the country.

8

Advance the well-being of all.

We are all in this world together, and the only test of our
character that matters is how we look after the least fortunate among us.
How we look after each other, not how we look after ourselves.
That's all that really matters.

Tommy Douglas

For all the debate on the topic, an observer might assume that universal health care is a new concept, yet appreciation of society's fundamental obligation to care for the health of its citizens has its roots far back in history. Marcus Tullius Cicero famously enshrined the principle in De Legibus, his treatise on the law of c.50 BCE with the phrase "*Salus populi suprema lex esto*," meaning the health of the people should be the supreme law. John Locke echoed that injunction in his influential *Second Treatise on Government*, as did Thomas Hobbes in *Leviathan* and Spinoza in his *Theological-Political Treatise*. Often now shortened to *Salus populi suprema lex*, this prime directive appears on the coats of arms and mottos of states, cities, towns, universities, and associations throughout the world.

Most of us know that without our health we have nothing, both on our own and as members of large societies. It follows then that our well-being as nations depends on our careful attention to and protection of the health of all citizens. Our progress depends on it. When global health crises such as the pandemic occur, nations have a clear if painful opportunity to review their health-care priorities with a view to improving outcomes for all.

What Canada Learned from COVID

While Warren Buffet may have been talking about the health of individual businesses when he observed, "You only learn who has been swimming naked when the tide goes out," the insight applies equally to the health of individual groups within society. Not all communities are created equal. During the pandemic, we learned just how marginalized, underserved, and therefore vulnerable certain groups in Canada have become. Seniors took the heaviest toll, with citizens over sixty-five years old suffering more than 80 per cent of all COVID deaths in the first year. Three out of four of these were already compromised by ailments such as heart disease, stroke, cancer, asthma, diabetes, dementia, and anxiety disorders, so higher rates of death among the elderly were to be expected. But the substandard care that so many of the victims received in their retirement and so-called assisted-living facilities increased their exposure to contagion and worsened their chances of recovery. As we heard in dismal story after story, too many of these elder Canadians died alone without family to comfort or care for them and, in some cases, without anyone knowing for days that they had died.

Other groups, too, suffered unduly. Indigenous communities, low-income workers, immigrant workers, people living in racialized neighbourhoods, and the poor and homeless also bore the brunt of the pandemic, suffering high rates of infection, damage, and death. Too many of these citizens were tied to low-paying, low-benefit service jobs with little institutional protection, with the constant necessity to earn a living rather than take reasonable precautions. The degree and consequences of social inequity in Canada came as a shameful surprise to many once COVID hit.

There were other revelations. The Canadian response to the pandemic was slow and uneven. Health is a provincial responsibility, and there has been little consensus across the nation on what actions should be taken at any given moment in the progress of COVID with its many variants. Some provinces had travel restrictions, others had curfews, some mandated the wearing of masks and social distancing while others left the matter to choice. Some closed restaurants, others left them open. Some demanded proof of vaccination in public spaces, others didn't.

Variety, of course, is a feature of life in a confederation, but not all responsibility rests with the provinces. The duty of pandemic monitoring and warning lies logically with the Public Health Agency of Canada (PHAC), particularly through its Global Public Health Intelligence Network. Even though the network was Canadian bred and led, conceived in 2000 in concert with the World Health Organization, the office has been sorely understaffed, with the key position of chief health surveillance officer left vacant since 2017. Despite being recognized by the World Health Organization as the leading agency in the early detection of emerging plagues worldwide, the network was about to be eliminated altogether when COVID hit. Little monitoring was undertaken, therefore, in the immediate years leading up to the outbreak, and scientists in other government departments have since spoken of their deep concerns that their own warnings and advice to PHAC were largely ignored. The agency had also failed to manage the national stockpile of personal protective equipment (PPE), even though PHAC officials had known for a decade that there were serious problems with supply chain and inventory management. I am a fervent believer—as are most Canadians—in the need to keep our institutions active, effective, and responsible. In this case no one bothered, and who knows how many of the thirty thousand Canadian deaths thus far could have been prevented if warnings had come earlier and if better coordination had been made between the many departments, agencies, and facilities that bear responsibility for health care?

Another concern has been Canada's ongoing instinct to look to its own interests only, circling the wagons, hoarding pandemic PPE supplies, and channeling curative vaccines into our own country only. As we came to understand in early 2022, by which time vaccination rates had reached an effective level even as the Omicron variant moved in, COVID is now a disease of the unvaccinated. It is within unvaccinated populations that variants evolve, so if we do not ensure that the whole world is vaccinated, the pandemic will rage on in one form after another. In many parts of the world, alas, vaccination rates are almost negligible. As I write, while just over 84 per cent of Canada's population five years and older is fully vaccinated, twenty-eight of the world's countries have fewer than 5 per cent of their own citizens inoculated and thus are breeding grounds for new variants. We have a long-standing moral obligation and a pressing medical reason to contribute, yet Canada so far has made only a modest contribution to the world vaccination effort. That must change.

Other effects of the pandemic caught us off guard too. Businesses were pummelled and, despite a COVID relief program that ranked in the world's top twenty as a percentage of GDP, many businesses simply failed. The toll on restaurants was particularly visible, with continuing closures and many bankruptcies. There are over a million small businesses in Canada with fewer than a hundred employees, and by 2020 a quarter of those were reporting revenue decreases averaging 30 per cent year over year. Many of them were family operations without the resources to weather a multi-year reduction in sales. There was a devastating toll on charities as people cut back on contributions, forced to keep their money close to home. Education systems were largely unable to make the transition to online learning without a huge drop in the quality of teaching. Young people, whose mental well-being is highly dependent upon social interaction and acceptance, suffered in silence, and it may be decades before we know how deep are the scars. Similarly, the pressures of isolation saw marked increases in substance abuse, domestic violence, self harm, and suicide. And, almost a side note, active interest in arresting the tide of global climate change waned, even as the doomsday clock ticked its dreary way toward midnight.

Yet for all the confusion, error, damage, and sorrow of these pestilent times, a vast number of innovations have been possible, innovations and successes that otherwise might never have arrived. Vaccines to tackle COVID were developed with record speed. Before this pandemic, the fastest evolution of any vaccine from initial viral sampling to approval was for mumps, which took four full years to be engineered, validated, and approved by Canada's centennial year of 1967. In the fight against COVID, the Pfizer vaccine took the same journey in under eleven months. That speed of advance has allowed us to reimagine what the near future of vaccine development may hold. Many contend that the COVID-19 experience will almost certainly change the future of vaccine science. Dan Barouch, director of the Center for Virology and Vaccine Research at Harvard Medical School, said in *Nature* magazine, "It shows how fast vaccine development can proceed when there is a true global emergency and sufficient resources. New ways of making vaccines, such as by using messenger RNA (mRNA), have . . . shown that the development process can be accelerated substantially without compromising on safety."[1] We can now expect that other vaccines could be evolved within similar timeframes, mitigating diseases such as malaria, pneumonia, tuberculosis, and any subsequent global pandemics. Beyond the lifesaving vaccines themselves, we've also figured out how to make rapid testing available on a large scale, overcoming the frustrating test shortages that left many Canadians uncertain and stressed. As my friend Harry Rakowski, a wise thinker and prolific writer, and clinician investigator at the Toronto General Hospital Research Institute, put in his New Year's message for 2022, "We have antiviral drugs on the cusp of approval that will reduce the risk of overwhelming hospital and ICU capacity from the small number of people getting seriously ill. Domestic production of these essential drugs is finally on the horizon."

A happy accompaniment to that news was the fact that women practitioners stood at the forefront of many if not most of these innovations. While women account for 70 per cent of the world's healthcare practitioners and social workers, they are too often denied public credit for their leadership. Yet with COVID we've seen pioneers such as German-Turkish scientist, physician, and business entrepreneur Özlem Türeci earn world attention as her biotechnology company BioNTech developed the first messenger RNA-based vaccine approved for use against COVID-19. American biochemist Jennifer Doudna and French biochemist Emmanuelle Charpentier became the first two women in history to be jointly awarded the 2020 Nobel Prize in chemistry for their development of CRISPR gene editing. Hungarian biochemist Katalin Karikó with Drew Weissman developed the method of utilizing synthetic mRNA to fight disease that became the basis of that new vaccine. American teenager Anika Chebrolu won the 2020 3M Young Scientist Challenge for identifying a lead molecule that can selectively bind to the spike protein of the SARS-CoV-2 virus, a discovery that pharmaceutical researchers believe will lead to an effective treatment for COVID in the future. In Thailand, Ramida Juengpaisal built a national COVID tracker that aggregated information about the virus and helped to stop the spread of misinformation about the virus and its treatment in Southeast Asia.

Many women politicians themselves became inspiring examples of strong and capable leadership during the pandemic. Women heads of state in New Zealand, Germany, Slovakia, Finland, Taiwan, Scotland, Iceland, and Denmark stood out for the impressive effectiveness of their response. I've already mentioned physician Bonnie Henry, who has been praised worldwide for her early handling of the crisis in her role as provincial health officer for British Columbia. Women such as these around the world have taken the lead and helped us rise to the challenges we faced with nerve, insight, and compassion. Countless young girls will now be empowered by their examples to move more confidently into leadership roles.

A further example of rapid adaptation to COVID-19 was the response of Canada's universities, who doubled down on their mission by moving 1.4 million students online in only ten days while making dramatic investments in mental-health supports for students including, in some provinces, twenty-four-hour online counselling. Summer schools were mounted where professors learned to rethink and retool their pedagogical approach for online classes. Despite the challenges, the rates of enrolment, retention and completion of university programmes all rose.

Vivek Goel, president of the University of Waterloo, observed, "If the pandemic was only a biomedical problem it would have been solved a year ago." Ironically, the pandemic gave society the clarity to focused critical attention on vulnerable populations, and we have tackled the rise in rates of mental illness and domestic violence with creativity and love. We've adopted safer health practices to ensure the health of those confined to our prisons. We have recognized the importance of trust in our political leaders, including those serving in federal, provincial, territorial, and local governments. We have shown our support by giving them our attention, patience, and cooperation. We have gained deeper understanding of the relationship between animal habitat, world climate, and disease. As we retooled many of our businesses to produce personal protective equipment at wartime levels of productivity, we also made huge advances in online business and digital work life, with all the attendant complexity.

We've become more inclusive and varied in our definition of community and are working at last to find better ways to serve marginalized groups such as long-term-care residents and the homeless. We've witnessed and admired the leadership of Canada's medical and science community. We've celebrated our doctors, nurses, and all the health-care professionals and volunteers who support them by writing notes, sending thank-you letters, telling their stories on air, and giving shout-outs on social media, even marking the end of our work days with applause from the open windows of our homes around the world.

Lastly, and close to my heart, we have seen the kindness, care, generosity, welcome, and gratitude that people have given to one another exercised in every corner of the world. By doubling and tripling our volunteer efforts, we used the pandemic to completely restructure the nature of employee–community engagement. Humankind has a natural and deep instinct to help in times of turmoil, and help we did. With that, I'll leave the conclusion to Harry Rakowski.

"Although we still face many problems as individuals and as members of the world's community, we can best overcome them by building on the compassion and resiliency that so many of us showed in the face of great adversity. We need more kindness, compassion, and curiosity."

Let us keep those these qualities at the forefront of our actions.

The Public-Health Rectangle: Canadian since 1776

When Cicero penned *Salus populi suprema lex*, he set forth the guiding principle on which a nation's health system must be built. While the duty to ensure people's well-being may be discharged uniquely in any jurisdiction, experience over centuries has proved that health systems work only when they live up to that principle by attending to four distinct priorities. Just as four sides must be joined to form a square, empathetic health care of a population occurs only when all these interrelated qualities are hardwired into the system: Careful attention to population health, a wise steward's regard for cost effectiveness, broadly based satisfaction of the patient, and concern and respect for the provider. When the square is intact, any variety of improvements and initiatives based on new science and evidence-based policy can be undertaken. The result will be a dynamic, responsive, effective system that transforms empathy into action.

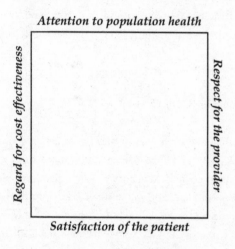

Health care that is accessible, affordable, and of high quality is a basic human right, and, by acknowledging that right, we shoulder our responsibility as a collective to advance the well-being of all individuals. Canada's recognition of this right and our willingness to act as stewards of a universal health system is part of our shared history. I wrote earlier about how First Nations communities put a high value on compassion to the vulnerable, knowing that staying healthy is both an individual and community duty. For immigrant colonists from Europe, Indigenous medicine was in many ways a vast improvement over the protocols they had known in Europe. High standards of hygiene among Indigenous bands made for a healthy environment, and deep knowledge of herbal remedies and treatment practices made it possible to treat their ill and wounded with impressive effect. Importantly, they willingly shared their medical knowledge with all they met.

Then in the colonial era, one particular incident offered early evidence of the empathetic attitude that set health care in Canada on its distinctive path. During British attacks against the French at Louisbourg during the Seven Years War, the surgeon Philippe-Louis François Badelard had fled to Quebec to continue his practice, but was captured there by the British. His reputation as a deft (if cranky) surgeon had preceded him up the St Lawrence, so the British asked him to continue

Hippocratic Oath, Revised

Do no harm was the basis or the original oath proposed by Greek physician Hippocrates around 400 BCE. Since then the oath has been updated many times and still inspires all members of the medical profession to serve with empathy. This version was conceived in 1964 by a dean of the School of Medicine at Tufts University and was widely accepted and is still in use today by many medical schools.

- I swear to fulfill, to the best of my ability and judgment, this covenant:
- I will respect the hard-won scientific gains of those physicians in whose steps I walk and gladly share such knowledge as is mine with those who are to follow.
- I will apply, for the benefit of the sick, all measures [that] are required, avoiding those twin traps of over-treatment and therapeutic nihilism.
- I will remember that there is art to medicine as well as science, and that warmth, sympathy, and understanding may outweigh the surgeon's knife or the chemist's drug.
- I will not be ashamed to say "I know not," nor will I fail to call in my colleagues when the skills of another are needed for a patient's recovery.

acting as a physician to patients both British and French, the only difference being that he would do it as a member of the Canadian militia. Badelard agreed and soon became a revered member of the growing Quebec community. In 1776, Quebec governor Guy Carleton asked Badelard to help solve a medical mystery that had been puzzling residents upriver in Charlevoix, as it had their neighbours throughout the Baie de St. Paul on which Charlevois lies. A strange disease had come

- I will respect the privacy of my patients, for their problems are not disclosed to me that the world may know. Most especially must I tread with care in matters of life and death. If it is given me to save a life, all thanks. But it may also be within my power to take a life; this awesome responsibility must be faced with great humbleness and awareness of my own frailty. Above all, I must not play at God.
- I will remember that I do not treat a fever chart, a cancerous growth, but a sick human being, whose illness may affect the person's family and economic stability. My responsibility includes these related problems, if I am to care adequately for the sick.
- I will prevent disease whenever I can, for prevention is preferable to cure.
- I will remember that I remain a member of society, with special obligations to all my fellow human beings, those sound of mind and body as well as the infirm.
- If I do not violate this oath, may I enjoy life and art, respected while I live and remembered with affection thereafter. May I always act so as to preserve the finest traditions of my calling and may I long experience the joy of healing those who seek my help.

upon them, claiming a disturbing number of victims. The symptom cluster was distinct; a sore throat would lead quickly to agonizing joint pain and ulceration of the genitals, ending with wholesale disintegration of the victim's bone tissue and death. Practitioners in Charlevoix had so far not been able to determine either the cause of or cure for of the ailment. The only diagnostically significant detail was that the malady had appeared not long after the arrival of Scottish soldiers in the area. Badelard made the mystery his central focus from 1776 to 1784. He named the infirmity le mal de la baie St-Paul and travelled from parish to parish treating its victims and looking for its source.[2]

He solved it. It was a new strain of venereal disease, brought by the Scots militia. Once he was sure, he set down measures to prevent the disease, including a modest diet light on meat, and measures to treat it, including the ingestion of mercury, which worked well as a cathartic (the way ipecac does today) even though it made people's teeth fall out. But it's neither the diagnosis nor the treatment that intrigues me most; it's the way Badelard and Carleton went about

Who becomes a hero in Canada?

I came to believe that health services ought not to have a price tag on them, and that people should be able to get whatever health services they required irrespective of their individual capacity to pay.

TOMMY DOUGLAS, 1979

Tommy Douglas was voted "Greatest Canadian" in a 2003 CBC Television competition. As premier of Saskatchewan, Douglas led the campaign for state-funded health insurance in his province. As Charlotte Gray writes in her book *The Promise of Canada*, "His success provided the model and the project. Alarmed that one in twenty residents were being felled by the disease, the doctor and the governor agreed that all patients should be given immediate medical treatment—without exclusion, cost, or judgment. Everyone got treated, no one got charged, no one got blamed.[3] Then Badelard wrote a paper describing the disease and detailing best practices to prevent and treat it, a paper that was widely shared in Canada and is now remembered as the first medical-research treatise in the country.

So here in Charlevoix in the late eighteenth century we have the genesis of Canadian universal health care—available to all at no direct cost to the patient and with research shared openly to improve care everywhere. The fact that the decision to handle the issue in this novel way sprang from collaboration between a French medical expert and an English administrator also makes me proud, yet another of countless proofs that one of the key ingredients of our unique culture in Canada is the fortuitous and unbeatable combination of our varied cultural inclinations and strengths.

momentum to the federal Liberal Party to do the same for the whole country." I think Canadians' esteem for Douglas arises from our support for state-funded health insurance: We realize just how much good it has done for us individually and as a country. We also realize what our support for it says about us as a people—that we are smart and caring, that we are empathetic and that we value fairness. Government (that is, Canadians together) can be a force for good; it can improve the lives of every one of us. As Charlotte Gray put it: "The fight to introduce medicare into Saskatchewan remains a turning point in Canadian history. Other countries might regard homicidal clashes as founding moments in their national psyches. In Canada, the battle was fought with stethoscopes."

That early strategy had two additional underpinning tenets: heal all and do no harm. For a doctor treating an ill or even apparently healthy patient, the doctor ensures that whatever intervention is undertaken does not worsen the condition of the patient, respecting the natural response of the body to heal itself and restore its normal equilibrium. Healers, while fulfilling an immediate obligation to heal their patients, recognize that the illness of one may infect others and ultimately a whole community. In the reverse case, an illness prevalent in many throughout the community may infect each individual in that community, including the single most powerful or protected individual. As John Donne wrote, "No man is an island entire of itself."

Two centuries later, the government of Canada drafted (and all provinces endorsed) an approach to health care dubbed the health-field concept. In 1975, following an in-depth study of the underlying causes of illness and death in Canada, this new prevention protocol was outlined in a document called *A New Perspective on the Health of Canadians*, and relied upon constant coordination among healthcare professionals working concurrently in the fields of human biology, environment, lifestyle and healthcare organization. This holistic approach was a first for Canada and other countries, and I think it followed directly, if slowly, from the approach to public health care we adopted in Charlevois back in 1776.

Public health policy that mandates rational, non-judgmental inquiry leading to broad treatment and prevention is, for me, one of the most admirable innovations of that period in our history. Today, in the midst of our own novel, virulent, and global pandemic, we must hold ourselves to the same standard. We must harm no one by our actions, instead working to heal all through sharing our knowledge, medicines, and treatments with all citizens of the world at no cost to any victim. As we proved two and a half centuries ago, it's the smart, caring, and Canadian thing to do.

Universal? Not always.

Canadian physician and writer Vincent Lam has long made the connection between good health and social well-being. Among other examples, in his 2011 biography of Tommy Douglas,[4] Lam channelled Cicero when he wrote: "In a civilized society, health care should be considered essential to individual and social well-being, and viewed both as a public right and a collective obligation." Canadians may think of the need for universal health as self-evident, yet the sentiment is not universally accepted. Comparing practices here in Canada to practices in the United States often spawns more confusion than clarity, but many diligent observers have been compelled to contrast Canada's state-funded system with the United States' employer-based health insurance. Writing for the *New York Times*, professors and authors Anne Case and Angus Deaton make a strong and specific connection: "Employer-based health insurance is a wrecking ball, destroying the labor market for less-educated workers and contributing to the rise in deaths of despair." In their 2020 bestseller about the decline of American society,[5] they defined such deaths as those resulting from suicide, drug overdoses, and alcoholic liver disease, citing peer-reviewed studies that conclude when joblessness increases, so do the number of deaths of despair. The tragic irony in the United States is this: American health care itself is a prime cause of rising rates of deaths of despair. Employer-based health insurance is an impetus for employers to reduce the number of less-skilled workers they hire by outsourcing, offshoring, or automating their roles. Health care is not something that the free market can deliver in a socially tolerable way.

In such a regime, the lowest paid do not enjoy insurance, cannot afford private treatment, and, often, cannot even risk taking time off to seek any treatment at all. In such systems, these most vulnerable groups can't get health services they need when bad things happen, and they perish. Here at home, we've opted for a different approach, but we cannot be smug; we have many regrettable Canadian proofs of the link between poor socio-economic status and health outcomes.

One of these proofs comes from a collaboration between the *Hamilton Spectator* and the McMaster University Health Services and Hospital, whose surveys established a link between low-income postal-code districts in Hamilton, Ontario, and the highest frequency of emergency-room visits and other highest scores of morbidity and mortality. Named CODE RED, the Hamilton study tapped into the large body of Canadian scholarship that also reveals major gaps in Canadian health care. Put bluntly, poor people are doomed to poor health. As one might expect, data proved the opposite for high-income postal codes. When the articles appeared in 2010, they drew wide attention and some astonishment among Canadians, although they came as little surprise to those living in the low-income districts themselves. CODE RED provided hard data for government and agencies to address problems of poverty and health, mobilized other agencies to help people in need, and became a key issue in the municipal election. The series received international attention and has been integrated into the curriculum of a number of university courses. Among the many awards and honours given to the *Spectator*'s team of journalists, the judges of Canada's Michener Award for Journalism presented them with the Governor General's Award for Public Service and Integrity in Journalism. When reporter Steve Buist accepted that Michener Citation of Merit in June of 2011, his brief remarks ended with a sombre reminder of the inequities that exist within our own health system here in Canada: "What's most notable—and discouraging—about our findings are the staggering variations that exist across the city from best neighbourhood to worst. It's not an exaggeration to say that some parts of the city have Third World health conditions and Third World lifespans—a sobering concept for Hamiltonians to consider." It's not just some parts of the city as Buist put it, it's some parts of the whole country. As we continue to learn, the suffering among those within impoverished and vulnerable groups (named above in this chapter) is far greater than among those better off, and, if we don't change that, we're all going to pay the price.

Collaboration on Concussion

Sharon Jr., our middle child, early on showed herself to be both healer and helper. We have one marvellous photograph of her sitting cross-legged on the kitchen floor with ten slices of bread around in two rows of five in front of her flanked by a large jar of peanut-butter. She was making sandwiches for her elder and younger sisters' school lunches, while the family dog salivated nearby. Just six years old, she built a system to do the job she figured needed doing, unasked. Everyone got fed and, as I recall, none of the girls choked on dog hair. It was no surprise to any of us that Sharon Jr. ended up as a medical doctor, given her trademark combination of acute curiosity and compassion, and extraordinary discipline, and yet her path to become a medical professional was indirect.

At Harvard she earned her undergraduate honours degree in arts, majoring in government and played two varsity sports. From there she went to Cambridge to study law. She returned home to McGill and completed a master's degree in law and bioethics while also serving on the research ethics board of the Douglas Hospital. She took several science courses with excellent grades and similarly high scores on the Medical College Admissions Test, and then applied to McGill medicine. She was not admitted. Her grades were fine, but the interviewing committee expressed a concern that, with such a varied background, she lacked a laser focus on medicine. At the time I was McGill's former principal, so I guess her rejection proved the independence of admissions decisions. But as Sharon's subsequent career trajectory demonstrated, her breadth of education and experience plus her determination to ask questions and answer them were important assets that would help her become a leader and innovator in medicine. She unites all four aspects of the four-sided health-care model we described above.

With a glowing recommendation from McGill's former dean of medicine, for whom she worked as a part-time research assistant, she went to study medicine at Dartmouth College, one of the smallest medical schools in the United States. It is a jewel, whose dean of admissions told her they admitted a group of students each year with non-traditional backgrounds—this was a risk, but one they stood behind. She flourished there. Her master's of law thesis had addressed legal and ethical dilemmas in modern medicine, in which she had taken a profound interest while working with the former dean of medicine on examining, modernizing, and teaching professionalism for physicians.

Years earlier, Sharon Jr. had been deeply moved by the death of her grandmother, Joan Downey, of congestive heart failure. Studying law at Cambridge at the time, she got the news that Granny was failing, and booked the first flight home from the United Kingdom, calling in on one of her stopovers to talk to her grandmother but, alas, arriving too late to be at her bedside. From that point on, her mother and I could see Sharon Jr.'s awakening drive to move from law on its own to law and medicine combined. She would say it was also observing important decisions around allocating health-care resources being decided in the courts in England during her studies that helped her appreciate the value of a strong health-care system in a society.

Sharon Jr. married the Yale- and Columbia-trained physician Roger Zemek, who did additional training in development pediatrics and then a fellowship in pediatric emergency medicine at McGill, and who was happy to settle with Sharon Jr. in Ottawa. Today they are physicians and researchers in the University of Ottawa's medical faculty and hospital system. Sharon is the scientific director of the Montfort Hospital Research Institute, one of the university's teaching hospitals, while Roger is the director of clinical research at the Children's Hospital of

Eastern Ontario (CHEO). He majored in mathematics at Yale and, with his colleagues, conducted the largest study of pediatric concussion in the world. As the evidence from that study and many others examining concussion changed the standard of care and identified gaps in the care available, Sharon Jr. and Roger drew on their expertise and experience working with interdisciplinary teams to create a better approach to one of the most inconsistently treated illnesses that children and adults suffer: concussion. With Sharon Jr.'s older sister Alex as CEO, they created a health-care team approach that offers evidence-based multidisciplinary collaborative care. Appropriately named 360 Concussion Care, their operation also functions as a living lab, constantly learning from each patient to drive improvement of health outcomes for those who suffer a concussion. To this truly entrepreneurial endeavour, Alex brings valuably broad experience, having taken arts and then law degrees at McGill, followed by two years studying Chinese at the Beijing Language Institute, then practising communications law while serving two terms as senior policy adviser on law, health, and education to the premier of Ontario, and then serving as CEO at Catalyst, an NGO advancing leadership opportunities for women, and finally as a vice-president for public and government relations for CBC, all before leaping into innovation as CEO of 360. Leading a new "start-up" enterprise, Alex is both innovator and manager, and at times has been the note taker and person answering the phones, able to adapt to the requirements of the job to get it done.

Concussion is tricky in both diagnosis and treatment, because every patient has a unique injury and a unique cluster of presenting symptoms they manage in the environment of their family, friends school, work, and activities. As such, each patient must also have a personalized treatment plan and some require access to a diverse team of collaborating specialists, ideally soon after an injury if not recovering well, all to be achieved within a national health-care system known for its provincial peculiarities, isolated silos of specialty care, public funding of some services and not for others, and long wait times. In that context, 360 Concussion Care serves each patient as both healer and advocate, making a diagnosis, creating a bespoke medical plan, and helping their patients receive coordinated care from specialists including occupational therapists, physiotherapists, social workers, neurologists, psychologists, and whoever else is needed to return the patient to robust health as rapidly as possible.

Alex brought an extra dimension to the subject of concussion. It is described in *Inconceivable*, her non-fiction book published in 2021. I read the manuscript three times in its various drafts and was moved to tears each time. My proposed title for it was "The Other Side of Sorrow" because the story, one of the saddest tragedies imaginable, ends in three-person-inspired joy.

Alex was unable to get pregnant when she and her husband David started trying to have a family in her early thirties. Alex endured many years of unsuccessful fertility treatments. All failed. She and David opted to work with a surrogate mother to carry their child. Their surrogate became pregnant and carried a beautiful baby girl to full term. The day after her due date they got the exciting news that labour had begun. They jumped in their car to drive the hundred kilometres to the birthing hospital to welcome their baby.

Disaster again greeted them at the hospital door. Their baby, Sam, died in childbirth.

I spoke to Alex often through the difficult months and years that followed. When I saw Alex she always had a tenacious thrust to her chin but a grim look of despair in her eyes.

She and David grieved the loss of Sam profoundly. They also made the decision that the only way forward for them was to try to become parents again. They worked with two surrogate mothers, one in Ontario and one in Green Bay, Wisconsin, who both became pregnant. But once again dark clouds appeared. One of the surrogates went into labour eleven weeks early and delivered baby Georgia twenty-nine weeks into the pregnancy and weighing under three pounds.

Three months later, Alex and David brought Georgia home from her extended stay in the neonatal intensive care unit and prepared for the arrival of her sister Sadie in Green Bay. David stayed home with Georgia and I drove Alex to Green Bay for Sadie's birth. We drove Sadie, at one day old, almost twenty-four hours through a raging snowstorm to bring her home on Christmas Eve.

Almost two years later, a quite incredible event occurred. Alex found herself naturally pregnant, and on Christmas Day Lucas was born.

Our cup runneth over!

Alex's book *Inconceivable* is hard to believe on several counts. Her personal story is deeply moving in its demonstration of courage and determination and is very personal. It is also an education around the prevalence of infertility, its painful impact on people struggling with it, and the need for better access to help for people who need help building their families.

Alex served as executive director of the policy team for Ontario premier Dalton McGuinty for five years. He created a task force to review fertility and foster care and adoption, and as a result Ontario instituted some groundbreaking and compassionate policy reforms.

Alex brings personal experience, creativity, and wisdom in her new enterprise with concussions.

I say all the important things in life I have learned from my children. And from whom did they learn? That's easy. Their mother.

I was thirteen-year-old Sharon Sr.'s first date; we were married when she was twenty and she had her five daughters in seven years; the last three were by Caesarean section, ending her baby-making days.

While raising our five daughters in the fifty-six years since our marriage, Sharon has been an incredibly loving and innovative partner: to a young law professor, a law faculty dean, and a president of two universities, and as the governor general's first lady. She has been simply extraordinary in these posts. She is curious, caring, and strategically and intuitively wise. She has brought these character traits to all the institutions we have served during our journey, and most important, has been a wonderful mother to our five daughters (and along the way to many of their friends). In another important sphere of creative activity, she completed her diploma in physio and occupational therapy at the University of Toronto, an honours bachelor of science degree at Western University, and a master's and doctoral degree in rehabilitation medicine at McGill. And through it all she has been a relentless supporter of mental health, both to bring it out if the shadows and to develop with so much hope the remarkable advances we see in diagnosis and cure.

Sharon tells something of her story in a trilogy of historical fiction books, the third of which is now more than half completed. The books chronicle the lives and triumphs of three strong courageous and remarkably resilient women. The first, entitled *Matrons and Madames*, features her grandmother, widowed through the gassing death of her Scottish engineer husband in the trenches in World War I and devastated by the loss of her baby son in the 1919 influenza. She immigrated with Sharon's three-year-old mother to Lethbridge, Alberta, to become the first woman superintendent of the hospital there. The second book, *Patchwork Society*, is her mother's story, that of a single divorced woman transposing her life from society star in Sault Ste. Marie to intrepid social worker—the first in that challenging northern region—while also raising Sharon and her sister. The third book is Sharon's journey and navigates through the dramatic social changes during her lifetime. I'm terrified about this one because she knows all my foibles and frailties, most of which I dearly hope she will adroitly conceal.

I see in her stories the characters of our daughters. These three books give us another angle from which we see her inspiring efforts to help build a smart and caring Canada.

The health of people is the true wealth of nations.

A year after CODE RED was published, two American economists completed their own survey of what happens when some citizens and not all citizens get to make choices about the distribution of benefits and resources within their country. Their evidence-based conclusion was summed up in the first three words of the title of what soon became their bestselling book, *Why Nations Fail: The Origins of Power, Prosperity, and Poverty*.[6] Their thesis is that regimes in which all citizens participate and from which all citizens benefit simply do better than others. Ultimately, regimes that control who makes decisions and who gets rewarded all fail.

With surgical precision, the authors slice into dozens of alarming examples from history that support their contention, and they echo the thoughts of some three hundred scientific works to support their thesis. This book is a great read, and I heartily suggest you find a copy if you're wondering why it matters to you that people in one postal code of Hamilton, Ontario, die earlier on average than those in another, or why undrinkable water on a First Nations reserve is indeed a national threat, or why immigrants, the unemployed, the homeless, and incarcerated criminals should all receive the same level of health care that you do.

As the authors reveal, it matters because these are all situations in which choices have to be made about who gets what. And when one group does not get something that everyone else does, it's invariably because they weren't in on the decision-making. Without giving everything away, the book suggests that the approach can either be one of inclusion or extraction. People are allowed to be in on decisions or they aren't. By now you know my position on the necessity of inclusion, and this book furnishes compelling proof that the choice to be extractive destroys economies, societies, and empires. Civilization is indeed a garden in a jungle; it must be carefully tended to survive. I propose that the health of all those living in that garden be our first priority.

Empathetic things to do when you intend to Advance the well-being of all.

. . . as an individual

Head up your own health team.
No one has greater influence over the state of your health than you. Cultivate healthy habits. Be responsible for your own diet, and exercise, and be responsive about your physical and mental health, seeking guidance from your broader health team of physicians, therapists, pharmacists, and caregivers when you might need them.

Think always about equity.
Treat people as whole people, not simply as members of a particular group. Advocate for balance and fairness in our health-care system. Identify people who are still being left behind; reach out to the them, and put them in touch with the agencies, institutions, and services that are ready and able to help them secure and maintain their health.

. . . as a community

Cherish and respect our healers.
Health-care professionals are among the most admired groups in Canada. When physicians, nurses, and pharmacists are considered as one group, they rank as the single most trusted authority in Canada. They've earned that respect from the public, and they should have that

respect acknowledged by community leaders, who can tap into their unequalled expertise and influence to effect lasting improvement.

Recognize the interdependence of all actors in health care.

Every great community health system recognizes the need for swift and transparent communication among a myriad of health-care experts, from doctors and nurses to counsellors and midwives. Build community forums and invite all participating members of the health community to have a voice.

. . . as a nation

Prove that public health is your country's highest ideal.

Recognize health care as a fundamental human right and social responsibility. Remember the motto *Salus populi suprema lex*, and provide the funding, muster the resources, build and constantly improve the system, and educate the populace to value their health and the health of all their fellow citizens in all things.

Pay attention to the quality of our health institutions.

The Commonwealth Fund, a health-care measuring institution, ranks Canada fourth from the top in resources invested in its health system as a percentage of GDP and second last in system performance. The United States is highest in investment by far, yet lowest in performance by far. Ranked in order of performance, the other countries in the survey as are: Norway, Netherlands, Australia, United Kingdom, Germany, New Zealand, Sweden, France, and Switzerland. Canada should always ensure the high quality of its health care. Avoid complacency. Look to see what necessary services are required, then work to strengthen our health institutions in ways that fill the gaps.

Challenge the medical profession.

While leadership in matters of health policy may come from elected officials, true inspiration to follow it will come from practitioners in the healing professions. Challenge and encourage them to lead in a responsive and innovative way.

9

Be in the business of trust.

I've always been fascinated by business and learned early on that many people in business don't do it very well. About as vague a noun as you can get, business is just a catch-all term for the many ways people go about exchanging what they have or can do for things they need to have or wish to get done. The key to a thriving business, of course, is figuring how to do that well enough to generate a reliable source of income. Given that some seven thousand Canadian businesses tumble into bankruptcy every year and another twenty-thousand or so just quietly shut their doors, one can assume it's not easy to pull off.

That revelation came with my third part-time job at age twelve, working after school on weekdays, all day on Saturdays, and all day through the summers for a local family that ran an automotive dealership shop in Sault Ste. Marie. As their eager gopher, I earned twenty-five cents an hour for fetching, sweeping, scrubbing, moving, hauling, washing, tidying, filling, emptying, and other such grunt work for which I was qualified. When the garage was particularly busy, I was also tasked with ferrying cars from where they had been parked around the corner into the garage bay itself, then driving them back again once they were ready, though the experience was postponed until I was thirteen.

When I came to work full-time in my first summer there, I was tasked with greeting customers as they came in, writing down the car trouble they were having or the maintenance they required, and passing those requirements to the chief mechanic, who was also the service manager. He would meet with or call each customer with an estimate once he knew what was needed. A gifted technician whose work was impeccable, the service manager had deep knowledge, high standards, and an almost unbearable personality. His routine with customers went like this. 1. Look at the requirements. 2. Inspect the car. 3. Give an estimate. 4. Refuse to explain. 5. Refuse to negotiate. 6. Suggest they go elsewhere.

The owner, a mechanic himself who had all but retired, helped out around the shop. He was a gentler soul but seemed unconcerned that his service manager was letting customers know they were stupid, a habit that frequently drove them to the competition; at the very least, it would induce them to authorize only a minimum amount of work. No wonder. His standards might have been the highest in town, but he had given them no context in which to understand the need for the repairs he prescribed, and no reason, therefore, to trust the estimate.

The place was jam-packed that first week of summer, and the service manager was too busy under the hood to speak to customers or phone them, so I was asked to take the extra step of explaining the estimates to the car owners. I put down my broom and jumped on the phone. With the owner over my shoulder, I made about a dozen calls that day, and my routine was this. 1. Introduce myself. 2. Tell them how many repairs were recommended. 3. Explain why each was needed. 4. Tell them the possible maximum cost of each step, erring on the high side. 5. Acknowledge that the total was expensive, even if necessary. 6. Invite them to choose only some of the repairs if cost was an issue. 7. Tell them that if we found something undetected and expensive I would call them back to have them authorize any extra cost.

What happened that day amazed both me and the gentleman at my shoulder. In almost every case, when invited to choose which of the services to authorize, the customers said, "Do them all. I trust you." Even when I promised to call them back if we found something else wrong, they most often said, "Just go ahead. I trust you." They didn't trust me, of course. I was just a thirteen-year-old kid. But they did trust the business because of what I had said. I didn't have any detailed insight then into why they had chosen to trust the estimate, but having heard the word *trust* so often that day, I couldn't help but conclude that business must depend on it.

Since then, I've spent my life around and in corporations. Even though my visible career has been in academic and government circles, everything I accomplished depended on the involvement and contribution of businesses in every sector, so I kept my eyes open. In time, I sensed the heady mix of risk and freedom that entrepreneurs feel, their fortunes rising and falling on the merit of their own instincts. Yet, unlike my curmudgeonly mechanic boss, those who prospered never considered their customers to be stupid or miserly but rather saw them as intelligent people with legitimate needs that plenty of competing businesses were perfectly willing and fully ready to meet. In almost every case, they understood that the trust of their customers was a gift freely given, and they worked relentlessly to earn it.[1] Recognizing the wisdom of this awareness, I began to say that the business of business is trust.

As my journey of learning about business progressed, I met people running larger and larger operations and saw how those who succeeded tended to be equally ambitious and humble; while ready to make big bets, they always sought advice on matters they did not understand. They didn't want to hit any wall that others could already see. In time, I was asked to join the boards of some of these businesses as a director, just one member of a group entrusted to offer guidance to the CEO and executive team from a slightly removed, likely unbiased perspective. That made me an insider. As a director, I then had the great learning opportunity to see how business works in disparate sectors and disciplines. I'm constantly impressed by the ingenuity and, to be candid, honest dealing with which most businesses undertake their operations.

I learned about the building-materials trade as a director of Masco, plumbing and water systems with EMCO, textiles with Dominion Textile, distillery products and entertainment with Seagram's, online learning with D2L, the Internet with OpenText, senior living and mental health care with RBJ Schlegel, solar energy with Aspire International, financial services with Canada Trust, publishing and media with Southam, insurance and investment management with Fairfax, information technology with CGI, telecommunications with Alcatel, aerospace with SPAR, and securities as a public director of the Montreal Stock Exchange. In every company, in every boardroom, I asked myself the question I began to ask myself at age thirteen on that crazy Saturday at the garage: What are we doing to earn people's trust in us? Before long, I asked the question out loud. As I heard from C-level executives how their businesses interacted with their customers, staff, suppliers, and shareholders, I learned of countless strategies for building authentic trust, strategies backed by dozens of metrics to help companies monitor their performance in things like customer experience, satisfaction, and retention. But my interest soon lighted on the deeper question: What precisely is trust? I knew it had a lot to do with the confidence one has that someone else will behave as expected, no matter how conditions change, but what is it that leads to such confidence in the first place? My curiosity had an ulterior motive; I'd long suspected (fretted, really) that erosion of trust is the first omen of the eventual failure of a society, and I wanted to know a lot more about how to restore it.[2]

In my journey, I was intrigued by something Stephen M.R. Covey had written about trust in business, as I fancied it applied to trust in every realm. He penned his insights in his 2006 book called *The Speed of Trust*. If you're not yet familiar with that particular work, you probably know his father's bestseller, *The 7 Habits of Highly Successful People*, which has sold 25 million copies since its first printing in 1989. In *The Speed of Trust*, Covey Jr. shares a formula that would stir any entrepreneur's interest:

trust —> lower cost + faster speed

meaning, the more trustworthy your business is considered by its customers, the cheaper and faster you can do business. So trust, he contends, leads to increased profit. To me, Covey's most helpful insight comes after that, as he describes the four building blocks of trust. The first two are the integrity and intent of the person representing the business at any given time. If that person appeals to the customer as honest (integrity), and seems to truly want to help meet that customer's expressed need (intent), those two blocks are now in place. The third and fourth blocks relate to the performance of the business itself. If customers believe your company has the ability to live up to its promises (capacity), then trust grows deeper, whether you've been asked to source certain materials on their behalf, build particular products for them, deliver their packages on time, or shovel the snow off their driveways after each storm. Lastly, if your company's track record is solid (results), they have empirical proof that supports their instinct to trust you. Here are the four buildings blocks at a glance.

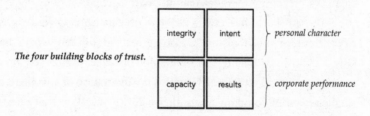

The four building blocks of trust.

I'm struck by an interesting difference between the set of two building blocks on top and the set at the bottom. The lower blocks, related as they are to corporate performance, are pretty easy for a customer to verify. Before ordering anything from a small local business, prospective customers can ask around about the company's reputation, find articles about them online, call the Better Business Bureau, or, if still unsure, google that company's name with the word *review*, or, when suspicious, with the word *fraud*, *scam*, or *complaint* just to see what comes back. In large public companies, there are myriad ways to verify a company's claims; most countries have securities commissions that set stringent requirements for frequent, detailed, and honest reporting of a corporation's plans, affiliations, results, returns-on-investment, and the like. So whether a business is small or large, it's not hard to learn about its capacity and results.

The personal qualities in the top two blocks, however, are trickier to validate. How do you know if a sales rep is exaggerating? How can you tell if a price you've been quoted is fair and guaranteed not to change later? How can you be sure the products a company offers are well made? In short, how can you tell in a brief exchange whether the people you interact with in a business are on the level? With the upsurge of online scams, and the continued success scammers have tricking their victims into assuming (or disregarding) the trustworthiness of their dodgy offers, it's clear that many people make leaps of faith based on faulty gut instinct.

Because businesses can be fooled too, especially when dealing with suppliers, arranging mergers, teaming with partners, and hiring staff, the corporate world has a wide variety of mechanisms to verify integrity and intent, mechanisms that vary greatly in different world markets. For business dealings in China, for instance, parties rely on an honour system called *guanxi*, by which the reputation of anyone referring a person or company to another will rise or fall on that referred party's performance. Thus, no one is willing to risk exaggerating the worth of anyone they propose. In Canada and the United States we conduct due-diligence investigations, and we call references to get the low-down on the person or company with whom we're thinking of doing business. So much emphasis is placed on this latter practice that people taking the calls have learned to be cautious in their responses. Lawsuits have been filed against former employers for defaming former staff by overstating their weaknesses when called for references. More surprising, perhaps, courts in some litigious jurisdictions are beginning to see cases in which companies that have hired an employee based on the glowing reference of a former employer now want to hold that employer liable for exaggerating the value of the staff member's performance.[3] Where business is concerned, trust is a weighty matter.

If you own or work in a business or institution serving the public, which most Canadians do, no matter what you offer, your first and most important job will be to build trust. It's not just to innovate new products or get out there on social media or build market share or drive profits. All these become more possible when you have the trust of others, yet are mere distractions when you don't. So your first thought about customers—both prospective and current—should be to ensure they never have to ask around about you or google your name to assure themselves that you are not fraudulent. The easiest, cheapest, most reliable way to avoid any confusion or suspicion is to tell the truth and be transparent. Let them know your results, both the good and the bad. Let them in on your true capacity, whether large or small on any given day. Help them understand your intent by stating it clearly in your mission statement and marketing materials and by describing precisely how you intend to do so in your dealings with them. And when you do those first three things without exaggerating, downplaying, misleading, or falsifying, they will come to know your integrity. And if Covey is right about those four qualities, trust will flourish, and your business will reap the rewards.[4]

So think kindly and creatively about your customers, your patients, your students, your parishioners, your subscribers, your passengers, your guests, your patrons, your fans, your members, and find ways to prove that their trust in you is deserved. Your doing so will be an act of empathy, even though being empathetic is not your ultimate goal. It is, however, the road that will take you there.

One over One in One

The advantages of building trust in businesses, as you would expect, are just as real for not-for-profit and public-administration organizations. One clear opportunity to reap such rewards became obvious to me on my second day as governor general. I walked into my office to find my desk overburdened with piles of dockets containing folders containing files containing regulations, orders in council, commissions, and all manner of letters to be signed. Pinned to each docket was a cover page with five or six signatures verifying that the item within had been read, considered, amended, and authorized for advancement to the next level of scrutiny. How odd. Why would it take a platoon of bureaucrats to prepare a document? Was there a reason for that? I asked around, and while no one knew for certain, all presumed there must be. Vetting at different levels of authority seemed prudent, and it's the way things had always been done.

I am not given to management by edict, so I considered a bit more and after some consultation concluded we should run a pilot project. For several weeks we implemented a system that we called "one over one in one." Our plan was to whittle the process down to just three components. First, only one person would be responsible for drafting the document from start to finish, seeking advice from others as required, but with sole authority to decide how then to proceed. The first one in our formula was just one signature, that of the author. While perfecting the document, the author could verify that it was ready for my signature and release, even if I wouldn't for some reason have time to read it line by line. The second one in the formula was my signature. The third one was the time allowed for the whole process—one day. We undertook, as a general principle, to have the required authorization or response to any document arriving at Rideau Hall sent within just twenty-four hours of its arrival. There would be exceptions, of course—complicated matters requiring more extensive consultations—but these too were managed on an expedited basis, with one person taking overall responsibility for the task.

The big change was that our senior colleagues, those who previously viewed the documents at different stages, shifted their roles from critical examination to coaching and mentoring those on their teams, the generally younger people now given responsibility for drafting the document. Those younger authors grew quickly in their writing skills, confidence, and pride in the quality and efficiency of the office, ultimately leading to greatly increased job satisfaction. This was two-way trust at work. It was only one change, but a dramatic change that began building a culture of pride across the whole team.

A second proof of the merits of the empathy–trust combination was also demonstrated in my early days at Rideau Hall. The secretary to the Office of the Governor General is the key figure overseeing all the staff at Rideau Hall. On my arrival as governor general, that post became vacant when the incumbent retired. To find a worthy successor, I sought advice from the clerk of the Privy Council,[5] who heads the public service and serves as the principal non-partisan adviser to the prime minister. The clerk is also the principal adviser from the public service to the governor general. I asked the clerk to identify a rising star from among those of his senior colleagues whom he regarded as potential successors. He recommended Stephen Wallace. Stephen had excelled at the Canadian International Development Agency, where among other roles he had served as the vice-president of the Afghanistan Task Force. As a senior public servant, he had been assistant secretary of government operations at the Treasury Board Secretariat, and an associate deputy minister for the Department of Canadian Heritage. He was fluently bilingual, honest as the day is long, smart, and gracious. We reached out to Stephen and invited him to come and talk to us about the position of secretary.

There was not a history in the office of the governor general of regularly developing a strategic plan to govern operations in both the long and short term. During our selection interviews, I informed Stephen about this and asked how he would go about working on a strategic plan. He advised that he had already given that some thought and could produce a sketch over the weekend, but he then quickly added that this would not be the strategic plan I wanted. I was intrigued. He said, "Give me three months so we can consult directly with all the staff at Rideau Hall. We will want to invite each and every person there to give their input. Then the plan we arrive at together will be smart and will be owned by the entire team." I'm pretty sure I had made my decision before he even finished talking. We offered him the job. To our delight, he enthusiastically accepted. Stephen is the ideal public servant, epitomizing as he does the leader-as-servant philosophy, carrying his high intelligence lightly, exuding a keen curiosity while encouraging advice and engagement from others. With the two most important qualities of all—kindness and thoughtfulness—he set a new standard for collegial management. He began with the conviction that building one's people is the surest way to build one's institution, and that required implicit respect for each team member's talent and commitment. He treated everyone with empathy at all times, working always to see their perspectives before offering his own. That was the route to building a trusting team, and it was the team as a coherent whole that ensured the successful execution of the dynamic plan created. I was pleased but hardly surprised that for the last two years of our mandate, very much with Stephen's leadership, the Office of the Secretary to the Governor General was selected as the employer of choice among all the agencies and ministries of the Government of Canada operating in the national capital region.

Stakeholders vs Shareholders

Did you ever expect a corporation to have a conscience,
when it has no soul to be damned, and no body to be kicked?

EDWARD, LORD THURLOW, C. 1790

Over the past two or three decades, those who study business, especially publicly traded corporations, have wrestled with two basic questions: What is the purpose of the corporation? Who is the corporation? In corporation-law statutes and judicial decisions, these what and who questions are usually answered by specifying the duties of directors who, acting together as a board, oversee the corporation. They are obliged by law to ensure in their oversight that they "act bona fides and in the best interest of the corporation." This statement of obligation, however, neither answers the two questions nor helps directors understand their duty.

In much of the last century in Canada, that duty was presumed to be owed to shareholders, with directors' chief responsibility being to drive maximum profit to those shareholders. Recently, judicial decisions in Europe and subsequently in Canada have broadened the scope of duty by declaring it to extend beyond the interests of shareholders alone and attending to those of stakeholders. These include employees, creditors, suppliers, and communities in which the corporation operates and, even more broadly, society as a whole. Thus, corporations are presumed to have a role in ensuring the public good.

More recent still, the movement from shareholder to stakeholder responsibility has embraced three comprehensive if somewhat loosely defined categories: environment, society, and governance—or E.S.G. Environment includes sustainable economic development and response to climate change with mitigating strategies. Society includes the public good of the countries in which the corporation operates and the welfare of the citizens who are impacted directly or indirectly by it. Governance demands not only a company's observing all legal requirements but also ensuring that its internal rules and overall culture build and reinforce trust in the corporation. These three priorities, of course, do not stand alone. Financial viability is presumed to be a central focus of any corporation's activity; if it is not viable, it cannot be in a position to take on any of its other responsibilities.[6]

Not all buy into this evolving view of responsibility to stakeholders, particularly in the United States. Many continue to see modern capitalism as properly and exclusively focused on profits, with companies bound to reward their shareholders—the de facto owners—to the exclusion of anyone else. These apologists often cite Adam Smith, whom they describe as the father of capitalism, and often quote passages to their advantage from Smith's seminal book *The Wealth of Nations*, which was published in 1776. They imagine Smith's invisible hand as the guiding influence that maintains a balance through market forces alone, rewarding with profits those corporations that deserve to prosper while driving those that do not into bankruptcy. What these advocates forget are, first, that Adam Smith did not hold the chair in economics at the University of Glasgow but rather the chair in moral philosophy; second, his most famous book at the time, written some years earlier, was entitled *The Theory of Moral Sentiment*; third, his notion of an invisible hand was more of a shroud or envelope circumscribing the market to promote fair dealing, regulatory intervention to avoid monopolies, avoidance of collaboration and pricing conspiracies, and punishment of fraud, all ultimately working together (when and if they do) to engender trust. Alan Greenspan contended that our market system depends, critically, on trust, and, as he specified, particularly trust in the word of the colleagues with whom we do business. As chair of the U.S. Federal Reserve, Greenspan was dogged in his promotion of a more equitable definition of the corporation. Now often named as a modern father of capitalism himself, Greenspan emphasized the necessity of building authentic trust to guide Smith's invisible hand.

As we continue to see the development of E.S.G. and stakeholder capitalism in Canada, we understand that it is built on trust and executed through regard for the interests of those beyond the shareholder.[7]

Selective empathy doesn't work.

Several years ago I had the opportunity to join a team of advisers helping one of Canada's major banks become more empathetic. On that team were two distinguished professors from the Harvard Business School and a few seasoned Deloitte partners. The bank's leadership had been alarmed to discover that a considerable percentage of their customers found the experience of dealing with the bank's branches to be transactional, offhand, impersonal, and, therefore, unsatisfying. They were also concerned about the recent tragedy at Wells Fargo in the United States, whose strategy of aggressive cross-selling (adding new services to existing accounts) yielded widespread neglect of customers' interest first in the bank–customer relationship. Wishing to build the trust of those people lest they jump ship, they vowed to make interactions at the branch level warmer, kinder, more human. The joint task force of bank execs and advisers concocted a broad range of interventions to encourage and empower staff to treat customers with greater empathy. It built a set of metrics to monitor the degree to which the trust of customers returned or were retained once the new behaviours had become the norm. The bank adopted the control-group method common to scientific research; they monitored results in two hundred branches, running the change campaign in half of them. The other hundred went about business as usual.

To everyone's surprise, by the end of the campaign they had measured no significant increase in levels of customer trust in any of the branches. That was a poser. So the team regrouped, but this time took advice from the people actually doing the work. They engaged with tellers, loans officers, financial advisers, accountants, and branch managers to find out why nothing had improved. They quickly identified the problem: the focus of the trust-building campaign had been entirely external with no emphasis given to building empathy internally. So while customer-facing staff had been doing their best to listen actively and serve customers with individual care, they had no power to change any process at the branch, and no systems for acting on what they had heard. They had learned to listen empathetically, but no one was listening empathetically to them.

Equipped with this knowledge, the bank redesigned the program, placing equal emphasis on behavioural empathy and trust building within the organization, this time with particular concentration on employee-to-employee communication. They ran the program again, with one hundred branches carrying out the revised program while another hundred carried on as before. Bingo. Substantial improvements began to pop up in all the metrics, which had been broadened to track shifts in inter-employee trust as well.

The experiment demonstrated that you can't be empathetic in just one area if you hope to make a difference; you have to see things whole. If a business wants its employees to build trust with its customers or partners—which all business should—then just as much effort must be made to encourage and empower employees to be empathetic with each other. Similarly, don't think of the culture of an organization as separate pieces of a pie each with a different flavour. Culture is and should be comprehensive and inclusive and, to quote an old saw, "Culture eats strategy for breakfast." George Shultz dubbed trust the *coin of the realm*. As U.S. secretary of state, treasury and labor, and as the president's chief of staff in both democratic and republican administrations, Shultz observed that when trust was in the room, good things happened. When trust was not in the room, good things did not happen. As he concluded, everything else is details.

Empathetic things to do when you intend to Be in the business of trust.

. . . as an individual

Know that empathy is the beginning of trust.

. . . and be confident that trust is the foundation of long-term business sustainability.

Earn trust through action.

. . . certain that what you do will build people's trust in you more than anything you say.

Earn trust through consistency over time.

. . . knowing that Mark Carney was spot on when he said, "Trust comes in on foot but leaves in a Ferrari."

. . . as an enterprise or institution

See things far.
Value the long term over the short term. While the short term demands astute attention, make sure every step you take helps achieve your overall mission, purpose, intent.

See things whole.
Do not try to be selective about empathy. To build trust, empathy must be encouraged and supported in every corner of your organization.

Be transparent.

Honesty works miracles. Prove your integrity by being open about your capacity, results, and intent. Trust will follow.

. . . as a nation

Create a healthy, business-friendly environment.

Governments have a responsibility to make an environment where businesses can prosper. Recognizing that the public good is not necessarily the opposite of the business good, we must ensure that our laws, regulations, guidance, and relationships give businesses the room they need to flourish through operations that are equally innovative and empathic.

10

Look ahead and act now.

For the first six years of my life, my family lived in Sudbury, Ontario. My dad was retail manager of a hardware store plunked smack on the main street of our town. Business was booming. Although I didn't know it then, Sudbury at the time was Canada's unwitting, concentrated experiment in climate change and would offer a sobering demonstration of the effects of unbridled exploitation of resources, an example that would teach us all a painful lesson about stewardship of the earth.

Set in a basin with 330 lakes teeming with fish, all within easy travel, the area had sheltered and nourished Algonquin people of the Ojibwe nation for many thousands of years. Then in 1883, a blacksmith helping to excavate routes for the Canadian Pacific Railroad stumbled on rich deposits of nickel in the area. A remarkable substance, nickel is a shiny, silver metal that twinkles with a hint of gold in certain lights. It's hard and it's ductile, meaning it can be used to build things just as steel can, yet can be drawn out into wire just like copper. Rust resistant, it also makes an ideal and impenetrable coating for other metals, which is how it came to be the cladding of choice for military artillery. The 1883 unearthing in Sudbury changed life in Northern Ontario just as the discovery of gold in Timmins did sixteen years later. Sudbury's news caught world attention, and prospectors flocked in. Even Thomas Edison showed up to see how he could get in on the action.

By the time my family fetched up there in 1940, Sudbury had become one the world's top centres of nickel extraction and smelting. We lived in Copper Cliff, a suburb of Sudbury and the very spot where that blacksmith had first made history. Most of our neighbours worked for INCO and Falconbridge, companies that were especially busy now producing materials for the allied war effort. Above us all loomed The Beast, our pet name for the giant smokestack that carried droplets of toxic by-products from the smelting process away from our town and off over the land for miles around. Dispersing both sulphur dioxide and nitrogen dioxide, those droplets would later go by the name acid rain.

The effect of those toxins was evident all around us, as there was no longer any vegetation anywhere to be seen in our patch of the world. We all lived in a moonscape of blackened rock and dry dirt. Many were ill, and no one ever breathed easy. Nothing had changed by the time we Johnstons moved three hundred kilometres up the road to Sault Ste. Marie. Later, whenever our football teams travelled to Sudbury for games, we would cheerily pack up a small patch of green Sault Ste. Marie turf so that Sudbury kids could see what grass looked like. We were heartless, and not just on the playing field.

Sudbury's dismal record changed when an INCO VP by the name of Roy Aitken gathered a team to figure out a way to cap the stack and scrub gases on their way out of the smelters. Through the 1980s, the company committed $600 million to the effort, and it worked. Through a process called fixation, Aiken's team was able to convert emissions into solid sulphur that could be sold down-market for use in other processes. Once the system was in place, the harmless water vapour that remained was allowed to drift from the stack without risk of further contamination. That changed everything. Thanks to Roy Aiken's leadership, the support of INCO's executive team, the company's willingness to invest, and the sustained collaboration of all Sudbury smelters, Sudbury is once again lovely, lush, and green.

I think of that chapter in Sudbury's and Canada's history often these days. It's the reason I'm hopeful, even optimistic, about the ability of members of the human family to join forces and focus our efforts to tackle pollution, resource wastage, habitat destruction, and climate change with purpose and ingenuity. I earnestly believe we can restore our sorely damaged global environment to be lovely, lush, and green again.

But we'd better be quick about it.

"We don't have time," he said.

My first introduction to sustainable development came in 1987 in a curious way. One morning, just before boarding an aircraft while travelling in my role as principal of McGill, I took a phone call. It was the appointments coordinator at prime minister Brian Mulroney's office asking if I would chair a national round table on the environment and the economy. He explained that the prime minister had read and fully embraced a brilliant and far-reaching document just published by the United Nations Commission on Environment and Development. Chaired by Gro Harlem Brundtland, a former prime minister of Norway, the document was astutely titled "Our Common Future," but everyone in the know just called it the Brundtland Report. Its pages set out ambitious plans by which the world's nations could work together on a path to global sustainable development.

The prime minister was convinced that active, broadly based participation in the program was essential for Canada. I listened carefully, quickly learning more about the urgent need to make sustainable development the norm. I said I would be happy to consider it and would seek the consent of our board chair and our chancellor at McGill before taking on such a time-consuming, albeit part-time, commitment as this. "We don't have time," my caller said. Time was tight because the prime minister intended to announce the round table and its inaugural chair (me) at a press conference that afternoon.

But those words struck me as true on a much deeper level. Where environment is concerned, he was right: we don't have time. We need to make smart decisions quickly. So, without checking with anyone, I agreed to serve.[1]

We set up Canada's National Round Table on the Environment and the Economy (NRTEE) with sixteen members: four cabinet ministers from the federal government, four leading advocates from the environmental movement, four executive officers of major Canadian companies, and four willing souls from public institutions and the research community, one of whom was me.

We were most fortunate with the original composition. One of the four from both the public and environmental sector was Jim MacNeill, who had served as the coordinating secretary and rapporteur for the Brundtland Commission itself, having previously served as a deputy minister in the government of Canada and then as a senior official in environment at the United Nations. Jim held the pen for the Brundtland Report, so understood sustainable development better than any of us, and probably more than anyone else on the planet. We were also lucky in the prime minister's appointment of cabinet ministers, three of whom were Michael Wilson (minister of finance), Lucien Bouchard (environment), and Harvie André (natural resources). Wilson was a wise, constructive individual always open to various viewpoints. Bouchard was a committed environmentalist with a broad international perspective, having previously served as Canada's ambassador to France. André was an energetic entrepreneur and a realist.

At the initial meeting, one of the environmental-movement advocates chose to be quite strident, hinting that progress might be difficult given our markedly different perspectives. Harvie André calmly said, "Look, you have a choice: you can be like Lech Wałęsa or like Cardinal Richelieu." Asked to expand, he explained that Wałęsa, at the time leader of the solidarity movement in Poland, used the technique of publicly embarrassing the then government on every possible occasion. Cardinal Richelieu, the power behind the French throne in the decades prior to the revolution, used the opposite technique, moving his ideas and policies steadily forward by working collaboratively and quietly with the king and senior advisers. The four environment leaders led by Jim asked for a recess and after mere minutes returned to say, "Let's try the Richelieu route." We agreed on confidential discussions until we arrived at a consensus on any point. We could then issue documents and public statements on which we all agreed. From there on in, we enjoyed splendid collaborative and productive chemistry.

A side note: some months later, I accompanied Lucien Bouchard to a major international conference in Bergen, Norway. The objective was to have the world's nations develop a single, coherent plan of action to respond to the challenges detailed in the Brundtland Report. By the second day, it was clear that a substantial gulf separated the intentions of the United States and those of the European Union, whose delegation at the time was led by the Swedish and Austrian representatives. I watched as Bouchard slid gracefully into action, a Canadian Richelieu channelling Lester Pearson while exercising low-key, middle-power diplomacy to persuade everyone to get along. It worked. Bouchard managed to rally a number of previously reluctant nations and was able to bring both the United States and the European Union on side. It was Canadian statecraft at its best. We saw Bouchard off at the airport late on that Friday afternoon. He was travelling to the Canadian embassy in Paris to spend the weekend. Fresh from his successes at the international environment conference, he sent a telegram to the Parti Québécois on the occasion of its anniversary conference, congratulating those gathered at the conference, and then openly declaring that he was a sovereigntist, a declaration that surprised and enraged Prime Minister Mulroney. He remained in the embassy on the weekend. Faced with the controversy of the telegram and his disappointment on the progress of the Charlottetown Accord, he resigned from the cabinet and became an ardent leader of Quebec's sovereignty movement. It was a sad loss. While we were indeed separated by our vision of Canada's constitutional future, we had been unified in our shared vision of what the world's nations have to do to save the planet.

Another outstanding member of our round table was Judge Barry Stuart. Barry, whom I had known as a law student while I was a young professor at Queen's University, had since become a dear friend and godfather to our fifth daughter. Later, as a young law professor himself, he founded the Canadian Environmental Law Foundation and taught one of the nation's first environmental law courses—initially at Dalhousie University Law School and then at Osgoode Hall Law School. Like Jim MacNeill he was an impressive representative of our environmental leaders and was a master of collegial consensus. We were fortunate also in our business leaders, one of whom was social advocate, ethical innovator, and Shell CEO, Jack MacLeod. A lover of nature in all its variety and a true outdoorsman, Jack had more than once urged Sharon and me to join him and his wife to tent out among the wolves near Banff. He had wanted us simply to take in the splendid variety of flora and fauna in the Canadian woods. Alas, we allowed the urgent to drive out the important and missed the opportunities. Jack and an appointed team from Shell attended our meetings religiously and began identifying non-partisan research sources beyond those immediately available to government. This was of high value to us all. At that time Shell had begun to see an energy future beyond fossil fuels, and Jack was one of the evangelists who led the company's pivot to sustainable development. And, to our good fortune, we had Roy Aiken at the table, the former VP and senior engineer at INCO who had proved in Sudbury that environmental damage is reversible when you have the wit and the will to make it happen. And Jim MacNeill, as the intellectual leader of our enterprise, made a splendid contribution to our planning. What an extraordinary team. Sixteen different personalities and viewpoints.

The objective of the round table, which I now understand to be the proper objective of any round table, was to bring diverse and knowledgeable parties of interest together to consider a common issue and, by doing so, reach a common understanding of how to proceed to tackle a problem. This collaborative and empathetic approach led to creative and positive outcomes. Longevity was one of them; unlike most advisory councils, the NRTEE worked steadily and productively for two full decades, guiding successive governments and prime ministers. A simple but critical step was made early on. We arrived at an agreed-on definition of sustainable development that successive governments of Canada could apply as a litmus test for the merit of any proposed public legislation. Drawn from the Brundtland Report, that definition itself was legislated and is still the guiding principle on which the appropriateness of Canadian development is judged.

> Sustainable development is development that meets the needs of the present without compromising the ability of future generations to meet their own needs.

That was our first, very specific, recommendation, and I hope and trust we'll see visionary and strong policies coming soon that live up to the spirit of that definition and encourage Canadians to make wise lifestyle choices to cut carbon emissions in every area of endeavour. I was fortunate to have been a small part of the process that set the stage for such improvements.

In retrospect, I'm convinced that the success of our round table was possible because of three qualities of the round table itself, all of which related to the people we chose to bring on board and their manifesting of empathy. These three qualities could and should be echoed in every initiative that Canadians undertake or join as we better our stewardship of the planet to protect and sustain the health of our shared environment.

First was the great breadth of representation we gathered around the table. Inviting varied viewpoints from disparate interest groups, we were able to make sound recommendations without missing any relevant perspective, ignoring any critical research, or disadvantaging any particular group. By doing this, we lowered our risk of failing as we worked to identify priorities and opportunities for meaningful change.

Second was the openness all of them brought to the table. Every one of our members had the will and the talent to think broadly and understand and appreciate the differing opinions of the others, even as they respectfully presented their own interests.

Third, because we had people of wide influence around the table, the round table itself had wide influence. Great insight won't help if no one will take your call or read your recommendations, an unfortunate pitfall into which many dedicated activists have stumbled. But good news travels fast; Canada's quick advances helped inspire the creation of the Intergovernmental Panel on Climate Change, a body of the United Nations headquartered in Geneva. The panel's express purpose is to ensure that objective, scientific information on human-caused climate change is shared worldwide, with the objective of giving policy makers trustworthy data on which to base new practices and regulations to help stop and then reverse environmental damage caused by human activity. The panel continues to be a true leader in climate science, with its assessment reports subjected to what is considered to be most extensive review process in the world scientific community. All of us at the round table rejoiced when that panel came into being.

That said, there was one more important insight I came to in my four years as chair of that round table, an insight that grew as I studied hard data from all sectors of activity and all regions of the country; Canada's performance in the arena of environmental sustainability ranks far below what our record should be.

Individual actions will change the world.

The barriers to sustainable development operate on two planes: geographic and temporal. Geographically, it is hard to think globally and act locally, even though that is exactly what we must now do. And where time is concerned, humans are not very practised at planning more than a few years out, even though we need to be thinking generations down the road if we are to get this right. For some, it is a bridge too far. For them, thinking long term over several generations is like thinking about forever. It is difficult to take immediate steps to change the trajectory when you will not be around to see its curve. But we have to look ahead and act now.

A report published in late 2021 by the Berlin-based Hot or Cool Institute offered stark proof that Canada's per capita carbon emissions are worse than those of most other wealthy nations. After collecting recent data from ten countries whose cultures are markedly different, (Canada, Finland, United Kingdom, Japan, China, Turkey, South Africa, Brazil, India, and Indonesia), the institute was able to reveal how lifestyle choices have a direct effect on a nation's carbon footprint. Canada's standing as the worst offender on this table will come as a surprise to many Canadians.

We produce 14.2 tonnes of carbon emissions (CO_2e) per capita, four times as much as the average world citizen. Although we are home to only 0.5 per cent of the world's population, our CO_2e emissions make up a full 2.0 per cent of the world's total. I find the table really helpful, not as a slap in the face, but because it breaks down our emissions by activity. In a way, it's a roadmap for improvement, which is the institute's objective. They call their report "1.5-Degree Lifestyles: Towards a Fair Consumption Space for All," and their website (hotorcool.org) offers a growing list of practical suggestions for necessary changes and case studies of improvements made in each of the seven nations. Most environmental experts have concluded that the swiftest

Total per-capita carbon footprint by country and sector

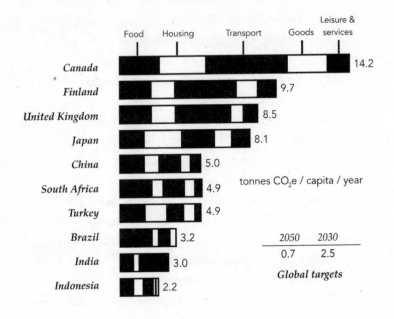

1.5-Degree Lifestyles: Towards a Fair Consumption Space for All

and most significant improvements will likely come from decisions made and actions taken in the world's cities, rather than the world's countries, so Canadian urbanites cooperating with their municipal governments now have great power in their hands. We should not have to wait for our provincial, territorial, and federal governments to enact laws and sustainable policy frameworks; on the contrary, there are countless lifestyle changes we can make as individuals that will make a marked improvement in our standing. According to the report, here are the most obvious things Canadians can do:

Food	Eat less meat and less dairy.
Housing	Share your home with others or get a smaller place.
Transport	Use public transport, carpool, or ride a bike to work.
Goods	Reuse, recycle, reduce.
Leisure and services	Choose physical exercise over motor sports.

Look ahead and imagine.

To preserve the health of the natural world—climate, air, land, water, animal life, and plant life—we must all learn to take the long view. I use a simple mental exercise to bring that view into focus. Try it now. Pick a year in the future, perhaps 2050 or 2075 or even 2100. Now cast your mind to that time and project yourself into it, imagining what conditions you will have to cope with as you go about your day. It's your future, so you can shape it any way you want, but don't just make this a wishing game. Use everything you've learned recently about the link between resource consumption and climate change to paint a realistic picture of how things might be.

Begin by standing outdoors near the place you live. Take a moment to observe your environment. Start with the air. Breathe it in. Is it clean? Is it hot? Feel that air on your body. Is it dry and burning or humid and sticky? Are you wearing protective clothing against heat, acid rain, or falling ash? Did you apply sunscreen today, and, if so, how many times so far? Is there an awning over you to shield from damage by ultraviolet rays? Are you wearing a mask to avoid contagion?

Look down. Does grass grow near your property or is the ground now bare? Do you have a garden with vegetables, or must you line up at a grocery store for everything? Is there still a hose for watering the ground, and is there a lock on that hose to prevent water theft? Do you have a driveway? Are there cars in it? How many? How big?

Gas, electric, or hydrogen powered? New or old? Are they owned, leased, or rented?

Now head indoors. What kind of dwelling do you live in: house, condo, apartment, or a rented room? Is your place spacious or small, messy or tidy? How many rooms? How do you heat them, cool them, light them? One bathroom or many? Lots of furniture? How many TVs, computers? What energy do you use to cook? Do you compost? What do you do with your garbage? Do they still take it away for you every week, or is that over? Do you have both a fridge and freezer? Peek inside. What kind of foods do you keep on hand? What kinds of containers are they in? Are your proteins meat- or plant-based? Check the pantry; are there shortages of any of your favourite foods?

Stop and listen for a moment. Is this place quiet, or do you have company? How many people live here with you? Is it just your own family, or have you taken in housemates? Do your parents live with you, or are you perhaps looking after someone else's children? Are they going to school, or is distance learning now the norm? Is everyone here in good health? If not, why not?

Now go into town. How far is it? Will you take that car of yours, carpool, or jump on public transport? Will the ride cost much? Will you need to refuel?

And are the children in this scene happy? Is their future assured? Are they grateful for how our generation responded to all the crises we face, or are they saddened and dismayed?

Simply imagining the kind of life you'd be leading in the future will help you come to a gentle awareness of changes in behaviour you could make right now to the way things are heading here on Planet Earth. So look ahead, but act now.

Insist on collaboration.

While we're convinced that individual actions are key to environmental repair, our best efforts must be led and supported by collaboration that is both multilateral and interdisciplinary. That can be tricky. While we have global organizations to study our global problems, as yet no government exists that can enact enforceable global legislation. Every nation is sovereign. Agendas are disparate, attention is scattered, and the quality of leadership varies from regime to regime, so the movement from social awareness to global political action remains elusive. Great strides can be made today, however, in the application of interdisciplinary wisdom. As we've seen, we can't successfully address any one aspect of climate change without full attention to the others. As with all life, our earth is a system of systems of systems linked by rhythms of cause and correlation that we yearn to understand better. Bringing our disciplinary insights together from all corners of the sciences (natural, formal, social, and applied) and from humanities (including law, history, languages, and the arts) is the only way to achieve and sustain the repair and redesign of our coexistence. The successes possible with such interdisciplinary attention are already visible everywhere. Just weeks ago, for example, scientists successfully isolated an enzyme that can break down plastics faster than ever observed before, even as bans on single-use plastics are changing the way people plan, buy, transport, and store their groceries. Working side-by-side, science and legislation are making great strides.

Our daughter Jen understands the intricacies of such interdisciplinary teamwork. When she joined Canada's ministry of natural resources as an environmental economist in 2017 after earlier stints in the environment ministry and the innovation sector of the industry ministry, she had already explored the practical advantage of creative alliances and consultative thinking, which is saying something, given the dogged individualism of her nature. Jen was not one to follow in anyone's footsteps. The poet of the family, Jen concluded early on that her view of the world was unique and valid. When offered piano lessons (under duress), as her older sisters had been (under duress), Jen wandered off and found a flute teacher who would let her play the songs she liked best, rather than zip up and down those darn keyboard scales all day. After high school, Jen avoided the big campuses, preferring to begin her undergraduate studies at Mount Allison University in Sackville, New Brunswick, attracted to its small-college, liberal-arts focus and close family environment. There she majored in modern languages, which had appealed to her ever since she (as her sisters before her) had attended both English and French primary and secondary schools in Montreal. Drawn to both German and Spanish, she moved out of the dorms into a small residence, more like a home, where the lingua franca was German. So her home life rolled along in German, while her spare time was conducted in Spanish—an ideal combination for her bohemian soul. For two summers, she headed down to Universidad de las Américas Puebla in Mexico to continue her studies in Spanish. There she made friends who were learning an impressive array of disciplines, including international business management, arts and humanities, social sciences, science and engineering, and economics. I suspect that's when she truly learned the advantage of welcoming multiple perspectives. The next few years saw Jen in disparate work and academic environments, closing the decade with a master's of public administration from Queen's, a master's of sustainable development from Waterloo, and consultative experience in Latin America and the Middle East on her resumé. The first of these was volunteering for a year in Costa Rica, helping an agricultural collective move its crops to larger markets through digital connections and to steer it through the Y2K digital challenge. She then spent a volunteer year in Jordan leading a youth program initiated by Jordan's king and queen to create a new generation of digitally literate young people. Before taking up the post in Jordan, Jen added Arabic to her growing collection of language competencies. This breadth helped her to learn which disciplines could be married and what circumstances influenced the reforms that will make effective and ongoing response to climate change.

As I write this, Jen has been making presentations to her senior officers in the energy efficiency program of Natural Resources Canada as part of the climate change strategy for the Canadian trucking industry. Given that transportation and electrical generation are the two greatest consumers of energy in Canada, trucking is one area in which we can make a huge difference, if we get it right. Merely changing legislation to force change would be fruitless. One nudge, as Nobel Prize–winning psychologists Daniel Kahneman and Amos Tversky have established, is more effective than many pushes. No one knows better what the appropriate incentives and relations should be than those in the industry itself, so Jen and her team are working to bring perspectives together from that industry, from other industries, and from many professional disciplines in many countries, and Jen's broad experience and innovative nature was key. Their aim is to help Canada build a flexible regulation strategy following broad consultation with the transportation and beyond, all supported by groundbreaking science and behavioural psychology. Collaboration works. Let's get at it.

Empathetic things to do when you intend to Look ahead but act now.

. . . as an individual

Have confidence.
We can save our environment, but that will happen only with universal, dedicated, and personal action. As governments find ways to legislate and as business retools for a green future, take initiative as one person, one family, one group of friends, or one street of neighbours to build a low-carbon lifestyle.

Find ways to make your own contribution.
Reduce. Reuse. Recycle. Favour physical activity over motor sport. Use public transport or shared mobility systems. Eat less meat, less dairy, and more veggies. Drive an electric car.

Take small actions to inspire your neighbours.
Cut your neighbour's lawn. Plant a tree and help it grow (somewhere that really makes a difference. (Bogs are important.) Start a community garden. (It will tie you to nature's life cycle.)

. . . as a community

Let your city show its leadership.
Recognize that the most important changes now will come from within the world's cities, not just the world's countries. Ensure waste collection

and improve waste treatment. Clean up parks and common lands and keep them pristine. Encourage community tree planting. Allow space for community gardens and support citizens as they grow their food.

Ensure community leaders are in touch with local environmental concerns.
Ask residents for their insights. Strike round tables at which citizens can resolve conflicting priorities as they give informed advice to their local governments about priorities to set, actions to take, and ways to make things happen quickly.

Let citizens see how it's working.
Make changes and let everyone know. Then celebrate local neighbour-hoods, communities, businesses, and interests groups that show environmental leadership.

. . . as a nation

Make tough decisions.
Adopt and enforce responsible building standards. Ensure public transport moves away from fossil fuels. Close coal-fire generating plants. Develop flexible regulations that establish limits and reduction targets with reliance on the marketplace and business to ensure an appropriate response. Focus on the most practical and realistic solutions that require government input, but seek private-sector input to help overcome myths while making strides in reducing energy use and lowering pollution. Whatever we do, we must recognize and publicize mutual vulnerability, then take strong action despite the objections.

Set a great example for the world.
Take Canada's per capita carbon emissions from 14.2 tonnes of carbon emissions (CO_2e) to 0.7 tonnes by encouraging and supporting

Canadian citizens to make deep changes in their lifestyles, and by adopting 80 per cent renewable energy goals in Canada.

Share our success around the world.
Once we have our own house in order, use soft power to exert influence; other nations will follow our lead.

Things we can do
as nations

11

Cherish the rule of law.

Among the many architectural attractions of Montreal that lure tourists and locals equally is rue Crescent. Now home to trendy art galleries, exclusive boutiques, bars, restaurants, and hopping nightclubs, the street attracts many people who go there just for the vibe. It has long been that way. From its creation in the 1860s, the once-curved-now-unbent street was studded with homes of the wealthy, punctuated over time by fine restaurants and cafés. Not all visitors will be aware that a brief incident on that street in 1946 sparked a long legal battle that closed more than a decade later in the Supreme Court of Canada. The case raised deep questions about the definition of rule of law in this country and rippled through time, eventually to be echoed even in the opening sentence of our Canadian Charter of Rights and Freedoms.

The day was December 4, 1946, and the weather in Montreal was pleasant enough. Enjoying temperatures just below freezing, the Wednesday lunch crowd at the Quaff Café on Crescent Street had made for good business, and the place was still packed at two in the afternoon when a squad of Quebec liquor police burst through the doors, moved past a room of quizzical patrons, and headed to the bar, where they announced their plan to confiscate every drop of liquor in the place. Owned for over thirty years by the Roncarelli family, Quaff Café by this time was in the capable hands of son Frank, an entrepreneur with a knack for publicity who had earned a fine reputation and considerable prosperity. As a Jehovah's Witness, Frank was a member of a religious group that, with only four hundred adherents in Montreal, had found little tolerance for their beliefs among a provincial population of over three million practising Roman Catholics. The cause of concern to the public was ongoing accusations by Jehovah's Witnesses that Catholicism itself was ungodly, a position vocalized in speeches and distributed door-to-door in pamphlets. Reaction was stern. As Justice Ivan Cleveland Rand later put it:

> The first impact of [the Jehovah's Witnesses'] proselytizing zeal upon the Roman Catholic church and community in Quebec, as might be expected, produced a violent reaction. Meetings were forcibly broken up, property damaged, individuals ordered out of communities, and in one case out of the province, and generally, within the cities and towns, bitter controversy aroused.

By 1945 provincial authorities, acting with the encouragement and approval of Premier Maurice Duplessis, determined to bring an end to the noisy campaign of the Witnesses. Citing a new city bylaw requiring that anyone have a licence for "peddling any kind of wares," police began rounding up men and women caught handing out leaflets in public spaces. The fine for such an infraction was set at $40, at the time equivalent to many people's monthly salary.

The accused, once charged and as directed by their church's headquarters in Warwick, New York, all pleaded not guilty and asked to be released on bail until such time as formal trials might be convened. Frank Roncarelli then ponied up tens of thousands of dollars to post bail. The transgressors, adamant in their cause, headed immediately back out to the streets where they resumed their evangelical campaign of criticism. The game of cat and mouse was now on. Even as prosecutors prepared an initial case to test how courts would consider the charges, local police were again dispatched to round up and charge the offenders. One singularly energetic orator was arrested and charged 103 times. For Duplessis, the matter had become a very public embarrassment, and he concluded that the political risk of failing to control the situation now outweighed the peril of being judged later for a heavy-handed response.[1] In the premier's view, Roncarelli's posting bail for all fellow adherents mocked the government, and he intended to stop it. Conversations began between Duplessis (who was also attorney general), provincial prosecutors, and the head of the Quebec Liquor Commission to explore the merits of yanking Quaff Café's liquor licence, which happened to be up for its annual renewal. They were hesitant at first, but when a fresh and bitingly critical pamphlet called "Québec's Burning Hate" openly accused leaders in Quebec of persecuting Christians, they decided to act.

The police moved to confiscate all Roncarelli's liquor, effectively destroying his business and thereby compromising his ability to bail out his buddies. Duplessis called a press conference to announce that Roncarelli's licence had been rescinded because of his support of the Jehovah's Witness church, a group he compared to the Nazis and the Communists. Rubbing salt into the wound, he vowed that Roncarelli would never again be granted a liquor licence in his province. By doing so, Duplessis implied that administration permissions such as liquor licences were in fact provincial privileges that could be withdrawn at the pleasure of the politically powerful.

That did it. With Roncarelli's establishment now dry, patrons who had weathered six long years of wartime rationing and shortages went elsewhere to celebrate, and the business failed. Six months later, Roncarelli was forced to put Quaff Café up for sale.

The issue was far from settled. Outraged by what he believed to be targeted, unjust punishment by the premier, Roncarelli filed a lawsuit against Duplessis personally, seeking $119,000 in damages as appropriate recompense. Thirteen years later, the case made its way to the Supreme Court of Canada, whose justices decided the matter in

Roncarelli's favour, albeit awarding him a lesser sum. Their written decision expressed their opinion that no law confers

> unlimited arbitrary power exercisable for any purpose, however capricious or irrelevant, regardless of the nature or purpose of the statute. . . . There is always a perspective within which a statute is intended to operate; and any clear departure from its lines or objects is just as objectionable as fraud or corruption.

It did not matter how objectionable, disruptive, or irritating the strident proclamations of the Jehovah's Witnesses seemed to Duplessis, his ministers, or indeed a majority of the citizens of Quebec. Although the written opinion of the Supreme Court described the Witnesses as a militant religious sect, they had broken no law, so no law could be bent to silence them. Justice Rand concluded that Duplessis

> through the instrumentality of the commission brought about a breach of an implied statutory duty. . . . It was a gross abuse of legal power expressly intended to punish him for an act wholly irrelevant to the statute, a punishment which inflicted on him, as it was intended to do, the distraction of his economic life as a restaurant keeper. . . .

The decision of the Supreme Court of Canada in the matter of *Roncarelli vs Duplessis*, [1959] S.C.R. 121, established in Canada a clear understanding that the rules we agree to live by must always be fairly applied. We live by the rule of law whose purpose is justice, and those in power must refrain from manipulating any law to suit their ambitions. Such behaviour, as the Court put it, is "just as objectionable as fraud or corruption." The unambiguous supremacy of the rule of law in Canada ratified in that case echoed through the decades, eventually in 1982 finding clear expression in the preamble of our Canadian Charter of Rights and Freedoms:

> Whereas Canada is founded upon principles that recognize the supremacy of God and the rule of law . . .

As the charter illustrates, all other rights and freedoms follow from these fundamental values. The Roncarelli case was an important milestone in establishing the empathetic responsibility of the state. It established the principle that the state in exercising its powers must walk in the other person's shoes, especially those of minorities and others who, because of their differences, do not fit easily into a majority population. The courts, made up of non-elected judges chosen for their knowledge of the law and their wisdom, could identify an implied constraint on government executive action, even if the power itself were contained within legislation enacted by the popularly elected legislature, unless it was exercised in a way that was neither arbitrary nor capricious nor unfairly oppressing a minority. Such restraint can trace its roots back to the Magna Carta in 1215, when English barons were successful in constraining the king's power to require them to raise a militia or to be taxed for that purpose without their consent in a public assembly.

Worth noting, the lawsuit by Roncarelli against Premier Duplessis was brought by Professor Frank Scott, later dean of law at McGill University who was among the leading constitutional lawyers of his time. He co-authored the Regina Manifesto, which became the founding charter of the Cooperative Commonwealth Party (CCF), forerunner of the New Democratic Party (NDP) we know today. Scott was not entirely persona grata with the merchant barons who dominated the McGill board of governors. His social-democratic views and activities often crossed swords with them where business philosophy was concerned. Little wonder that Scott had been passed over several times for promotion to the deanship of the McGill law faculty, but ultimately the strong support of the faculty members themselves convinced the principal, F. Cyril James, to refuse to pass him by once again. In the middle of the summer, Cyril James sought out Scott to raise the prospect of the deanship, only to discover that Professor Scott was touring in China. James then sent a telegram asking if he would like to discuss becoming dean of the law faculty, to which Scott allegedly replied, "Offer me the job and you will find out."

The Charter is our code.

Signed into law by Queen Elizabeth in April 1982, the Canadian Charter of Rights and Freedoms is a bill of rights housed within the Constitution of Canada. The Charter guarantees certain political rights to Canadian citizens and civil rights of everyone in Canada superseding the policies and actions of all areas and levels of the government. It is designed to unify Canadians around a set of principles that embody those rights.

The rights and freedoms enshrined in the Charter include the following:

Fundamental freedoms
Freedom of conscience
Freedom of religion
Freedom of thought
Freedom of belief
Freedom of opinion
Freedom of expression
Freedom of the press and of other media of communication
Freedom of peaceful assembly, and freedom of association

Democratic rights
Right to participate in political activities

Scott was also a much celebrated poet. He is acclaimed for his shortest poem, penned when he successfully liberated D.H. Lawrence's controversial book *Lady Chatterley's Lover*, which had been vilified by Roman Catholic bishops in Quebec, and under Duplessis banned from Quebec bookstores and libraries. Scott was successful in establishing that the publication ban was an arbitrary and indefensible exercise of power. *Lady Chatterley's Lover* became a bestseller. As a victory lap, Scott wrote: "I went to bat for lady Chat."

Right to a democratic form of government
Right to vote and to be eligible to serve as member of the
     House of Commons of Canada and provincial and
     territorial legislative assemblies

Mobility rights
Right to enter, remain in, and leave Canada
Right to move to any province to pursue gaining a livelihood

Legal rights
Right to life, liberty, and security of the person
Freedom from unreasonable search and seizure
Freedom from arbitrary detention or imprisonment
Right to legal counsel and the guarantee of habeas corpus
Rights in criminal matters such as the right to be presumed
     innocent until proven guilty
Right not to be subject to cruel and unusual punishment
Right against self-incrimination
Right to an interpreter in a court proceeding

Equality rights
Right to equal treatment before and under the law, and equal
     protection and benefit of the law without discrimination

No one is above the law.

In the case of *Roncarelli vs Duplessis*, Canadians were reminded that the law must not be misapplied as a tool of punishment. There is an important corollary to that principle: no citizen or corporation can be allowed to skirt the law to gain unfair advantage. To make sure that doesn't happen, our judicial system is designed to be independent from politics. The system is solid, but as we see repeatedly, that doesn't stop some from trying to get around it.

It is often said that a picture is worth a thousand words. While not quite a picture, one often sees in the entrance to courts across the land, or in a stained-glass window in the foyer, a statute or colourful depiction of Themis, the Greek Goddess of Justice. There are several features of her image that symbolize fairness, which is the foundation of Justice.

The composition of her figure perhaps illustrates the empathy and nurturing quality of constant attentiveness and careful listening. Her eyes are blinded with a scarf bound around her head. This signifies that justice is blind and objective. It cannot favour one against another and maintains a constant neutrality and non-partisan mien. Somewhat more complicated is the fact that the goddess is usually depicted carrying a set of scales with receptacles for weights on either side. This illustrates the intricate calibration that constitutes the weighing of evidence from either party to a trial, and that each item of evidence does not carry equal weight. These features emphasize legal customs emerging largely from a thousand years of the Westminster system.

Politics are absent. Judges are appointed by a consultative process which begins with a careful screening by professional bodies before a recommendation from the Attorney General is made to the Governor General, a non-elected official who carries out the non-partisan responsibilities of the King, who is the non-partisan head of state. They are expected to ignore political affiliations and ensure political positions or meanings do not creep into their judgements. They also respect the separation of powers. They are to interpret the law and not make it, which is the responsibility of elected legislatures.

Prosecutors are called Crown Prosecutors because they represent the impartial Crown and do not win or lose cases. Their job is to establish the truth through presentation of evidence and, in criminal trials, are obliged to disclose fully all evidence to the defended, especially including that which favours the defendant's argument.

The scales have different weight depending on the type of case. Thus, in criminal cases, the Crown must prove guilt beyond reasonable doubt because an individual's liberty is at stake. In civil cases—most frequently a contest between two individuals or corporations over property—the standard of proof is balanced between which of the two parties more persuasively meets the test of truth.

There are many other safeguards built into our system, but the important point is that the Canadian system is somewhat unique in how strictly it observes these requirements, especially as one views other systems around the world, including those prevailing in democratic regimes. Without indulging in criticism of our neighbour to the south, there is a different culture in their justice system, which springs from its roots in rejecting the Crown and creating a "We the People" republican system where partisanship is more evident. That said, the continuance of our Canadian system, which the Goddess of Justice personifies, is reliant on constant vigilance.

I often ask young people when I meet with them in a group or individually to discuss the institution of government: "How many fully functioning democracies exist in the world today? Is it 50%, 25%, 15%?" I pause for a few moments after hearing the guesses and say, according to the Economist Intelligence Unit, it is 8.3%. And the United States and France, often cited as the cradles of modern democracy, are not on the list. Then I ask: "And which are the top five?" Pausing again to accumulate a few answers, I reply: Iceland, Norway,

Sweden, New Zealand, and Canada. Sweden has a population of 10 million and Canada's is 39 million. The other three are much smaller. It is somewhat unique that a middle-sized country can function so well." Continuing with the guessing game, I then ask what is common amongst these countries, and answer that all but Iceland, which has a

Rules for Rule Keepers

The appearance of publicly funded police forces is a relatively recent event in the journey of civilization. While protecting the wealthy has long been a duty of private guards, the novel idea of a force trained and paid to serve all members of society was advanced in the United Kingdom only in 1829. Sir Robert Peel, then home secretary in the cabinet of the prime minister, the Duke of Wellington, proposed a metropolitan force to maintain safety within the community. Police in the United Kingdom today are still referred to as *bobbies*, for they follow Sir Bobby Peel's guidance; occasionally, they are referred to as *peelers*. The nine principles he set down to guide the police were so thoughtful and sensible that they are still practised today in democracies around the world as the tenets of community policing.

1. The basic mission for which the police exist is to prevent crime and disorder.
2. The ability of the police to perform their duties is dependent upon public approval of police actions.
3. Police must secure the willing cooperation of the public in voluntary observance of the law to be able to secure and maintain the respect of the public.

non-partisan president, are constitutional hereditary monarchies. The head-of-state institution provides a stability and certainty during occasional periods of chaotic political drama. These fully functioning democracies have a rigorous respect for the rule of law, grounded in justice, which is fairness and begins with empathy and reinforces trust.

4. The degree of cooperation of the public that can be secured diminishes proportionately to the necessity of the use of physical force.

5. Police seek and preserve public favour not by catering to the public opinion but by constantly demonstrating absolute impartial service to the law.

6. Police use physical force to the extent necessary to secure observance of the law or to restore order only when the exercise of persuasion, advice and warning is found to be insufficient.

7. Police, at all times, should maintain a relationship with the public that gives reality to the historic tradition that the police are the public and the public are the police; the police being only members of the public who are paid to give full-time attention to duties which are incumbent on every citizen in the interests of community welfare and existence.

8. Police should always direct their action strictly towards their functions and never appear to usurp the powers of the judiciary.

9. The test of police efficiency is the absence of crime and disorder, not the visible evidence of police action in dealing with it.

Of primary importance is that citizens at large in these special states expect that this is simply part of their culture and must be vigilantly stewarded and maintained.

The first medicine for society's ills is empathy, and at the heart of empathy lies fairness. The rule of law is our guarantee of such fairness, at least in matters of public contention, yet how precious and fragile it all can be. We must be vigilant.

Democracy requires more than a vote.

In 1995, the newly elected Parti Québecois held a referendum to determine whether Quebecers wanted to separate from Canada, the first vote on Quebec separation since 1980.[2]

A razor thin majority of 50.6 per cent of Quebecers voted against, while 49.4 per cent voted for secession. In the face of this narrow yet motivating defeat, the PQ vowed to mount an additional referendum. This prompted the federal government to ask the Supreme Court of Canada whether Quebec could, under domestic and international law, unilaterally separate from Canada. The request for clear judgement became known as the Secession Reference, which resulted in a historic opinion from our highest court on the interplay between democracy and the rule of law.[3]

The Quebec government took the position that secession is a political, not legal, question and, as such, is beyond the purview of the courts and strictures of the Constitution. Quebec had refused to sign the 1982 Constitution Act, and separatist sentiment had become further entrenched by the failed Meech Lake Accord and Charlottetown Accord negotiations, both aimed at bringing Quebec back into the constitutional fold. In Quebec, many contended that democracy alone—meaning a clear decision by a majority of Quebecers—was sufficient to warrant unilateral separation from Canada. As such, Quebec refused to participate in the Secession Reference, so the Supreme Court appointed a so-called friend of the court to represent Quebec's views.

When its opinion was presented, the Supreme Court of Canada affirmed that democracy requires more than a simple 50% + 1 majority rule. Court decisions interpreting our constitution show that democracy exists in the larger context of other constitutional values. Undertaking a delicate balance of law and politics, the Court set out the legal framework within which Quebec could unilaterally separate from Canada. It considered the legality, both under our Constitution and in the context of self-determination in international law. The Court set out unwritten core values in accordance with which the Constitution, and any act of secession, must operate: federalism, democracy, constitutionalism and the rule of law, and respect for minorities.

The rule of law requires order and due process, while democracy enshrines the political will of the people. Stating that any secession must factor in these fundamental principles, the Court concluded that unilateral secession by Quebec is illegal. Importantly, however, the Court also determined that the rest of Canada had a duty to negotiate the terms of secession in the event of a clear democratic expression of will to separate. To balance these two counterpoints, the Court read in conditions that would allow for self-determination within the constitutional framework. The Court then passed the torch to the political actors to work out the process for secession—most notably to define a clear majority vote on a clear referendum question—and to settle on a process for secession negotiations in the event of a vote for separation. In 2000, the federal government enacted the Clarity Act. This legislation set out a framework and delegated responsibility to the House of Commons to determine what would constitute a clear question, and it set out the factors for determining whether there was a clear will to secede.

The sober and lengthy legal reflection on this matter was deliberate; Canadians had observed what can happen when force, rather than law, is used as the means of enforcement. Just over a century earlier, the American civil war (1860–65) had been the chosen response to the question of whether thirteen states could separate from the union, which the government determined they could not. The ensuing civil war saw more Americans killed than in all previous and subsequent military battles combined. Keenly aware of that outcome, Canada addressed the possible separation of Quebec with legal means alone, not force.

Empathetic things to do when you intend to Cherish the rule of law.

. . . as an individual

Recognize the precious gift of living in a civil society guided by the rule of law.
Trust in the legal system and those who make it work, but acknowledge that the law requires constant and vigilant cultivation.

Uphold the law at the ballot box.
Cherish the 1982 Charter of Rights and Freedoms as a creed for our personal protection, then prove your respect for those rights and freedoms by making an informed vote whenever a vote is called for.

Get involved.
Join a local organization (e.g., condo organization or school board) and participate in the process of community deliberation with fairness to all as your guiding principle.

. . . as a community

Hear both sides of any case.
Study every topic openly to appreciate the possible effects of any impending decision. Only when you get all the facts can you avoid arbitrary application of any rule.

Use powers well and fairly for the common good.
Be guided by the public interest and the justice of the system. Never apply or fail to apply a law merely to serve the preferred interest of any individual.

Monitor and measure anything your community wants to improve.
Do not rely on anecdotal evidence alone. You must monitor and measure anything you hope to improve. Only empirical data fairly gathered will show whether your management has been effective.

. . . as a nation

Create laws that are fair to all.
Be sure the laws that govern society are sound and good and based on the principle of fairness. Amend or reject any proposed law that favours one group over another or bestows advantage with bias.

Act transparently.
Any decision made behind closed doors is prey to bias. While national security may require some secrecy in some circumstances, let the public see and understand how the law is fairly, consistently, and equally applied to all citizens. Three Ts aptly summarize the process: truth, transparency, trust.

Hold our leaders responsible.
Executive privilege is a slippery slope. Appointed and elected representatives have both a legal and sacred obligation to protect the public interest. Make sure your government has no tolerance for preferential treatment or self-interest.

12

Right the wrong.[1]

Whenever the phone in our house rings at 11:30 p.m., I twitch. One night in 1975, my unease proved fitting. There had a been a murder, and my name had come up.

The caller was Anna, a friend from our church back in Toronto, a woman I knew when Sharon and I lived there. I had met her when we both volunteered to support a group of families in one of Toronto's many low-income neighbourhoods. Most of those families were new Canadians, recent arrivals with limited language proficiency and only a slender understanding of Canadian habits, systems, and rules. Often, their most pressing need was for advocacy, for someone to help them access the many services already in place to support them but that were shielded by approval processes impenetrable to newcomers. Margareta, a woman living in that community, had just called Anna. When she heard her caller's predicament, Anna decided to reach out to me, even though by then we had moved from Toronto to London, about two hundred kilometres down the road.

I've changed some names and nations here, but the features of the case were as follows: Margareta and her husband, Anton, had emigrated earlier from Slovenia. Margareta's sister Zala had come to Canada around the same time, and they all shared high hopes of supporting each other as they built new lives in their new home. Zala landed a good job right away; once established, she travelled back home to marry her fiancé, Franc, who was then just finishing his compulsory military service. Franc joined her back in Canada not long after. Margareta and Anton had a tougher time getting on their feet, but eventually Anton was hired as a labourer by a local construction firm. The work was tough, sometimes dangerous, but the security of a steady job allowed Margareta and Anton to begin a family. Tragically, just after the birth of their daughter, Anton was killed in an on-site accident. Now a young widow in a foreign land, Margareta was forced to work as a domestic to pay for the necessities of life, as humble as they would certainly be.

By then, her brother-in-law, Franc, was also working in construction. As a two-salary family, Zala and Franc hoped to purchase a modest home in a low-income neighbourhood, intending to improve their circumstances over time. Then they had a daughter of their own. When finally able to buy their first residence for their growing family, they were ecstatic, despite the fact that the place they could afford was tiny and jammed up against the equally tiny homes of their new neighbours. They couldn't even nudge their car out of their driveway without having to cross over part of one neighbour's drive in the process.

That particular neighbour had come from Croatia long ago, bringing with him bitter memories of earlier disputes between the two nations. When his new Slovenian neighbours began cutting across his property, the elderly man decided to make it tough on them. Whenever he caught Franc or Zala trying to get in or out of their own drive, he clenched his fist and yelled at them, which, as intended, made their lives miserable. One day, when Zala and Franc returned home with their little girl, they found the border of their driveway blocked with a huge concrete slab that had been cemented in place to prevent removal. After parking their car on the street, Zala took their two-year-old daughter into the house while Franc headed to the garage for a sledgehammer, with which he then demolished the obstacle. His neighbour, incensed, stormed out and threatened, "I will get you for this." Franc waved him off and went back indoors, presuming the matter concluded.

The family resumed its routine. After half an hour, Zala went out for groceries while Franc stayed home with their daughter. Just after she left, two men bearing baseball bats strode up the walkway. They were the neighbour's two sons, somewhat inebriated and summoned from another neighbourhood to settle the argument in their father's favour. They smashed through Franc's door with their bats and came upon the man standing with his daughter clinging to his legs. They attacked, with one man taking a bat to Franc's head. Franc had armed himself with a butcher's knife, which, when set upon, he thrust into the chest of one man, then into the ribs of the other, where the blade snapped off. The first man died instantly. The other sank to the floor, a blade deep in his ribs.

When the neighbour feared that his sons wouldn't be coming out of the house next door, he called the police. They came, conducted an investigation, took Franc into custody, and charged him with murder. Zala called her sister, Margareta. Margareta called Anna. Anna called me. Her worry was that the family might not be properly represented, for they had the typical newcomers' unfamiliarity with the legal world, and no money.

I contacted a fellow lawyer at a law firm for which I had worked one summer, then headed from London to Toronto to get involved. The next morning we met with the family. As we expected and as they admitted, without the funds to engage a seasoned lawyer and reluctant to deal with someone outside their community, they had retained the only lawyer they knew, a young man who had handled their real estate transaction when they bought their house. He had little experience, let alone in defending a client on a serious criminal charge. He was sure, however, that he could manage the case. I wasn't.

With Zala's permission, I called Martin Schweig, a lawyer I had met while doing school-recruiting work on behalf of the Harvard

Club of Toronto. He had played hockey at Harvard, as had I, returning afterward to complete law school in Toronto, after which he practised with a major criminal defence firm. Eventually he hung out his
own shingle as a criminal lawyer. Martin was a crackerjack.

His first challenge was to obtain Franc's release on bail, which
required securing a second mortgage on the house, which he had to
do with Zala, as Franc was in custody. The second was for him to
communicate frankly with Franc, his new client, a man of limited
English who distrusted anyone he didn't already know. Little wonder,
given everything that was happening.

But Franc shared few details with his new attorney and even fewer
with the police, claiming to have no recollection of anything that happened after the first blow of the baseball bat to his head. So Martin
asked me to serve as co-counsel, hoping that my connection to Anna
and his sister-in-law might induce the man to trust me enough to
relay the details of the incident. It did not and he would not. Franc
had no faith in any system. Like so many who come to Canada from
troubled shores, his relationship to the state was one of deep suspicion
and disdain. He expected nothing but to be disposed of by an uncar-
ing, contemptuous, and likely corrupt system of justice. He chose to
be tried by a judge, not a jury, and declined to take the stand in his
own defence. He felt powerless.

For seven days he sat in silence as the trial unfolded, waiting for the
hammer to fall and for his life, his wife's life, and his daughter's life to be
ruined. Bad enough that his family would be destitute without his
income; it was also understood that as a resident not yet a Canadian
citizen, he would be deported to Slovenia if found guilty. But that is not
what happened. The judge in this case was a patient and experienced
professional who saw his task as getting to the truth. So too was the
Crown attorney, who, with meticulous care, followed all the rules of due
process, including scrupulous disclosure of all evidence, incriminating
and non-incriminating alike, bent as he was on presenting the facts of

the matter with neither bias nor exaggeration. In no way was he seeking a slick courtroom victory. As defence attorney, Martin of course was eager to share any detail that would give the judge a true portrait of the man in the dock, though Franc would disclose nothing. Even as the accused sat silent, these members of the court took seven full days to get to know him, his background, his relationships, his circumstances, his work habits, his finances, and the many pressures under which his family lived. They asked about Franc's marriage, his childhood, his friendships. They explored the relationship between the neighbours to understand how the acrimony between them had become so deep. They asked the neighbour about his own past, trying to get at the prejudice that drove him to send his own sons to do violence, and in doing so to sacrifice a life, a burden he would carry every day forward. Clearly, the court wanted far more than the mere facts of the case. Working together under well-established rules of evidence, guided by an expert, curious, and compassionate judge, they assembled a complete picture of the accused's circumstances, pressures, values, and character before the judge reached a verdict on the charge of murder. It was just two words long: not guilty.

Not guilty. Imagine that. The judge would not even consider the lesser crime of manslaughter, nor did he make any overt finding of self-defence or undue provocation for the accused. He simply declared the accused to be not guilty, affirmed that the man was unlikely ever to offend again, and ended the matter there. I have no idea what went through his mind in coming to his decision, but I came away from this challenging situation profoundly impressed with our system of justice. For five days I had seen a room full of people listening, conversing, appreciating each other, all in an effort to fully understand the circumstances of another human before reaching a judgment. That is the very definition of empathy in action.

We are fortunate in Canada that lawyers who choose careers as prosecutors almost always maintain a high level of professional conduct and integrity.[2] Our judges are still chosen on merit, not political connection, from among the most respected members of the profession and typically accept a substantial diminution in their compensation as they leave the practice of law to sit on the bench. These are the people who, on behalf of Canadian society, resist judging anyone until they have taken the time to enter their worlds, understand their circumstances, and see matters from their perspectives. They exhibit the kind of selfless character we must treasure and perpetuate if justice is to be done. What a lesson that has been for me.

The Path to Fairness

I have always found that mercy bears richer fruits than strict justice.

ABRAHAM LINCOLN, 1864

It is the duty of the state—in our constitutional system "the Crown"—to protect both person and property. The due process of this responsibility requires that the Crown meets its duty with a basic fairness, and also with scrupulous attention to procedural requirements and guidelines. Basic fairness requires constant effort to establish and improve the social conditions that incent or do not discourage criminal behaviour. When an alleged crime occurs due process must be rigorously pursued, and when a conviction is recorded, sentencing is based in fairness with due consideration of deterrence, restitution, rehabilitation, and reintegration as its aims.

In Canada's case there is at least a millennium of history underlying our Criminal Code and the many other laws that impose sanctions or imprisonment, fines, restitution, and injunctions to deter unlawful activity. That history has produced a number of fundamental fairness principles. You probably know them all. They include the following:

Justice is blind. No party is favoured; beginning with the sovereign, no person is above the law. That's why the statue of justice is blindfolded.

Each person is presumed innocent until proven guilty, and, in the case of most criminal charges, beyond a reasonable doubt.

The accused cannot be compelled to testify against themselves. Just as important, negative inferences cannot be drawn by a failure to testify.

An accused is entitled to judgment by a jury of peers—ordinary citizens who commit to consider evidence without bias.

Everyone must abide by strict rules. Police must follow the law in their investigation. Prosecutors, called Crown attorneys, must adhere to strict rules in charging and trying. The case must provide all relevant evidence to the accused and have it tested in courts open to the public and presided over by an expert, impartial judge. Under Canadian law, prosecutors are not tasked with winning a case as such, and unlike the practice in many U.S. jurisdictions, judges and prosecutors in Canada are not elected but appointed. As we saw in Franc's murder trial, they work as agents of the Crown to ensure truth be told, and that justice be done and be seen to be done. The statue of justice carries evenly loaded scales in her hands for that reason.

After any trial that ends with a verdict of guilty, sentencing is considered and decided. In earlier times, the goals of sentencing were limited to deterrence and restitution. In Victorian England, for example, guilty prisoners might be incarcerated in jails, sometimes in the rotting hulks of decommissioned ships, and in many cases sentenced to transportation by sea to a penal colony such as Botany Bay in Australia.[3] While the practice seems bizarre to modern observers, it helps to know that, at the time, criminality—the inclination to commit crimes—was itself considered to be a contagious weakness of character. They sent criminals to the other side of the world so that ordinary citizens could not be infected. I fancy that vestiges of that fear still lurk in our tendency to lock prisoners away from society behind thick, guarded walls, even for minor crimes on occasion.

In Canada in the 1870s, missionaries of a Toronto group providing spiritual care to prisoners in local jails discovered that the men needed far more support than religious services, and the movement to see offenders as humans in need of rehabilitation began. Programs of support were created to help prisoners reintegrate into society after they had done their time. Eventually the group joined with others under the banner of the John Howard Society, a nod to the pioneering English prison reformer of the eighteenth century. As they canvassed neighbourhoods for support, members of the society began to speak in public and circulate information that raised awareness of the deeper issues, eventually shifting public opinion to a more realistic, humane view of the circumstances that lead to crime, which in turn led to openness to the idea of rehabilitation of an offender. In 1939, Canadian parliamentarian Agnes Macphail launched the Elizabeth Fry Society to offer the same support to inmates of women's prisons.

Empathy After Crime

Men and women have spent centuries seeking justice, and Canada over time has made considerable advancements in the way we approach and ensure deterrence, restitution, and rehabilitation. In the past fifty years, we have also made great leaps in the important process of reconciliation between those who have committed crimes and the victims whose lives they have affected. In 1974, a probation officer named Mark Yantzi and a prison support worker named Dave Worth were working on a case in Elmira, Ontario, when they both realized that the system needed changing. Two youngsters had been arrested and charged after vandalizing twenty-two properties in their community. But to Yantzi and Worth, it seemed pointless just to lock the kids up when they had affected so many families. Both men had learned from First Nations colleagues that there was a better way; traditional restorative justice focused not on punishment but rather on making things right again. So, seeking true justice and a more powerful remedy, they asked the court's permission to arrange a meeting between the young offenders and their victims, hoping that reparation—the making of amends for wrongs committed—might follow. When the judge agreed, the men turned to local First Nations leaders to better understand the mechanics and lessons of restorative justice practised by countless generations of Indigenous communities in Canada. In this case and in many that followed, the modern application of First Nations experience met with outstanding success. Wrongs were righted, wounds were healed, and restorative justice again found favour, paving the way for more formal legal recognition of traditional restorative justice practices in Indigenous communities in Canada, the United States, Europe, Australia, and New Zealand.

The idea is to bring together the person harmed and the person who caused that harm in a supervised meeting, often facilitated by many members of the community. There they can talk about what happened, what damage was done, both material and emotional, and determine together how the person who caused harm can repair that harm, or at least try to. This model of justice is focused not on punishment, but on making things right and, where possible, reintegrating the person who did the deed back into the community, hoping he may return with insight and skills that will lead to better behaviour.

One of the deep benefits of restorative justice is the empowerment that the community feels as members work to settle their own disputes. At the personal level, those who are harmed get to voice their pain, describe the impact of the crime on their lives, and identify the needs they have now that they didn't before. The guilty person (whether charged, accused, or formally judged as guilty in court) gets to feel the impact of their actions and may choose to acknowledge that impact honestly. With the help of community members in the room, all parties can then come to an agreement about what should be done next. When it works, they create a plan together that is restorative (thus the name), realistic, fitting, and fair. That may help everyone involved move toward healing, and even forgiveness, as the community takes responsibility for the reform of the accused's behaviour.

At its heart, restorative justice assumes that a relationship that has been fractured by an action can now be restored by new actions, even though only over time. It recognizes that rifts are harmful, especially in small communities, that mere punishment seldom helps anyone, and that creative mending of broken relationships is a powerful catalyst that can build strong new bonds. It creates an environment in which the wrongdoer can show proper respect by listening deeply and by responding honestly even when disagreements still exist. Skilled

Saying *Sorry*—The Canadian Thing to Do

Canadians may be teased worldwide for our habit of apologizing, yet I think our inclination to do so is an indication of great strength, as expressions of humility usually are. For us, apology is not admission of error, but rather good manners and an invitation to communication, a means of connection and reparation. In the past decade, the law has finally caught up with our tendency to apologize out loud. In almost every Canadian province and territory,[4] it is now prohibited to use someone's apology as proof or even indication of possible guilt in any matter. For instance, Ontario's Apology Act, passed into law in 2009, defines apology as

> an expression of sympathy or regret, a statement that a
> person is sorry or any other words or actions indicating
> contrition or commiseration, whether or not the words
> or actions admit fault or liability or imply an admission
> of fault or liability in connection with the matter to
> which the words or actions relate

facilitators can guide participants to offer that respect one to another, suggesting mid-course corrections when anyone wobbles.

But it's not merely an exercise. For the process of restorative justice to work, everyone involved has to understand and admit their personal responsibilities in the events that went down. It sometimes emerges that the victims themselves, often unknowingly, had treated the wrongdoer unfairly, dismissively, or even cruelly before the crime was committed. So the process demands that every party do the soul searching required to discern where they may have played a part in the unfolding events. Only when all those who need to take responsibility do so willingly will the process work.

and then goes on to decree that an apology made by or on behalf of a person in connection with any matter,

a) does not, in law, constitute an express or implied admission of fault or liability by the person in connection with that matter;

(b) does not, despite any wording to the contrary in any contract of insurance or indemnity and despite any other Act or law, void, impair or otherwise affect any insurance or indemnity coverage for any person in connection with that matter; and

(c) shall not be taken into account in any determination of fault or liability in connection with that matter.

This simple yet powerful edict encourages all Canadians to express their empathy freely in any situation.

Then comes a plan for repair, but only once respect and responsibility have been authentically expressed can any discussion of reparation take place. Repair, of course, is never fully possible. Stolen goods may be returned, damaged property may be replaced or fixed, but the shock of assault, invasion, or intimidation may linger long. The person who caused harm is expected to repair the harm that they did to the fullest extent possible, knowing well that not all of the harm can be repaired. The repair principle replaces thoughts of revenge and punishment, instead focusing on moving forward in a more positive direction. It is through working to repair the situation that the person who caused harm is able to regain their self-respect and respect for others.

Finally, and ideally, the members of the community will then allow the person who caused harm to accept responsibility and begin a process of reintegration into their midst. This is not just a grace to the wrongdoer; it is the moment of healing for all.

It strikes me that our justice system not only reflects our national character but also reminds us and guides us to follow our better instincts in all conflicts, no matter how small. Every transgression has a backstory, every failing an aspect of confusion. As we move to solve the many problems we face as a human society, we must work to overcome our differences, heal our separation, restore our faith in each other's potential, and deepen our respect for each other's novel ideas. Our own justice system here in Canada proves every day that we can do just that.

The Power of Positive Empathy

Another observation of the effect of positive empathy can be made in the distinction between the rule of law and justice, where law is the body of static statements found in constitutions, in legislation, in government regulations, and in judicial decisions, and where justice is the exercise of the values underlying those statements. Without the values that promote justice, rules can be misapplied. When that is done deliberately, it can be thought of not as the rule of law but rather the law of rule. Justice based on fairness is a central requirement for a healthy society, and for the rule of law to be just, it must reflect the best values of the society it serves.

If I were to start a new law school, I would inscribe one general question over its entrance: "Is law just?" and of any student examining any specific law in any class or legal-aid assignment, I would ask, "Is this law just?" That would induce the student to explore a law's history, to consider what harm or problem it was intended to remedy or contain, to examine the prevailing social circumstances when that law was promulgated, to trace its evolution and to judge whether it has been successful in mitigating or containing as intended, and to assess in retrospect whether it was fair at the outset and whether new social conditions had emerged that required amendments for that law to be just now.

I would also organize several opportunities for social evenings in the first week of the law school to have the students watch and discuss two classic movies that raise the dichotomy between justice and the rule of law: *Judgment at Nuremberg* and *To Kill a Mockingbird*. The first tells the story of the judge who had been the leading constitutional scholar during Hitler's Third Reich in Germany before the Second World War. He was subsequently charged with murder and tried in the post-war Nuremberg trials. At that trial, he refused to plead innocent or to employ the defence that he was simply following the rules laid down by Hitler's government. He accepted guilt for being an opponent of justice during Hitler's regime. *To Kill a Mockingbird* illustrates a trial in America's deep south in the 1920s, a trial at which all the rules of procedure are followed, yet at which an all-white jury still finds a Black man guilty of murder even when the evidence shows he is clearly innocent.

I experienced the power of positive empathy myself in my first week as the new dean of the Western University Law School in August of 1974. It began with a telephone call. My secretary said, "The chief justice of the Supreme Court of Canada is calling you." I picked up the phone and Chief Justice Bora Laskin said, "I want to thank you for taking on the challenge of the deanship at Western. You have a big job ahead of you. How can I help?" I replied that the thoughtfulness of his call was in itself touching and that it was, as such, help of the best kind. His response was quite typical of the chief justice—a swift move into action. He indicated that he wanted to help stabilize the culture at our law school, an institution that former Justice Ivan Rand of the Supreme Court had founded. Chief justice Laskin knew we were going through a difficult period. One problem was that a large number of our faculty members were spending more than the one day a week they were allotted to engage in remunerative legal practice. The understanding was that these law teachers would take on only such work as informed and enriched their teaching and research. Unfortunately, for many of our teachers, these paid activities were now occupying far more than a single day each week, and much of the work was routine stuff that paid well but enriched little. The chief justice offered a wise remedy. He explained that the Supreme Court did not begin fall hearings until the third

Justice Ivan Cleveland Rand

Long celebrated for his championing of civil liberties, Justice Ivan Cleveland Rand[5] presided on the Supreme Court of Canada until the day he turned seventy-five. He had been the swing vote in 1949 on the three-person United Nations Commission (with the two other representatives of the United States and the United Kingdom) that created the modern state of Israel. As a lawyer from New Brunswick, he had joined the Supreme Court of Canada while judges still served for an unlimited term. Shortly before his seventy-fifth birthday, however, Parliament passed a law imposing retirement at age seventy-five. That law was not to be applied retroactively and week in September. He would ask one of the nine justices to spend the first two or three days of September right after Labour Day as our "judge in residence," joining in law school lectures, participating in seminars, meeting continuously with small groups of students and faculty. With the justice's presence, the chief justice proposed, teachers and students alike might be inspired to bring greater focus to their work. He was right. The participation of such an accomplished jurist instantly elevated the professional atmosphere of the school. It was a dramatic success, a tribute to the perception and engaged character of Chief Justice Laskin, and one more proof that positive empathy is a transformative force.

Justice Rand was grandfathered in, but he was so offended by the assumption that judges lost their ability to function well after age seventy-five that he resigned from the Court on his seventy-fifth birthday. Then he immediately founded the Western University Law School. He did so with aplomb, teaching twice as many courses as the other regular professors to fill the gaps where they did not have specific expertise. In addition to his commitment to civil liberties, he was a champion of rigorous physical exercise and chose his apartment eight kilometres south of the campus so he could walk each way every working day of the year—rain, snow, or sunshine. A brilliant, productive, and inspiring Canadian, Justice Ivan Rand got Western University Law School off to a flourishing start.

Empathetic things to do when you intend to Right the wrong.

. . . as an individual

Recognize the precious gift of living in a civil society guided by the rule of law.
Trust in the legal system and those who make it work, but acknowledge that the law needs constant amendment and improvement as society changes.

Distrust your negative opinions.
Gut instinct may work well in matters of intimate relationships, but it is unreliable when judging the actions of your neighbours, acquaintances, and colleagues. Any negative opinion quickly reached is often little more than an expression of your implicit bias. Don't jump to conclusions.

Presume innocence.
Most people are well meaning even when misguided. Give everyone the benefit of the doubt until you know the full circumstances of any event in which they are involved. The news is usually good.

Avoid cynicism.
Given the multiplicity of motives that go into any human decision, do not lazily ascribe the least noble of these to someone else's chosen path, lest they return the favour. Listen well and seek to understand.

... as a community

Encourage diversity of opinion.
Seek the broadest range of opinion on any topic. That is the best way to shed light on the opportunities and pitfalls of any proposed community project or undertaking.

Protect, prevent, and resolve.
To be safe and nurturing, every community must protect the safety of its members by preventing crime, abuse, and neglect. But don't just enforce the law; go further and help resolve the many differences that arise between those of varied backgrounds, circumstances, and ambitions. In all public dealings, seek to heal differences and find the path to the greatest common good.

Develop and support your police.
Despite recent urges to reduce police budgets in the wake of incidents of poor police behaviour, the vast majority of police officers are capable, dutiful, and honourable servants of their communities. Remind your police of their role, train them in the latest concepts and techniques, and support them with frequent public praise for their contribution. And remember Sir Robert Peel's nine principles of policing, firmly rooted as they are in community service.

... as a nation

Work tirelessly to make your justice system truly just.
Build a system that is consistent across all sectors. If you are tough on drug dealers and soft on white-collar embezzlers, you will destroy your system's credibility for all groups equally.

Make criminal justice restorative.

Give guidance that leads to sentencing that contributes to all four priorities: prevention of crime, restitution of damage, rehabilitation of the offender, and reintegration for the continued health and integrity of the community.

Change to inspire.

Seek constantly to improve the administration of justice with particular attention to fairness, while accommodating shifting societal conditions and pressures. Avoid any system that merely imposes sanctions for misbehaviour. Under such systems, society cannot improve.

13

Protect the most vulnerable.

The test of a democracy is not the magnificence of buildings
or the speed of automobiles or the efficiency of air transportation,
but rather the care given to the welfare of all the people.

HELEN KELLER, 1935

Never once did it occur to me that I would, could, or should be the governor general of Canada. In retrospect, it was statistically more likely that I would end up orbiting the earth as a Canadian astronaut than serving as the Queen's representative within our constitutional monarchy. I knew something about the post, having studied constitutional law, and in my time keenly observing many lively, often heated, debates over membership in and management of the confederation that binds our provinces and territories into one wobbly, wonderful package.

I had not studied in any depth the post of governor general, but my crash course in learning about the job, which began in June 2010, was a revelation. I came to admire the wisdom of many previous governors general, impressed by the profound effect of their perspectives on the progress and health of our country. Through my exposure to Canadian English history, I had known Samuel de Champlain[1] as a conquistador who came from France to plant the flag, convert the Indigenous people to Christianity, and send furs and fish back to France. I was so utterly mistaken. It was David Hackett Fischer's book, *Champlain's Dream*, that dramatically altered my view. Champlain's founder's dream was for an inclusive Canada. His vision of a diverse, tolerant, and welcoming society had not been shared by the many other Europeans who had previously tried (and all failed) to establish a permanent colony in this land. I had become mesmerized by the novels of John Buchan Lord Tweedsmuir, among them *Sick Heart River* (1941), which he wrote while serving as governor general.[2] That tale reflects his fondness for Canada and the restorative power of our country's natural beauty. I had developed great respect for Vincent Massey, a high-ranking member of the first generation of Canadian foreign service officers and a great diplomat, who had also learned the value of sharing one's fortunes as a member of a large, wealthy, and endlessly generous family. As our first Canadian-born governor general, Massey transformed the vice-regal office into a uniquely Canadian institution, opening up Rideau Hall as a non-partisan gathering place for all Canadians. I was humbled too by Georges Vanier, a deeply religious and kind-hearted soul, but also a distinguished warrior who had been wounded severely, losing a leg in battle in northern France in the Great War, and then served as a diplomat in the foreign service, as had Massey. His selfless words still move me: "I know of no occupation more noble than service and no calling higher than service of the public." And I came to a deep and quiet admiration for Roméo LeBlanc, whose own modesty and humility led him to create the Caring Canadian Award, a program that celebrates the open-hearted. So yes, I learned about the role of the governor general, and I have held those who have shouldered it in high regard. But me? Governor general? Never.

Never say never. The request came in a phone call from the director of public appointments at the prime minister's office in the summer of 2010. He told me the prime minister was researching the recommendations of a five-person committee of knowledgeable Canadians with a clear understanding of the job who had been asked—without calling for application—to identify who across the country might be suitable to consider as Canada's twenty-eighth governor general.[3] The question was simply put: "Would you consider serving as governor general?"

I said, "Let's be practical; you will be putting together a long list. Why don't you list me as uncertain, and if, by some strange quirk, my name survives to a short list, give me a call." A few hours later, the call came back. "It's a short list."

I figured I better take this seriously, so I suggested a period of prudent reflection. "Give me a week to ponder and consult with my wife and the three or four friends I usually talk to about important personal decisions." The reply was swift: "Oh, no, sir, you can't discuss this with anyone." My reply was equally swift: "Well, you better count me out. I could never agree without at least consulting with my wife. Otherwise, I would be packing my own bag and going to Ottawa solo. That would make for a mighty lonely five years at Rideau Hall."

The caller said, "Can I get back to you, sir?" Fifteen minutes later, he rang to say, "It is a very, very short list. Confer with your wife but please not with anyone else. And would you come to Ottawa Saturday evening for dinner with the prime minister and his wife?"

Sharon was not keen on the idea. Our life in Waterloo had been more than comfortable. Yet by then I had been a university president for twenty-six years. I had served for three consecutive, five-year terms at McGill and was coming to the end of a second six-year term at Waterloo. I had loved serving in this way, but believed that no one should do that type of job forever. There are always brighter, younger minds ready with new ideas to help shape our universities appropriately for a different era, and the university is an institution that requires constant evolution, and refreshing, just as its culture must emphasize constant improvement. Sharon and I talked at length. She was not enamoured of the idea and was happily settled in our Waterloo life, but, ultimately she concluded that we both felt serving the public would continue to be our priority. This new job would be fully devoted to such service. I was up for it, but Sharon's perspective was key. If we accepted, we'd be moving to Ottawa, farther away from our kids and grandkids, and we'd be working and living at two official residences—Rideau Hall in Ottawa and La Citadelle de Québec. As Sharon put it, "It wouldn't be easy living over the shop." Her decision was crucial. In retrospect, I can't imagine doing the job without her committed partnership, and, as events turned out, she was simply magnificent.

Our dinner with Stephen and Laureen Harper helped clarify our decision. Mr. Harper was open and direct. Importantly, as a student of government himself, he recognized and affirmed the separation of the offices of prime minster and governor general. They were in place for different reasons, focused on different but complementary tasks. As Bagehot wrote, the separation of head of government and head of state is key to the balanced and measured approach that makes the Westminster system work. The head of governance branch handles the business of government through elected representatives, while the head of state honours the dignity of government and is non-political, as intended, for the due protection of the constitution. There would be no political pressure on what must be a non-political role. I disagreed with several of Prime Minister Harper's priorities, and would continue to, but I also respected his integrity. Moreover, I began to think that my own sensibilities, exercised as they would be in this uniquely non-political leadership role, might possibly add something useful to the national temperament, and the lessons I had learned from exploring the accomplishments of previous governors general affirmed that. Sharon too found herself turning to the idea. For her, such service might be a fitting way for us to acknowledge and repay—at least in part—the many advantages that the country we love had given us, advantages it works to offer all its citizens. She had a particular focus on mental health and, while at Rideau Hall, would be able to vigorously promote mental health awareness and remediation. It was our turn to give back. Service, Sharon says, is love made visible. So we packed up our farm in Waterloo and moved to Ottawa.

Seeing Canada with Eyes Wide Open

Serving as governor general with Sharon as vice-regal consort put us in a privileged position from which we could see the country in ways not open to most Canadians. We were taking up this role at a point in my life where I could approach my work with some maturity and self-awareness—two qualities to which I had aspired but did not possess even a decade earlier. My experience had given me perspective with which I could carry out the office's many ceremonial and diplomatic matters while looking deeper at the social and economic realities under which many Canadians live. I had no political role, no right to offer any opinion on what the government should focus on, but I did form the opinions that I've been sharing here.

As I went in, my dedication to service was strengthened by deep pride of country. Being hatched and raised in Canada has been a blessing for me. The family I was born into had little money, but the high expectations of my mother, the encouragement of my school-teachers, and the guidance of my sports coaches instilled in me a dual sense of purpose and optimism. After that, the generosity of my neighbours during my childhood and of those granting scholarships during my student years made it possible for me to excel. All in all, our country's values, institutions, and people made it possible for me to enjoy a rewarding life.

This is so true for so many Canadians and explains why Canada routinely ranks as one of the most liveable nations in the world, as judged in a host of comparative assessments by international organizations. One of these is Overall Best Countries, the annual ranking by *U.S. News & World Report*, an American media company set up in 1948 to add consumer advice and analysis to its core offering of news. The company's Overall Best Countries ranking is a thorough analysis of quality of life across ten broad categories, each with metrics in many discrete sub-categories rating relative cost of living, infrastructure, education, citizen safety, ease of doing business, degree of corruption, transparency of government processes, and so on. Since the program was initiated in 2016, Canada has placed in the highest three ranks every year, reaching top spot in 2021. That year's citation emphasized that Canadians pride themselves on encouraging all of their citizens to honour their own cultures, that our national policy of multiculturalism celebrates the country's diversity, and that Canada is a high-tech industrial society with a high standard of living. The analysis continues by stating that Canada is known to be good for business and is highly rated for being non-bureaucratic, free of corruption, and guided by transparent government practices. Beyond the essential benefits of broad access to food and housing, solid education, universal health care, and employment that sustains a reasonable quality of life, Canada also enjoys intangibles such as job security, political stability, individual freedom, and environmental quality.

Much cause for pride. Yet much more room for improvement, as we must all admit. In my life, and particularly through the lens of my work at Rideau Hall, my eyes were opened by meeting and getting to know many Canadians whose lives were less than ideal. And through Sharon's focus on and work in mental health, I had already become well aware that many suffer in darkness, either because they cannot access the help they need to overcome their mental conditions and distresses, or because they have been stigmatized and sidelined by the ignorance and fear of those around them. We had also in our time met so many who lacked jobs, income, security, education, clean water, access to the Internet, transport, and even appropriate health care. We knew of immigrants who, despite Canada's reputation for welcome, had not yet been able to get on their feet despite working two and three jobs every day and night. We had known military families whose sons and daughters had perished on foreign shores or come home broken by horrors they had seen in the ragged corners of the world. We had visited communities right here in Canada where natural disasters had ripped people apart, destroyed their livelihoods, and thrown their futures into question. We knew victims of racist attacks, human trafficking, domestic violence, and all the woes that humans in their ignorance can visit upon others. And we had seen so many children in so many communities who, simply because of want of education, were doomed to lives lived far below their own beautiful potential.

So when I took up my own duties as governor general in October of 2010, Sharon and I knew that we had been given a rare opportunity to inspire Canadians to help improve conditions for these vulnerable people. Well aware that I was not blessed with any genius, I figured that my contribution—if I could make one at all—would come from dogged hard work, and I knew going in that the success of that work would depend on my stating my hope for our country in simple words. Those words came to me early on. It occurred to me that our future would be brighter if we learned to be smart and caring at the same time. That combination struck me as the surest way to make improvement. If we are smart but not caring, we can be prosperous but only as individuals, and if we are caring but not smart, we will be appreciated but unable to make enduring change. If we could be both at once, I reckoned, we would have the wit to work out our problems and the heart to know who and how best to help. At my investiture on the first day of October, I put it simply:

> We are a smart and caring nation. A nation where all Canadians can grow their talents to the maximum. A nation where all Canadians can succeed and contribute. There is much work to be done to fully achieve our vision.[4]

Smart and caring; in a way, these were the two values that grow from learning and family, values that I had already chosen to feature as the central two elements of my official coat of arms.[5] The motto placed below that coat of arms was *Contemplare meliora*, Latin for my hope that we can all envisage a better world. And then I set to work.

My assignment was to fulfill the fundamental responsibilities of the office: meeting the constitutional duties of signing legislation, orders, and commissions into law; proroguing and dissolving Parliament; protecting the constitution; serving as commander-in-chief of the Canadian Armed Forces; representing Canada at home and abroad; encouraging excellence and achievement through the honours system; and, through it all, bringing Canadians together. Dream job.

As I soon learned, I hadn't truly anticipated the pace, which kept me hopping. In my seven years in the post, as commander-in-chief I made 12 formal visits to Canadian Forces bases in country, visited our troops abroad 7 times, including 2 visits to Afghanistan (the first of which was within six weeks of taking the job), and attended some 330 military events to honour those who serve our country so selflessly and professionally. I led 56 Canadian missions abroad, 12 in North America, 6 in South America, 3 in Africa, 18 in Europe, and 17 in Asia. At home, Sharon and I helped uphold Canada's reputation as a warm, welcoming country by hosting[6] a total of 62 dignitaries on state, royal, and working visits to Canada and greeting 276 foreign heads of mission to Canada during 64 letters-of-credence presentation ceremonies. Then, through the presentation of medals, awards, and decorations for everything from bravery and scientific achievement to artistic excellence, we celebrated Canada's best and brightest. With the fantastic support of the Chancellery of Honours, we engineered what one reporter called the biggest renewal of the Canadian Honours System in 50 years, which included rebranding and reintroducing such honours as the Sovereign's Medal for Volunteers and the Meritorious Service Decorations. I cheerily invested more than 1,000 deserving individuals into the Order of Canada, all of whom were aptly described by the motto of that order, *Desiderantes meliorem patriam* (they desire a better country).[7] Certain that celebrating great achievement is the best way to inspire such achievement in others, I attended more than 30 honours ceremonies in towns and cities across Canada and presided over more than 100 such ceremonies at our two official residences. I approved the presentation of about 17,000 governor general's academic awards and three new honours to celebrate contributions in critically important arenas: the Sovereign's Medal for Volunteers, the Governor General's Innovation Awards, and the Academic All-Canadian Awards, which each year recognize about 3,500 Canadian triple threats—university students who excel equally at varsity athletics, academic studies, and volunteer activities.

With Sharon's expertise and leadership, we visited 150 mental health organizations in Canada, hosted 9 dedicated mental health events at Rideau Hall, visited 6 military family resources centres to learn about health issues—from the stress of military life and absences to the pain of living with PTSD. And in 2016, under the auspices of the Canadian Alliance on Mental Illness and Mental Health, Sharon became the patron of the Champion of Mental Health Award for Youth, which was named after her.

And having been so inspired by Vincent Massey's insistence on opening up Government House at Rideau Hall as a gathering place for all Canadians, we put great emphasis on inviting the public to come and see what Sharon and I called the Home of the People of Canada, referring both to the residence at Rideau Hall and to that at la Citadelle. During my time in office, more than 1.5 million Canadians accepted the invitation, all thanks to the gracious and entertaining guides who, with our superb security staff, made all those visits warm and memorable.

And all the while I talked and talked and talked, giving some 1,400 speeches—always in both official languages, intent on sharing the story of Canadians' achievements and innovations with anyone who would listen.[8] And yet, despite this crazy schedule, I was still able to spend much of my time, as was Sharon, just listening. As I declared in the opening chapters of this book, listening is the greatest tool of learning and communication we humans can deploy. So much becomes clear when you ask absolutely anyone this six-word question: "So how are you getting along?" and then let them speak.[9] We asked it of health-care workers, of midwives, of miners, of homeless teenagers, of band members on reserve, of farmers, of prisoners, of terminally ill patients, of seniors in long-term-care homes, of factory workers, of sex workers, of recent immigrants, of the kids of military families, of wounded veterans, of orphans, of small business operators, of elected officials at every level of government, of volunteers, of inventors, of victims of abuse, of teachers, and of children in daycare centres. From the first day on the job, we were astounded by how open people were, how honest, how unexaggerated, how caring, and, in so many and varied ways, how vulnerable. And we came to one overriding conclusion: wherever dire need exists in populations of our country, the most logical remedy will usually be government action. I don't mean handouts. I don't mean charity alone, for in vulnerable populations you will always find others being charitable, trying to help, trying to change lives for the better by giving their neighbours a hand up. But for the kinds of problems that plague many in society, that is never enough. The permanent fix must always come from a societal action, and government is the mechanism through which society takes action. In a civilized society, it is the job of government to protect the most vulnerable. We need that job done, we expect it to be done, and we have the right to vote out any government that does not take that duty seriously.

Clarity from the Pandemic

In my time as governor general, I learned much about our vulnerable populations, but what I know is no secret. Thanks to COVID-19, it is now more obvious than ever where the problems are. The pandemic has laid bare many of the inadequacies of our country, especially our failure to protect the most vulnerable among us. The aftermath of this health crisis is the moment when we Canadians can put right our failings—to build a better normal and not merely revert to the old one. Empathy means listening to, learning from, and, in some cases, learning yet again from people whose backgrounds and experiences differ from our own, especially people who are vulnerable. We must take and retake note of the voices of the elderly, of people of colour, of people with low incomes, and of Indigenous peoples, particularly women. Their vulnerability was revealed to us most acutely during the pandemic.

Turning empathy into action means putting right our clearest failings, and we must do that at all levels of government: federal, provincial, and municipal. It's obvious now. We must fix how we attend to people in long-term care. We must remove the insecurity of people living at the poverty line. We must end the discrimination people of colour suffer as a result of surveillance, policing, and manipulation or neglect of health data. We must heal the divisions separating us from our Indigenous citizens by following through on the wise and practical recommendations of the Truth and Reconciliation Commission and the National Inquiry into Missing and Murdered Indigenous Women and Girls. We must prove we abhor acts of violence based on religion, ethnicity, and sexual orientation by strengthening laws and making sure they are applied. We must give women victims of domestic abuse the tools they need to escape the horrors with which they live, and we must hold their abusers to strict account. We must fix our environment, lower our consumption, find truly sustainable energy, come down hard on online fraud and extortion, put an end to homelessness, ensure food security for all citizens, improve and protect the quality of our water. . . .

I could go on for pages, not because there is so much wrong with Canada, but because there is so much opportunity for progress. We are already an extraordinary country, as we have seen, empirically and consistently among the three best countries of the world in which to live. Changing conditions, especially for the most vulnerable, is how we stay so high on that list. We do that by being vigilant about what we must do, by electing people to form governments with the expertise to make the necessary changes in ways that are affordable and sustainable, often through institutions, agencies, and suppliers with boots on the ground where they are needed. Government is essential, and, in Canada, government works, precisely because it can be changed by the people it serves. That messy reality is the very definition of democracy.

Scuffle in the Corridor

When truckers rolled their rigs into Ottawa in late January 2022, the people of Ottawa, Ontario, and, eventually, all Canada reacted in ways as varied as anyone could imagine. The protesters came into town hauling a variety of messages, for while they spoke of unity they represented a disparate range of groups and interests. They did, however, rally under the spoken demand that the prime minister and the federal government put an end to all vaccine mandates in the country. Over 90 per cent of employed truckers in Canada had already themselves been vaccinated by that time, but the protesters were frustrated, they said, by what they felt were draconian border regulations imposed by both Canadian and U.S. authorities, measures that made it difficult for them to move cargo between the two countries without long and expensive delays for testing and for isolation when required. Some people in Ottawa welcomed the convoy with enthusiasm, many waving Canadian flags on overpasses as trucks passed below on their way into town. Others were distressed, especially as rigs began to fill Ottawa's downtown streets and neighbourhoods with a non-stop blaring of air horns that eclipsed all other sounds. Supportive citizens appeared downtown to show solidarity, even as shops and restaurants, which were only barely surviving lockdowns as it was, shuttered their doors once again to avoid the invasion of maskless crowds that might threaten their health and the health of their customers. With few exceptions in the first two weeks, political representatives stayed clear, most citing refusal to be drawn in by the mob. The absence of leaders struck some as prudent and others as cowardly. Local and national media portrayed the protests as legally allowable but confused, seldom interviewing organizers of the event to seek out their positions, in part because there were many leaders of many different groups within the protest. The resulting lack of representation in mainstream media then fuelled the truckers' contention that they were being deliberately misrepresented, with supportive social-media producers declaring this neglect to be part of a deeper plot to silence the truckers altogether.

Looking on as an observer on the outskirts of town, for I admit I did not venture in during those early days, I was struck by two questions: First, how had such deep division arisen in Canada, a nation long celebrated (and certainly within these pages) for its tolerance of diversity and respect for civil order? Second, how had the protestors come to distrust the processes of government—the way decisions are made within democracies—so completely that they agreed among themselves to usurp the public conversation to try to bully governments across the country to carry out their will? Those questions were soon joined by a third: How did the government then conclude that invoking the Canada's Emergencies Act was an appropriate and proportional response? One can't help pondering whether such exaggerated actions by citizens on the one hand and the somewhat tardy response of government on the other are omens of impending societal collapse.

Analysis of these events and answers to these questions will roll out over the coming years, as similar analysis will in the United States, where such discontent (or manipulation, depending on how you see it) led to an attack on the Capitol in January of 2021. The phenomenon hasn't been limited to North America. Mimicking the Canadian model, even waving Canadian flags as symbols, Freedom Convoy protests have been staged in France, New Zealand, Austria, and other countries in which people have elected to force changes in government policies through sustained disruption of day-to-day activities in major centres and border crossings.

In democracies, citizens are assumed to have made a compact with government. On one side of the social compact, governments pledge to muster resources and take action for the greater public good, from maintaining a fair system of justice on the one hand to defending the nation with military force on the other. On their side, citizens agree to exercise their right and responsibility of suffrage by electing to office those who will faithfully represent their interests and priorities. Those priorities evolve over time, so, as conditions change, governments change which activities are prioritized and the degree to which they are addressed. Representative governments, by their nature, tend to be responsive, forever playing catch up, their agendas invariably a lagging indicator of public will. When any government falls too far behind, or when it is seen to no longer be in step with public will, the public becomes disenchanted and exercises its will at the ballot box.

To avoid being out of touch, governments have a duty to consult before they act. While having a duty to be responsive, they must also lead, shaping public opinion and spurring public action. Finding the proper balance between listening and leading can be difficult. Does all good leadership involve consultation? If so, what kind of listening must government undertake and how much is enough? At which point should consultation become action? And are there situations in which consultations are unnecessary or perhaps unwise? These can be tough questions for governments to answer.

In their book *The Narrow Corridor: States, Societies and the Fate of Liberty* (2019), economists Daron Acemoglu and James Robinson (of *Why Nations Fail* fame) emphasize the importance of a counterbalance between a strong state and a strong civil society. When the state grows too strong, or the demands for individual liberty become too extreme, the corridor between them disappears and the state begins to fail. The use of Canada's Emergencies Act to end the Freedom Convoy vividly evokes the concept of the narrow corridor between a despotic Hobbes' leviathan state on one side and civil society gone amuck on the other. Back in 1988, Parliament had enacted the Emergencies Act, a law authorizing the federal government, during national emergencies, temporary use of measures to ensure safety and security that would otherwise be unconstitutional and unlawful. This new act replaced the War Measures Act enacted during the First World War, which had long been criticized for its sweeping unilateral powers to suspend constitutionally protected rights and freedoms.

The Emergencies Act is considered a tool of last resort, to be used only when no other federal or provincial laws are adequate to respond to the crisis at hand. On February 14, 2022, the minority Liberal government invoked this tool of last resort for the first time in Canadian history in response to the Freedom Convoy trucker protests both in Ottawa and at a number of cross-border bridges. The prime minister announced his decision by saying, "It is not something to undertake lightly, and it's something that needs to be momentary, temporary and proportional." The Emergencies Act authorized police to block off public assembly in certain designated areas such as Parliament Hill and international bridges, required banks to freeze convoy leaders' accounts, and compelled any crowdfunding platforms used for convoy financing to meet the terrorist-financing and money-laundering reporting requirements of Canada's financial intelligence agency. Was the government right to use those powers in this case?

It's worth remembering that the act exhaustively defines and, by doing so, greatly limits the context in which the federal government can invoke its measures. In can be used only to respond to five types of emergencies: national, public welfare, public order, international, and war. It may be invoked only temporarily, and its measures stay in place for only thirty days. While a prime minister may make the call, parliamentary approval is then required within seven days; should that approval not appear, the act is automatically revoked. In contrast to the War Measures Act it replaced, the Emergencies Act also limits the powers that can be used, and its executive orders and regulations require parliamentary review and approval through a majority vote in the House of Commons. As such, the cabinet cannot act on its own. Importantly, citizens can later challenge the lawfulness of the use of the act through the courts, which civil-liberty groups did in response to the Freedom Convoy measures.

In late April, the prime minister announced the creation of a Public Order Emergency Commission, which the act requires. The independent public inquiry into use of the act gave its commissioners the power to call witnesses and records so that the sequence and scope of events could be clearly established and considered. As we write this, no final report has been tabled, but the inquiry will offer Canadians the first formal insight into an event that took place within that narrow corridor between state power and civil liberty. We should all be deeply interested in the conclusions drawn and think hard about how we intend to proceed as a society.

Building Trust

It can be easy for governments and indeed for people to claim that some public questions or problems are impossible to answer or even to understand clearly or completely, so governments and the public need not act, need not feel pain or guilt, need not see the necessity of thinking about themselves or their country differently. Of course, as life speeds up, the fact and concept of government is increasingly expansive. Different governments—federal, provincial, regional, and municipal—have different responsibilities. Compounding the complexity are separations within some branches: executive, legislative, and judicial—each with their own responsibilities and powers. But one thing is certain: when governments act, they have an obligation to explain why they are choosing to act. On the flip side, when governments fail to act, they have an equal obligation to explain why they did not, could not, or should not. I think when governments act with empathy, they make themselves worthy of trust. Making themselves more worthy of trust is something all governments, public institutions, and public servants should be striving to do. Empathy means protecting the life, limb, and property of citizens, creating an environment for each of them to be treated with dignity and given the opportunity to reach their full potential. When that doesn't happen, trust erodes.

More than twenty years of data collected by the Edelman Trust Barometer has shown the continuing erosion of trust in authority around the world, but not all the news is bad. In May 2020, the Rideau Hall Foundation published a study conducted by Abacus Data to survey national opinion about how Canada's response to the pandemic changed public impressions of Canadian public institutions. For most Canadians, public institutions and government are seen as one thing. Since the pandemic hit, there has been a significant increase in the number of Canadians who say our country is headed in the right direction. Seventy-six per cent say Canada's public institutions have responded very well/well/as well as can be expected to the COVID-19 pandemic so far. Canadians who feel the country is headed in the right direction are even more optimistic and confident in Canada's public institutions. Overall public engagement has increased significantly. One measure we often track is "engaged Canadians," or those who are paying attention to news, politics, and current events. Younger Canadians continue to be the least engaged, even during the pandemic. One way to ensure our Canadian public institutions stay relevant and serve Canadians is to engage with them. Engaging with and participating within our public institutions can help to ensure the public institutions are looking out for our interests. Engagement also allows us to hold our public institutions accountable and ensure that they are continually serving the needs of all Canadians.

Our institutions, of course, are not buildings; they are groups of public servants dedicated to specific objectives. I have profound respect for Canada's public service and the work its members do on behalf of our country and its citizens. I have seen the excellence of Canadian public servants first-hand when I chaired, over a number of years, a dozen or so different national or provincial task forces such as the National

Roundtable on the Environment and the Economy, the Information Highway Advisory Council, the National Broadband Task Force, the Committee on Information Systems for the Environment, the National Advisory Committee on Online Learning, the Commission of Inquiry into Certain Allegations Respecting Business and Financial Dealings Between Karlheinz Schreiber and the Right Honourable Brian Mulroney, and the Leaders' Debate Commission. While working on these task forces, I learned that most problems faced by our governments are becoming more complex because our understanding of them grows more nuanced and because the number of people affected by them increases. Our ultimate success in tackling any problem we face will depend on how we acquire, analyze, and apply relevant knowledge. We must become smarter so we can be more caring. And service that enhances the public good must remain the constant duty of everyone in government.

Fair elections are meaningful tools to engage citizens and strengthen our democratic institutions. But how can you know whom to elect to make that happen? Only by staying informed. In 2018, the Government of Canada announced it would set up the independent Leaders' Debates Commission, and I was asked to chair it. The commission is meant to make the federal leaders' debates a more predictable, reliable, and stable element of federal election campaigns. Part of its mandate is to advance the public interest by ensuring that national debates before federal elections are as accessible as possible. We want to encourage the use of new media, reach new audiences, and ensure the debates are available in accessible formats. While we can't control what the leaders say and how they conduct themselves in these debates, we can control the format, producing what we hope will be conducive to exchanges among leaders that inform and enlighten viewers. Debates are just one forum thorough which Canadians can gain the knowledge they need to make informed decisions. But these are not frequent. In the interim, the greatest resource is the daily reporting of journalists, most of whom in Canada are expert, balanced, and trustworthy recorders of events, opinions, and, through it all, progress. To make competent decisions about leadership, every Canadian citizen must become a follower of sober, independent journalism, itself a hallmark of democracy.

Open journalism builds trust.

Independent media plays a critical role in democracies by giving citizens unbiased news, ensuring transparency where it might not always exist. Investigative journalism is a specialty discipline demanding high expertise and considerable resources. The late Right Honourable Roland Michener, Governor General of Canada from 1967 to 1974, knew and cherished the role of media, and in 1970 established the Michener Award for meritorious public service journalism. The Michener Awards Foundation's voluntary board of directors oversees the selection process for the award, while the Rideau Hall Foundation manages the operations and awards ceremonies. A critical requirement of the prize (which I call the Integrity Award) is the wider impact the investigative piece has on society and the community involved, usually by uncovering a truth or inspiring change. Here's some text from the website that references the importance of impact: "Entries are judged particularly for their professionalism, their impact on the public, and the degree of arms-length public benefit that is generated." The Michener Award submissions are judged by an expert panel of journalists who have worked in media outlets and in academia across the country. Here are notable, recent winners.

2020—The Aboriginal Peoples Television Network was announced as the winner of the 2020 Michener Award for meritorious public service journalism for its series, *Death by Neglect*, a stark and haunting investigation that delves into a First Nations child-welfare system in which three sisters took their own lives. Within weeks of APTN's broadcasts, investigations were launched into individual cases, families were reunited, new funding was announced for on-reserve child welfare, and a pandemic moratorium was imposed on Ontario youths aging out of care.

2019—The *Globe and Mail*'s "False Promises" delved into the systematic exploitation of temporary workers and foreign students by corrupt immigration consultants and employers. The complex and timely investigation spanned the country and resulted in real change, with the federal government introducing new open work visas to allow foreign nationals facing abuse to switch employers, as well as the passing of a new law allowing more stringent regulation of immigration consultants.

2018—Even with only ten dedicated reporters and editors, Saint John's *Telegraph-Journal* managed to place ambulance services front and centre as an election issue in the fall of 2018. The series starts with the tale of citizens being loaded into cars by concerned onlookers because ambulances (parked minutes away) failed to arrive. And as the investigation progresses, pushing past both stonewalling and misleading data, it reveals skyrocketing overtime payments, injuries, and mental-health issues on the front line. In announcing its overhaul of the ambulance system in 2018, the new government cited the *Telegraph-Journal*'s coverage.

2017—In a massive investigation, the *Globe and Mail*'s Robyn Doolittle tracked sexual-assault cases deemed unfounded that were handled by Canadian police, and showed that one in five such complaints were simply dismissed. The series spurred the federal government to pledge better police oversight, training, and policies, along with $100 million to combat gender-based violence. Statistics Canada promised to resume collecting and publishing unfounded rates. In all, some thirty-seven thousand sexual assault cases were reviewed and more than four hundred unfounded cases were reopened.

Empathetic things to do when you intend to Protect the most vulnerable.

. . . as an individual

Stay informed.

Your country needs your wisdom, and wisdom is the exercise of knowledge, so you must be knowledgeable about the issues of the day; the needs of the community; the best practices that have been adopted to solve problems in other communities; and the tools and talent available to make your neighbourhood, your town, city, province, and country a smart and caring place. Move beyond brief news reports and online posts to digest deeper journalistic pieces that examine issues from many sides and perspectives. As elections approach, watch and read leadership debates to better understand the personalities, motivations, values, and agendas of all those seeking your vote.

Stay involved.

Vote every time you can. Every government can be your government if you take an active role in electing a worthy representative to pursue your interests and make sure that your values are being understood and respected in the programs of government. If you are unhappy, speak out loud. There are many instruments in place by which an individual citizen can exert considerable influence on the political process: write to your member of Parliament, voice your concerns at public meetings, write heated letters to the editor. You have a right to be heard, people want to hear what you have to say, and there are many tools at hand. Use them.

Stay respectful.

Acknowledge and protect all the contributors to our civil society here in Canada, including governments, businesses, service clubs, charities, youth organizations, the military, the health system, and all the volunteer agencies and charities with the expertise and contacts to help the most vulnerable people in the community. The institutions of the country can always be improved, but they are still our best tools for solving inequities. Respect them, support them, help improve them.

. . . as a community

Encourage citizens to be involved in every aspect of community action.
The more people are involved, the more people will be creative, respectful, and protective of society and of the vulnerable members within it.

Drive community action.
Almost all community action should begin with consultation but then move quickly and resolutely to action that has a lasting impact. Organize community action in four phases: 1. thought, 2. trial, 3. action, and 4. traction, where traction is achieved by any set of protocols that can keep an activity sustained for long-term effect.

. . . as a nation

Be transparent.
Working behind closed doors, no matter how benignly, will raise suspicion among citizens that leads to distrust. Governments must become ever more transparent in order to have the trust they need to rally citizens to support and sustain necessary changes.

Design programs for the vulnerable.

When things are going well for people, they do not need government intervention. Government programs should be designed to help the vulnerable, mustering the resources of the whole country to focus attention on populations that need change in order to enjoy security and opportunity.

Carry through.

Trust depends on the perception of integrity, intent, capacity, and results. All of those can be proved by completing the tasks you promised you would undertake in order to get elected in the first place.

14

Do nothing about us without us.

I've never valued opinions quickly formed, especially my own. While they masquerade as conclusions of logic, they're usually little more than expressions of inherent bias. Thus they should be thought of as temporary positions and not taken too seriously. Long-held opinions, however, are not so easily discarded. Forged over time, they become part of one's world view. When we hang on to them, we invite them to influence all our other positions too, often wrongly.

Wisdom demands restraint—a damper on the impulse to react with emotion, preferring instead to think of any opinion (especially one's own) as an ideal opportunity to explore a topic further. Being human, however, I can't always resist forming opinions about things I've learned. Fortunately, as I get older, I'm beginning to see many things differently. Whenever I can be smart enough and humble enough to revise an opinion I've held for a long time, I think of it as unlearning. In my time I've had to unlearn a great deal.

One major unlearning was required to correct my faulty under-standing of the European colonization of Canada, in particular the influence exerted by Samuel de Champlain, aspects of which I've shared here already. Until 2010 I had assumed that the French had come to these shores primarily to take advantage of this land's rich fish and fur resources, which they managed to do first by setting up habitations that replicated the habits and values they had known in

France, and second by taking advantage of the knowledge, hospitality, and naïveté of the Indigenous inhabitants. Not so. Just before I was to be invested as governor general, I was given a copy of David Hackett Fischer's book *Champlain's Dream: The Visionary Adventurer Who Made a New World in Canada*. At Champlain's insistence, and according to his ambitious and compassionate vision, the colonies of Nouvelle France were established with high expectation of tolerance, diversity, inclusion, respect, learning, and equality of opportunity, still the hallmarks of Canadian society at its best. When I read this scholarly and riveting record of those years, I at last understood the origin of the unique nature of our national personality. My unlearning about Canada had begun.

In Chapter 5 I told the story of my gaffe as captain of the Cambridge hockey team when I did not insert a player on the ice during a varsity match with Oxford, thus denying him his colours, a revered symbol of team achievement. The opinion I held then, which I had not yet unlearned, was that winning should be the only object in competitive sport. As Vince Lombardi put it later, "Winning is not a sometime thing; it's an all-the-time thing." Looking back at my own narrow view and careless actions at the time, I now understand that building human character is the great object of sport, and that playing to win—not just winning itself—is one of the best ways, but not the only way, to make that happen.

My third great unlearning had to do with my way of thinking about the United States of America. Like most Canadians, I was always fascinated to know what makes our two nations and cultures different, but that restricted me to thinking no further than contrast and comparison: their football players are stronger than ours, our hockey teams are faster than theirs, their TV programs are funnier than ours, their politics are harsher than ours, their businesses are more ambitious than ours, our lives are less litigious than theirs, their rock music is more progressive than ours . . . and so on. I long assumed that comparison leads to understanding, but I now know that comparison leads only to categorization. Comparison furnished me with many things to say but little true knowledge of either of our cultures. Worse, it proved to be a barrier to authentic understanding and appreciation. I had to unlearn that habit. I try now to think more about what our individual cultures contribute to the world than just how they compare.

Next up, touring the country as governor general, I had the chance to meet thousands of people in different regions, and many hundreds of the conversations we had were relaxed and unrushed. These were happy examples of appreciative inquiry, the kind of conversations in which both parties ask questions because they wish to learn more, to let their knowledge appreciate in scope and value. Those discussions forced me to rethink my basic conception of how we Canadians make our society work. I had long harboured the notion, albeit vague, that we in Canada are bound by our common personality and manner, which is generally polite, respectful, tolerant, even humble, despite the odd outburst. True, those traits do operate in most of us, but I began to learn that what actually unifies us is something quite different. I had that feeling every time I met recipients of honours such as the Order of Canada, the Sovereign's Medal for Volunteers, the Arctic Inspiration Prize, the Governor General's Innovation Awards, and the Governor General's Academic Awards, the Governor General's Awards to Academic All Canadian Athletes, and awards for Bravery and Military Merit. Those individuals taught me that the unifying principle of Canadians is their fervent desire to make things better for others. We are a nation of helpers. I saw that principle in action in every imaginable context, and Canada is a complicated nation with a great variety of contexts to consider. We live spread out in wildly varied, often harsh climates, we hail from a vast array of cultural, ethnic, and linguistic backgrounds, and we make our livings across such a vast continuum of economic strata that you'd think we couldn't possibly share a world view. But we do. We all want to make Canada a better place, and most of us are actively engaged in doing so. A cynic might propose that by basing my view of a whole society on the character of the recipients of honours and awards, I was drawing conclusions from a skewed sample. My new and strong opinion is that seventeen thousand people in leadership and service roles desiring the same thing for their country is not a skewed sample; it is overwhelming evidence of an abiding truth.

One Thing All Canadians Must Now Unlearn

Reconciliation is not an Aboriginal problem;
it is a Canadian one. Virtually all aspects of
Canadian society may need to be reconsidered.

TRUTH AND RECONCILIATION COMMISSION OF CANADA, 2015

But the greatest unlearning of my life came recently. It has opened my eyes and heart to a new possibility, which in turn has deepened my confidence in our future together as a smart and caring nation. Even more, it gives us all as Canadians a new opportunity to set a bold example for the whole world, as we have done many times in our short history. I hope you will join me in it. We must at last learn to recognize and respect all Indigenous peoples in our country, and then we must prove that respect by forging an integrated society marked by harmony and true justice.

While long neglected and often even unacknowledged, the fracture between Indigenous and settler societies in Canada has gone unhealed for centuries. Many nationwide attempts to close the gap have been made, always beginning with research. The Royal Commission on Aboriginal Peoples was established in 1991 in the wake of the Oka

Crisis, a seventy-eight-day standoff between Mohawk protesters, provincial police, and the Canadian Army. The commission carried out extensive research and community consultation to study and survey historical and contemporary relations between Aboriginal and non-Aboriginal peoples in Canada. The ensuing report included dozens of recommendations for federal government action, most of which were never fully implemented.

In the past fourteen years alone, Canada has carried out two new surveys of Indigenous peoples and their lives in Canada. In 2008, the Truth and Reconciliation Commission was an honest and earnest effort by Canadians to confront reality and, in doing so, halt the erosion of trust between the country and Indigenous peoples and thus accelerate the journey toward reconciliation. A product of the Indian Residential Schools Settlement Agreement, the commission was created to gather the facts about the residential schools in Canada. Devised as tools of assimilation, the schools were developed and administered by the Government of Canada and the Anglican, Catholic, Presbyterian, and United churches. More than 150,000 children attended residential schools scattered across the country. Some 80,000 of these former students were still alive during the time of the commission. Many suffered physical and sexual abuse. All of them experienced some form of enduring trauma that stemmed from being separated—sometimes forever—from their families, communities, and culture. And as we've recently learned, or been forced to admit, more than 6,000 of those children died at the schools, buried on the grounds, many with no records of how they died or where they were laid to rest. Along with establishing the truth about the residential schools, the commission had a duty to assess the legacy of these schools and their treatment of students, recommend ways to heal the effects of that treatment, and outline steps that Canadians and their government should take to reconcile with Indigenous peoples, set out in 94 discrete recommendations.

In 2016, the National Inquiry into Missing and Murdered Indigenous Women and Girls was mandated to look into and report on the systemic causes of all forms of violence against Indigenous women and girls, including sexual violence. After more than two years of testimony from Indigenous knowledge keepers, experts, and more than fourteen hundred survivors and family members of the missing and murdered, at public hearings and evidence-gathering sessions across Canada, the final report was made public in 2019, defining the violence against Indigenous women, girls, and two-spirit, lesbian, gay, bisexual, transgender, queer, questioning, intersex, and asexual (2SLGBTQQIA) people as a national tragedy of epic proportion. Chief Commissioner Marion Buller declared that "despite their different circumstances and backgrounds, all of the missing and murdered are connected by economic, social and political marginalization, racism, and misogyny woven into the fabric of Canadian society. This truth is undeniable. The fact that this National Inquiry is happening now doesn't mean that Indigenous Peoples waited this long to speak up; it means it took this long for Canada to listen."

With the recommendations of these watershed consultations, our federal government has in hand all the evidence and advice it needs to act, and act it should. The time for research is over. Reconciliation is a long and difficult journey—perhaps even an unending one—that will require the active and ongoing involvement of all Canadians and all public institutions in Canada. In my view, it's the journey from recognition and respect as first steps to justice and harmony as destinations. This requires that each of us must unlearn our old prejudices and find new respect if changes in policy and practice are to have any lasting effect. But we do have evidence of that working, at least on one corner of our society, and one that I know well. The strides to respect and recognition made at our colleges and universities are leading the way for us all. These institutions are turning empathy into action by undertaking broadly based research and integrating exploration of

Indigenous cultures into their curricula, by offering substantial support for Indigenous students, and by sponsoring mentorship of Indigenous teachers.

Faithful Witness

Sharon and I were honorary witnesses to the Truth and Reconciliation Commission, and we soon came to understand that bearing witness is the epitome of empathy. As witnesses, we had three obligations: to observe keenly what we saw; to listen carefully to what we heard; and to share widely what we saw and heard, so that other people may understand what happened and act on that understanding—in other words, to be messengers and ambassadors for those who shared their stories and experiences.

That's a role all Canadians can and must play in some way in their own lives. Being honorary witnesses meant we had to observe and hear the truth revealed by people's stories to the commission, listen carefully to learn about other perspectives, particularly of those who suffered, and be faithful to what we learned, discovering together how we might partner to bring about more positive outcomes.

What Sharon and I discovered above all is that we must first unlearn—we must put aside so much of our cultural heritage about Indigenous people and learn afresh through their experiences. Canadians have ignored Indigenous voices for years. Even when we did listen to them, we did not act upon what we heard, or not to the degree we should have. We must listen, learn, and act, with a clear emphasis on action. And then we must teach the young—including emerging generations of Indigenous peoples—so they can teach the generations that come after.

A rewarding first step could be taking a course to understand the perspectives of Indigenous peoples. You might join the half million students who have enrolled in Indigenous Canada, a free online curriculum offered by the University of Alberta. Here's how the university describes it:

> Indigenous Canada is a 12-lesson Massive Open Online Course (MOOC) from the Faculty of Native Studies that explores Indigenous histories and contemporary issues in Canada. From an Indigenous perspective, this course explores key issues facing Indigenous peoples today from a historical and critical perspective highlighting national and local Indigenous-settler relations. Topics for the 12 lessons include the fur trade and other exchange relationships, land claims and environmental impacts, legal systems and rights, political conflicts and alliances, Indigenous political activism, and contemporary Indigenous life, art and its expressions.

Dan Levy, co-creator and star of the television comedy *Schitt's Creek*, has urged all Canadians to take the course, saying, "If 2020 has taught us anything, it's that we need to actively relearn history—history that wasn't taught to us in school—to better understand and contextualize our lives and how we can better support and be of service to each other." Join in.

The New Buffalo

When European settlers first swept west across North America in search of arable land, the continent was already occupied by some 1.2 to 2.6 million Indigenous people, living in tribes, bands, and community groupings we now respectfully and appropriately refer to as First Nations. Archeological studies indicate they had inhabited the region at least 40,000 years.

Along the western plains and into the foothills of the Rocky Mountains, these communities lived in harmony with the herds of bison that sustained them. First Nations people considered their relationship with these animals to be one of spiritual connection demanding deep respect. They saw animals as a sacred gift from the creator, and interacted with restraint to ensure the abundance and longevity of the herds. They hunted only when in need, and took enough only for their immediate requirements. From the bison came food, clothes, blankets, knives, and fuel. They employed every part of the animal for their survival, for to leave anything behind would be a show of disrespect.

Two species of bison roamed the land, and they went by many names. The Anishinaabe (a collective term for the people of the Ojibwa, Odawa, Potawatomi, Mississaugas, Nipissing, and Algonquin nations) referred to the plains bison as *bizhiki*. To the Nehiyawak (Cree), the plains buffalo went by the name *paskwâwimostos*, while the wood bison was known as *sakâwmostos*. The Niitsitapi (Blackfoot) knew them as *iiníí*, while in the Tsuut'ina (Sarcee) language the animals were called *xâní*. The Dakota (Sioux) of Manitoba and Saskatchewan, descendants of ancestors who had fled from slaughter by U.S. troops in the purges of the 1860s and 1870s, brought the term *tȟatȟaŋka* with them, which translates as "he who owns us," a humble admission of their dependence on the bison. The closely related Nakota (Assiniboine), whose language was similar, said *tataga*. When Champlain came to North America and was brought the hides of these bison to examine, he called them buffles, a derivative of the French *boeuf*, later adapted as "buffalo" by the English. I offer this not as a lesson in etymology, but rather to illustrate a principle I've learned to follow, that of honouring First Nations peoples by using the terms they have used to describe themselves and their world for millennia, rather than simply defaulting to the names they were given by settlers. So much to unlearn.

The attempted extinction of the buffalo in North America was a deliberate strategy to destroy the means of survival of First Nations people and thus render them incapable of sustaining their lives and defending their traditional territories. It worked. Assisted by the U.S.

military, the wholesale destruction of the species progressed at a furious rate, made possible by the Sharps rifle, which could kill a buffalo in a single shot from a moving train, which was how much of the slaughter was undertaken.

When Champlain arrived, we now estimate that there were 25 to 30 million buffalo in North America. By the late 1880s, there were fewer than 100 remaining in the Great Plains states of the United States, with perhaps 1,000 still alive on what we now know as the Canadian prairies. By 1884, there were no buffalo left in the Black Hills of South Dakota and Wyoming, which according to the Lakota origin story is the birthplace of the first humans and the first buffalo. There is a plaque on the site that declares, with dismal pride, that this is the

SITE WHERE THE LAST

BUFFALO WAS KILLED

IN THE BLACK HILLS

IN 1884 BY

JOE HEUMPHREUS

BOB PATTERSON

CHARLEY SAGER.

"Education is our buffalo" is a phrase now often used by First Nations elders to signify the importance of education for future generations of Indigenous peoples. Like the buffalo before it, education will be the means of survival, of sustenance, of community building, of spiritual focus, of wise discourse, of health, and of justice. But for education to work, it cannot be a government program handed down; it must be a comprehensive collection of honest, relevant, and insightful programs and practices designed and delivered with full involvement of Indigenous peoples at every step.

So turning empathy into action requires that we follow the admonition "nothing about us without us." The phrase has inspired people for four hundred years[1] to ensure that no policy or plan that will affect any group should ever be devised without the complete and direct participation of members of that group. Today in Canada the phrase honours the principle of co-creation by proposing that Indigenous peoples play a major role and have a final say in all programs, policies, and laws that affect them.

The Rideau Hall Foundation respects that principle in all its undertakings. We partnered with Mastercard Foundation, Yukon University, and Vancouver Island University to help Indigenous students at the two schools make successful transitions to their studies. This initiative, called EleV, is a prime example of listening, learning, and acting, of turning empathy into action. EleV programs were co-created by the schools and local Indigenous communities to take advantage of local strengths and to meet local needs. The programs are meant to enable students to achieve academic and economic success that is consistent with the vision of Mino-Bimaadiziwin, or "living in a good way." Another example is the Arctic Inspiration Prize. The Rideau Hall Foundation administers the prize, which recognizes and promotes the extraordinary contributions made by teams in gathering Arctic knowledge and applying this knowledge to benefit the Canadian Arctic, Arctic peoples, and therefore Canada as a whole. A particular focus of the prize is Indigenous people of the North—both as recipients of the prize and as the target of prize-winning initiatives, of which Indigenous peoples are contributors. As examples, $1 million was awarded in 2018 to the early childhood education program by Piruevik in Nunavut. A $500,000 prize was awarded to the Tr'ondëk Hwëch'in farm in Yukon that builds greenhouses and trains Inuit and Indigenous youths to become adept as greenhouse farmers. It is the oldest dairy farm in Yukon, supplying milk and dairy products to Whitehorse and smaller communities in the territory, substituting locally grown fresh food for expensive imported food products.

In other education initiatives, in 2017 the foundation was fortunate to engage Scott Haldane as its first full-time CEO. Earlier, as president of YMCA Canada, he was tasked by the federal government to establish a partnership with Indigenous communities to create the National Panel on First Nation Elementary and Secondary Education for Students on Reserve. The panel's final report in 2011 had set out five specific recommendations.

1. Co-create a child-centred First Nation Education Act.
2. Create a national commission for First Nation education to support education reform and improvement.
3. Facilitate and support the creation of a First Nation education system through the development of regional First Nation Education Organizations to provide support and services for First Nation schools and First Nation students.
4. Ensure adequate funding to support a First Nation education system that meets the needs of First Nation learners, First Nation communities, and Canada as a whole.
5. Establish an accountability and reporting framework to assess improvement in First Nation education.

Recognizing the importance of Indigenous teachers and the value they bring to their students and their communities, we became aware that the number of Indigenous teachers within Canada's elementary and high schools is in no way representative of those school communities. The urgency of the problem is compounded when teaching positions are left unfilled well into the school year, causing significant disruption for affected communities. Compared to their non-Indigenous colleagues, there are now only one-third as many Indigenous teachers as are needed to have the same percentage of Indigenous peoples in the teaching profession as their population represents. This gap leads in turn to an unrepresentative workforce and obvious inequity in the quality and relevance of education available to Indigenous youth. Through allyship[2] and by supporting Indigenous teacher education, the foundation in 2022 began investing in Indigenous education, and specifically helping underwrite efforts to increase the number of Indigenous teachers across Canada. Backed by a sizeable grant from the Mastercard Foundation, the program's ambitious and fully realizable objective is that, within ten or fifteen years, ten thousand Indigenous teachers will enter the teaching profession, ready to enter the Canadian school workforce in a variety of roles, from teaching to curriculum design to educational administration. It's a start.

The path to reconciliation will be long and winding, but we have clarity now that we did not have before. Even the Pope has apologized for the abuses of the past. With the ninety-four unambiguous recommendations of the Truth and Reconciliation Commission, we have a clear set of steps to follow. Progress will be incremental, but true progress is possible if we are earnest and tenacious. The new buffalo may one day roam free after all.

Empathetic things to do when you intend to Do nothing about us without us.

. . . as an individual

Unlearn before you learn.
Don't trust your present assumptions about the history or circumstances of Canada's Indigenous citizens. Unless you have been raised in a First Nations, Inuit, or Métis community yourself, your understanding of the issues facing Indigenous peoples in Canada may be flawed or incomplete. Drill past your current misconceptions to facts that you can verify, then build new knowledge on that foundation.

Take a course.
Learn about Indigenous history, values, and culture by taking a course designed and presented by Indigenous people themselves. Try an online offering such as those offered by the First Nations University of Canada, the Indigenous Canada online course of the University of Alberta, and Algoma University's courses in Anishinaabe history, philosophy, and world view.

Bear faithful witness.
Follow the three duties of witnesses of the Truth and Reconciliation Commission: observe, listen, and bear faithful witness. As both your knowledge of and respect for Indigenous culture mature, help others understand the truth about Indigenous Canada by telling them what you have learned.

. . . as a community

Act with deeper respect and great resolve.
Adopt the fundamental guiding principle of the Truth and Reconciliation Commission by "establishing and maintaining a mutual respectful relationship between Indigenous and non-Indigenous peoples in this country. In order for that to happen there has to be awareness of the past, acknowledgement of the harm that has been inflicted, atonement for the causes and action to change behaviour."

Make education a priority.
See education as the new buffalo for Indigenous peoples, and find creative ways to support of Indigenous Canadians in their effort to become teachers.

. . . as a nation

Do nothing about us without us.
The surest way to move past the failures of the past while creating new opportunities for the future is to ensure full participation of Indigenous peoples in the design and delivery of every program intended to support them. Ensure that all programs take a co-responsibility approach that will develop self-reliance. Be mindful that local ownership of all programs is essential, housing chief among them.

Negotiate faster.
Accelerate treaty negotiations and settlement of land claims while ensuring just and expeditious implementation of treaties already signed.

Move from study to action.
Take action on the recommendations of the final reports of the Truth and Reconciliation Commission and the National Inquiry into Missing

and Murdered Indigenous Women and Girls. Take action to improve housing, health, and education.

Focus on youth.

Focus on helping youth to develop the resilience and self-confidence they need for new careers suited to changing circumstances on reserve and off. Back motivational programs and make sure they are driven by Indigenous wisdom. Strive for equality of opportunity in education, being attentive to both inputs and outcomes.

15

Open more doors.

Immigration may soon grow from a national consideration to a global conversation. With the advance of climate change and the inevitable rise of sea levels, it is now understood that many of the world's coastlines will be considerably reshaped in the not-distant-enough future. Sea levels worldwide have risen some 240 millimetres since 1880. The rate of sea-level rise is accelerating, its increase having more than doubled from 0.14 centimetres per year during most of the twentieth century to 0.36 centimetres per year after 2006. The record was set in 2020 when levels raced up 91 millimetres in a single year. Even with steep reductions of greenhouse-gas emissions, global sea levels will likely rise another 300 millimetres (above 2000 levels) by 2100. In the worst case, that figure could be ten times this projection.[1]

How will these changes affect human populations? Given that flooding above high tide already happens three times more frequently now than fifty years ago, water damage to property is already common in low-lying areas and will become more so. But by how much? Until 2019, researchers tried to estimate the extent of the coming catastrophe by choosing a range of estimated sea-level increases, mapping the new high-tide data for each estimate onto averaged topographic charts, identifying general areas that will be underwater at each rise, and using census data to count the number of current inhabitants of lands that will then routinely be underwater. That method typically revealed that by 2050 some 80 million more people will experience at least one flood of their habitat each year. But a report published in *Nature Communications* in late 2019 revised that projection after researchers harnessed the power of artificial intelligence to build new, more granular representations of land elevation in the high-risk areas. Rather than just using average topography, their new tools could analyze discrete areas within cities and beyond to add to the total those in small, previously overlooked, low-lying areas. Their study revised the estimate of populations living in flood-affected zones from 80 million to 300 million people by 2050. Worse, it laid out a clear case—albeit a worst case—that by 2100, 9 per cent of the world's population will be living in annual flood zones. That means that, in the next 75 years, a billion of us might need to pull up stakes and move to higher ground.[2]

According to Benjamin Strauss, co-author of the 2019 report, Canada will continue to be on a great swath of that high ground, because our topography is still rebounding from the effects of the last ice age, with much of our land mass lifting at a pace that matches that of the rising oceans. We've been fortunate, and the question we must answer over and over is "Will we continue to share our good fortune with others?" That question will take on new significance if the global community cannot or will not reverse the effect of climate change and, as sea ice and glaciers melt, we witness history's most frantic era of human relocation.

Hell or High Water

But it isn't bad weather that most often chases people from their homes. In February and March of 2022, the first withering photographs of women and children being maimed and killed as they fled invading Russian forces in Ukraine sickened us all and reminded us that, while climate change may soon be the greatest cause of human migration, war will always be the most intense. With millions of refugees leaving Ukraine within mere weeks, the need for quick, organized emergency assistance from neighbouring nations was critical. Not since the Second World War had so many people in Europe been forced to flee so quickly. Those who made it to safety then had to consider the gloomy choice—return or resettle?

I had seen a similar group just eight years earlier. In 2016, Sharon and I joined a sizeable Canadian contingent on a state visit to parts of the Middle East. We were hosted in turn by Reuven Rivlin and Benjamin Netanyahu, respectively president and prime minister of Israel; Mahmoud Abbas, president of the Palestinian Authority; and King Abdullah II of Jordan. But for me the most memorable event of the trip had nothing to do with high protocol. One of our side visits in Jordan was to the Zaatari refugee camp, a sprawling, make-shift community in the northern part of the country. The camp sat on the outskirts of Mafraq, a city that had served for half a century as a base for the British military, then as a base for the Arab Legion during the 1948 Arab–Israeli War, then, in our time, as headquarters of the third division of the Jordanian Army. Just beyond that strategic post, nestled on the border with Syria, Zaatari had been designated in 2012 as the site of a camp to accommodate Syrians fleeing the violence of their civil war, which by then had been raging for a year. More than half a million people would die in that conflict, with another seven million displaced within Syria itself and almost four million more forced to flee across borders into Turkey, Iraq, and Jordan. By the time we visited, ninety thousand nationless people had made Zaatari their temporary shelter, not knowing then that it would become their permanent home. Despite the generosity and best efforts of the Jordanians, the UNHCR, and empathetic donors around the world, like any refugee camp Zaatari was as much a prison as a shelter. Conditions were harsh, accommodations were overcrowded, food supplies were humble, and medical treatment was spotty. While there were makeshift schools here and there, there was nothing beyond the equivalent of a high school curriculum and nowhere for a student to apply for work once schooling was done. No one had money and few had hope.

There were moments of joy, however. In one spontaneous and memorable event, Sharon and I came across a tiny soccer field, really just a tattered stretch of green carpet laid on a patch of dirt between two buildings. A band of pre-teens were tearing around on the pitch, shouting to each other, hurtling after the one soccer ball they had, all of them lost in the moment. Unable to resist, I took off my shoes, stepped onto the pitch, and joined these junior footballers in their game. Presumptuously, I took up position as goal keeper. Almost immediately, an eight-year-old saw an opening, an unsuspected opportunity, and moved on me with resolve, dribbling the ball to set up a shot on goal. Anticipating the trajectory of the ball even before it left his bare foot, I leapt out to the left of goal, hitting the turf and somersaulting into the dirt like I'd been taken out by a sniper. But I had been outplayed. The boy had faked the angle, driving his shot to the right instead for a clean goal. His hands shot up into the air with clenched fists, and he looked for all the world like Cristiano Ronaldo at a World Cup final. The entire field rose up in applause for the hero, who beamed back in silence. As I got back to my feet and dusted myself off to congratulate him, I had the immediate and sad thought this was probably the only such applause this boy would ever have for an accomplishment. What future had he?

We finished our journey to the Middle East in Jerusalem with a visit to the Al-Aqsa mosque, after which we proceeded to the Western Wall, specifically to the fifty-seven-metre stretch of lime-stone known as the Wailing Wall, the only remnant now of King Solomon's great temple. There is a time-honoured custom by which one inscribes a prayer or a message of hope on a small piece of paper, then folds and inserts it into a crevice in that wall with the expectation that the prayer will be answered. After a few moments of reflection, remembering the description of the temple as recorded in the Old Testament, and scouring my memory for what I recollected to be the prayer from that temple, I wrote simply, "May the peoples of all the regions and all faiths gather here in peace and harmony."

Whatever the calamity—be it hell or high water—displaced people everywhere in the world must rely on the kindness of strangers to survive, re-establish, earn their livings, move their families to their new homes, and continue to make their contribution as members of a new community. When that kindness is extended, it is always repaid. We in Canada have seen it time and time again. Our population has thrived through its openness to immigrants, most of whom have themselves been refugees. Canada historian Desmond Morton[3] is often cited as the observer who saw us as a nation of losers, implying that our shared experience of defeat in one form or another bound us together. Novelist Hugh MacLennan once wrote that all three of our first groups to settle "became Canadian because nations or factions to which they belonged had suffered total defeat in war." Immigrants have been and will always be key to our national character and prosperity.

A Long History of Refuge

Even the briefest scan of a chronological list of those we've helped is cause first for pride, because we cared to welcome them, and then for gratitude, because they gave our country so much intelligence, energy, talent, resolve, and loyalty in return. In 1776, 3,000 Black Loyalists came to Canada to escape the oppression of the American Revolution. In 1783, 35,000 Loyalist refugees fled to Canada from New York. In 1793, Upper Canada became the first province in the British Empire to abolish slavery, opening the country to the thousands of enslaved people who would escape to Canada along the Underground Railroad. In the late 1700s, Scots Highlanders settled in Canada as refugees of the Highland Clearances. In 1830, Polish refugees suffering Russian oppression came to Canada to build peaceful lives. They were joined in 1858 when fellow Poles escaping Prussian occupation arrived in a mass migration. From 1880 to 1914, Italians came to Canada having been thrown off their own farms by the so-called reforms of the newly formed Italian state. In that same period, Jews persecuted in the pogroms of what are now Belarus, Lithuania, and Moldova sought refuge here. In 1881, the mass migration of Ukrainians to Canada began, with 170,000 refugees escaping oppression by Austro-Hungarian imperial forces. After 1920, a second wave of Ukrainians arrived in Canada fleeing civil war, Soviet invasion, and Communist persecution. A third wave came at the end of the Second World War, joined by some 250,000 displaced persons from Central and Eastern Europe, victims of Nazism, Communism, and Soviet occupation. In the 1950s, Canada welcomed Palestinian Arabs who had lost their property and dwellings during the Israeli–Arab war of 1948. Middle Eastern and North African Jews fled to Canada in the three decades after 1950, and in 1956, 37,000 Hungarians arrived to escape Soviet domination. In the 1960s, Chinese refugees came here to escape the violence of the Cultural Revolution, and in 1968, some 11,000 Czech refugees fled to Canada during the Communist invasion. In the 1970s, 7,000 Chilean and other Latin American refugees were settled in Canada during the Pinochet regime. Through the seventies and eighties, 20,000 Soviet Jews settled in Canada. Thousands of Bengali Muslims came to Canada at the outbreak of the Bangladesh Liberation War in 1971. Tibetans came that same year to avoid further oppression by the occupying Chinese. The next year, 7,000 Ismaili Muslims came when all Asians were expelled from Uganda by Idi Amin. In 1979, Iranian refugees fled here after the overthrow of the Shah by an Islamic Fundamentalist regime. More than 60,000 Boat People found refuge in Canada in 1979 and 1980 after Communist victory in the Vietnam War.[4] They were followed in the 1980s by Khmer Cambodians, victims of the Communist regime there. In 1992, 5,000 Bosnian Muslims came to escape ethnic cleansing during the Yugoslav Civil War. In 1999, 5,000 Kosovars, mostly Muslim, were airlifted to safety in Canada. In 2006, Canada resettled over 3,900 Burmese refugees who had been living in refugee camps in Thailand for almost 20 years. From 2008 to 2015, 11,600 Bhutanese refugees arrived. In 2010, refugees from more than 140 countries were either resettled or were granted asylum here. In 2015, Canada began welcoming more than 23,000 Iraqi refugees and began resettling 25,000 Syrian refugees. In 2018, Canada resettled more than 1,300 survivors of Daesh, and in 2022, Canada set ambitious new immigration quotas to welcome some 400,000 newcomers each year.

While we should be rightly proud of our openness to newcomers, it's honest to understand that Canada's urge to welcome immigrants has been based in economics; a land this vast has always needed people to work it. Following suit, our recent significant increase in quotas is at heart an admission that our aging population needs an influx of young, active, hardworking, and fertile citizens to keep our economy stable.

The Fast Lane to Smart and Caring

Canada is smarter and more caring when we open the country's doors not only to more people, but also to more kinds of people from many different places and with an array of backgrounds, experiences, and talents. Empathy demands that we see beyond any obvious differences—race, ethnicity, religion, gender—and base our kinship instead on the values and ideals we share. Empathy allows us to more fully appreciate our differences and to see further beyond them. The thought to hold on to hard is this: we all belong here.

In Canada, our sense of belonging has been based on shared civic values from the beginning, and this concept has informed our approach to citizenship and immigration through history. We haven't always lived up to the ideal, but it has been an ideal since Confederation. Here you can be different and belong. All colours, all faiths, all sizes, all shapes. We are not a melting pot but a mosaic. George-Étienne Cartier, whom many consider to be chief definer of our Canadian philosophy at the time of Confederation, insisted upon that ideal as the way to ensure that the French were not assimilated into this new political order. In his pivotal speech of the day, he said, "I view the diversity of races in British North America in this way: we are different races, not for the purpose of warring against each other, but in order to compete and emulate for the general good." Writing in her marvellous book *The Promise of Canada*, Charlotte Gray contends, "It is Cartier that we can thank for developing the government structure that in our country's early years allowed two very different groups of immigrants—the French who had started settling the St. Lawrence Valley three centuries earlier, and successive waves of British who had scattered elsewhere, particularly after the mid-eighteenth century— to live alongside each other. . . . Cartier explicitly spoke of 'a political nationality' in a speech that has an astonishingly modern ring of inclusivity, even if the groups mentioned don't seem particularly diverse today." Cartier insisted that Canada embrace either a political or a civic nationality but not an ethnic one. Only then could French culture survive on the continent, and only then could subsequent people cohabit the country and protect their culture. Nothing has changed. The benefit of openness to difference and celebration of diversity is still the key to our future as a nation that is both smart and caring. Every new citizen gives us a new advantage.

As governor general, I had the honour to preside over citizenship ceremonies about once a year. These ceremonies symbolize Canada by respectfully honouring the many paths taken by those who choose to immigrate to our country while at the same time celebrating their imminent contribution to our society. The credit for making these events inviting, dignified, and celebratory goes to Adrienne Clarkson; as one feature of her post–governor general legacy, Adrienne founded the Institute for Canadian Citizenship dedicated to making life better for immigrants. Thanks to Adrienne's institute, there are now about seventy-five such ceremonies in a year, each attended by about fifty new citizens of all ages, joined by family members who are joyful to be with them as they take on their new responsibilities as Canadians. When I began each ceremony, I would say to those assembled, "Guess what? You are all bilingual today. We are going to recite the oath in French and English." Surprised (and occasionally worried) looks followed. I would then voice each phrase of the oath in French, pause, and then have the new citizens repeat the phrase, and then the next, and so on to the end of the oath. Then we would switch to English and repeat the process. When we were finished, they were Canadians. What was most touching about the ceremonies was watching as many of the children helped their parents recite some of the trickier parts of the oath in one of the languages with which the parents were not so familiar. The whole event was therefore marked by respect, humility, and humour, which I figured was about as Canadian as we get.

The Canadian Citizen: A Recent Concept

For the longest time, Canadian law simply didn't recognize any one of us as Canadian citizens. People born in Canada after Confederation weren't deemed Canadian citizens at all; they were all just British subjects. So when I was born in 1941, even though I was born right here in Canada, I wasn't considered by law to be a Canadian citizen. It wasn't until 1947 and the passage of the Canadian Citizenship Act that we set out the definition, terms, and conditions of citizenship in Canada. The legislation's architect and champion was Canada's secretary of state, Paul Martin Sr. He was inspired to create the act after a visit to the Canadian military cemetery at Dieppe, where he saw vivid proof of the common sacrifice recently made by hundreds of young Canadians for their country. Martin's experience, while profound, wasn't wholly unique. Throughout the war, education programs and awareness campaigns nurtured in Canadians—both newly arrived and native-born—a growing awareness of their shared identity and collective responsibility in building a smarter and more caring country. The Citizenship Act would further infuse in all Canadians the transformational power of a shared identity. As Martin put it, "Citizenship is the right to full partnership in the fortunes and future of the nation." Writer and historian Andrew Cohen identifies the act as perhaps our country's most potent instrument of nation building, "part of a process of national self-definition that would lead to a native-born governor general, a new national flag, a reworded national anthem and a renewed constitution." The Citizenship Act inspired Canadians to create a citizenship based not on blood and tribe but on rights and obligations, a citizenship that embraces and includes rather than rejects and excludes. It's also why we allow all Canadians to enjoy dual citizenship. Having dual citizenship doesn't make a person any less Canadian. On the contrary, it is just proof of our ability to appreciate and see beyond our differences. That's empathy in action.

What We Learned from Syrian Refugees

Between November 2015 and February 2017, Canada took in some forty thousand refugees from the Syrian civil war. About fourteen thousand of them were sponsored privately. Like the flight of Vietnamese refugees before and the Ukrainian exodus after, the Syrian refugee crisis was a telling moment for our country. After the visit that Sharon and I made to the Zaatari camp, I made a point of calling John McCallum the day after he was sworn in as minister of immigration, refugees, and citizenship. I asked whether the office of the governor general, with its convening power, could do anything to help with the integration into our country of the thousands of Syrian refugees that his government had pledged to welcome. The minister observed that the task was a daunting one, that he would appreciate any help our office could provide, and that he was open to any suggestions. I proposed convening a conference at Rideau Hall that included many of the groups involved in handling Syrian refugees. We strongly emphasized the involvement of groups undertaking private sponsorships of refugee families, an approach that was pioneered in Canada. The gathering would enable the groups to meet face to face, exchange ideas, and strategize about how the process could work better right away and be sustained over time. It would also shine a public spotlight on the crisis and the actions Canada was taking—to declare, in effect, this is something that is important for our country to do. The conference was a success. It was the first time many of these key players had actually seen one another. They were also able to see the different parts that made up the whole process and determine how that process should work if it were to be successful.

We decided we would build on our success to use the convening power in yet another way; we would celebrate some of the communities that had already done a notable job in welcoming and integrating Syrian refugees. One of these communities was Oakville, Ontario. We gathered one evening in a local auditorium with about three hundred volunteers engaged in making private sponsorships work in their town and a hundred or so refugee families. The evening began as a minister, priest, rabbi, and imam delivered a blessing on the event and on all those gathered there. I got up afterward to say a few words. I said how lovely it was to hear a blessing from representatives of several of Canada's religious traditions. I also pointed out that, acting as a single, coherent group, the congregations of these religions sponsored many refugee families. They pooled their finances and the best of their other resources as one unified, multi-religious band. The members of the mosque, with their knowledge of the language of the refugees, took on responsibility for communications. The members of the synagogue made sure the young people were integrated into local schools. The Catholics looked after securing homes for the refugees, and the Protestants worked on finding them jobs. Great teamwork.

Some voices in our country were raised against Canada's efforts to welcome the Syrians, a few even declaring that terrorists were using the crisis as an opportunity to infiltrate the country. Yet Canada had taken deliberate steps to mitigate this risk. The United Nations Human Rights Council had recommended to Canada only refugees whom the council had identified as legitimate and truly needy. Our country also sent our own security people to the refugee camps to screen prospective refugees. And in a decisive step, we made a point not to take single men. As a result, the refugees coming to Canada were the most vulnerable people we could find. The crisis tested our country in another way too. Some said that our country's cities have more than enough homeless people who are looking for roofs over their heads—why were we taking in and committing to house more? My answer to that question—and many others like it—is that our response need not be an either-or proposition or a zero-sum game. There is nothing stopping Canadians from succeeding in addressing both of these problems.

Not a Spotless Record

For many years, racism was entrenched in Canada's immigration policy, and our behaviour was narrow, punitive, and wrong. Canadians can now study the dark side of immigration history thanks to the Canadian Museum for Human Rights, the first national museum to be located outside Ottawa, appropriately in Winnipeg, a city with an impressive record of welcoming immigrants to our country. While a visit to the museum's beautiful new building in Winnipeg is worth the effort, an online exploration can be deeply rewarding. One of the topics you can read about is the way in which Canada discouraged Chinese immigration. This from the museum exhibit:

> Unfortunately, many white Canadians were hostile to Chinese immigration. In 1885, immediately after construction on the Canadian Pacific Railway was complete, the federal government passed the Chinese Immigration Act, which stipulated that, with almost no exceptions, every person of Chinese origin immigrating to Canada had to pay a fee of $50, called a head tax. No other group in Canadian history has ever been forced to pay a tax based solely on their country of origin. 'It was an attempt to basically discriminate against the Chinese,' Dr. Yu, who had produced the historical notes, explained. '. . . it was a way to alter the flow of migrants to the new Canada to be weighted towards European and in particular British migrants.' In 1900, the head tax was raised to $100. Then, three years later, it went up to $500 per person. Between 1885 and 1923, approximately 81,000 Chinese immigrants paid the head tax, contributing millions of dollars to government coffers. One of those who paid the tax was Dr. Yu's maternal grandfather, Yeung Sing Yew, who immigrated to Canada in 1923. Yeung was also one of the last Chinese immigrants to pay the head tax; the year he arrived in the country, the Canadian

government passed a new Chinese Immigration Act, which came to be known as the Chinese Exclusion Act. Under the new act, Chinese immigration to Canada was completely banned. This legislation was kept in place until 1947, and its effect on Canada's Chinese community was devastating.

Chinese are just one of the ethnic groups we tried to keep out. In 1907, Canada limited the immigration of Japanese men to four hundred a year. In 1914, hundreds of Sikh and Hindu would-be immigrants were refused entry to Canada when the ship they were aboard, *Komagata Maru*, arrived in Vancouver. Canada closed its doors to Jewish immigrants from Nazi Germany in the 1930s, going so far as to deny entry to more than nine hundred Jews aboard the *M.S. St. Louis* and force them to return to Europe. This entrenched racism extended to people within our borders. Indigenous peoples were denied many rights, including (until 1960) the right to vote unless they gave up their treaty rights and Indian status. In 1942, Canadians of Japanese origin were forced to leave their homes, farms, fishing boats, and businesses of all kinds in coastal British Columbia, including Vancouver, and move to internment camps in the provincial interior and even to farms in Alberta and Manitoba.

Canada didn't end discriminatory immigration quotas until the 1960s when, at the time, 87 per cent of immigrants were still of European origin. Then in 1962 we amended immigration policy and began to assess applicants based on skill, irrespective of ethnicity, race, or country of origin. All the news wasn't good; a clause in the new regulations clarified that only immigrants from specific desirable countries could sponsor their adult relatives. In 1967, further immigration reforms established an objective points system, with applicants awarded points based on education, language fluency, and job skills. That changed everything. Between 1970 and 1979, we witnessed a remarkable shift; immigration from Asia skyrocketed, with 27 per cent of all new arrivals originating from East India or South Asia. In the same period, 48 per cent of immigrants to Canada were members of visible minorities, while only 13 per cent of new arrivals were from the United Kingdom.

We have learned from our historic mistakes and our racist and anti-Semitic policies. We have also learned from our successes. We showed our desire to act out of empathy and not to repeat the cruel actions of earlier times.

New Residents, New Challenges

In February of 2022, just one week before millions of Ukrainians were forced to flee their own nation, Canada's federal government unveiled a plan by which we would keep ramping up the number of new permanent residents in Canada. The plan called for recruitment and immigration of 431,645 permanent residents in 2022, 447,055 in 2023, and 451,000 in 2024. After that, the government intended to stabilize intake at an aggressive annual rate of over 1 per cent of Canada's population by 2024.

The opening of Canada's doors is more than laudable; it is critically important to the welfare of the country. Such an intake would be key to Canada's pandemic recovery. Despite Canada's economic rebound since the onset of the pandemic, there were still many hundreds of thousands of jobs in all sectors waiting to be filled when the plan was announced, and no economy that is chronically short of workers can ever achieve its potential. But it's the long-term benefits of increased immigration that matters most. Canada's population is aging; by the end of the 2020s, our worker-to-retiree ratio will descend to three-to-one, far too low to sustain our health care system, keep our public education system properly staffed, and ensure the social services and benefits funded at different levels of government will continue.

With declining birth rates in every province, we need more workers and young families to come to Canada, and soon. But the influx must be brilliantly managed. While there is a huge list of applicants for permanent and temporary residence, the backlog in processing their cases accounts for more than 1.3 million of them. Some of these files are years old. Many applicants may since have found their opportunity elsewhere. More than half of the anticipated entrants will come from economic streams, meaning they want to be here for reasons of economy, not of asylum. But with forty thousand Afghan refugees and an ongoing wave of Ukrainian refugees, there is plenty of work for Canada and Canadians to do to make sure both groups get the assistance they need to get on their feet quickly. This will require settlement assistance, language training, and much more money for public services, housing, and infrastructure. It also means we'll have to rethink our glacial processes for approval of foreign professional credentials. In the heat of the pandemic, we were disappointed to watch tens of thousands of trained and experienced health care workers with foreign credentials standing impotent on the sidelines while frontline workers with Canadian credentials exhausted themselves to the point of burnout.

That said, we are heartened, excited even, that Canada is once again showing the world that we see the wisdom, practicality, and moral value of opening more doors. As a nation, the most empathetic gesture we can make is inviting others to join our family, share our fortune, and build our future together.

Empathetic things to do when you intend to Open more doors.

. . . as an individual

See the benefit.
Recognize that self-interest for Canadians is to welcome people who bring their special gifts. We cannot enjoy the standard of living we enjoy now without immigration.

Go to a citizenship ceremony.
Take the time to witness the earnest enthusiasm of those who will help us build a better country.

Sponsor a refugee.
Get involved in the sponsorship of a refugee. There are countless ways to help, and Canada.ca has all the details.

. . . as a community

Fight ignorance.
Acknowledge that our history is not all that old. Good advice (Cartier and Champlain) is still relevant, and bad habits (racist attitudes and laws) are still operating.

Be kind to those at home.

Be sure to apply the lessons of immigration success to local populations such as Indigenous people that have had to fight systemic discrimination.

. . . as a nation

Be fair and transparent.

Continue Canada's emphasis on immigration that invites people of merit without discriminating on any basis of ethnicity.

Communicate the benefits.

Let all citizens understand that in Canada our quality of life depends absolutely on our inviting more immigrants to bring their energies and special talents to build and sustain our economy.

Accelerate the process.

We need to speed up the process from immigration to citizenship. We especially need to speed up certification and accreditation for professionals.

Epilogue

Look skyward.

On Christmas Day 2022, a magnificent instrument lifted away from our planet, bound for a patch of space 1.5 million kilometres from Earth known as Lagrange Point 2, or more informally L2. That spot had been mathematically calculated back in 1750 as the location nearest us where gravitational forces and the motion of an orbiting body would likely cancel each other out, making it possible to rest there without expending any energy. Until this year, L2 had been visited only in the imaginations of physicists and dreamers, but, just thirty days after its December 25 launch, the James Webb Space Telescope came to a stop in that quiet corner of space, alone in perfect stillness, ready to peer out into the distance with an unobstructed view. An array of mirrors, aligned by a Canadian-designed sensor system, can now focus and amplify faint amounts of light onto a camera, allowing us to see for the first time both deep down into our past and far out into our future. By following its gaze, we will learn where we came from, not just at the birth of our species but also near the birth of our universe. By studying images captured by this ingenious device, we will also be able to pinpoint habitable planets and perhaps resolve the ancient question of whether life exists beyond our own solar system. Not since Sputnik soared into orbit in 1957 have we been given such a stellar opportunity to rethink our role in the cosmos.

The knowledge coming from these explorations will open our eyes and hearts in astounding new ways. Yet as marvellous as it is, the

James Webb Space Telescope is only one of an endless stream of coming innovations by which we will transform our world and our relationship to life around us. There are 8 billion people now on this planet. Einstein said that a human could expect to have only two truly great ideas in a lifetime. Let's do the math; in the span of the next generation—just twenty-five years—together we will conceive some 16 billion truly great ideas. They must all be shared, for it is knowledge wisely applied that will be our salvation.

As humans, our growing sense of interdependence, our love for each other, and our reawakening ambition for our common welfare will spark all the empathy we need to address our many problems and set ourselves on a better course. Success will certainly follow if we learn to turn that compassion into action. We must be deliberate, not allowing ourselves to be distracted from the great conversation in which we are now all engaged. Above all, we must refuse to let any influence turn us from respect of our fellow citizens. No manufactured rift, no tempting entertainment, no online misleading, no furious yet meaningless conflict can be allowed to divert us from the common aim that now unites us as what we truly are—a world of creatures with contrasting backgrounds, beliefs, inclinations, habits, and preferences united in the single purpose of making a society that accommodates, supports, and celebrates all. In this, Canada has an advantage. We have set an example of the embrace of diversity that can be echoed planet-wide—a proven formula that can guide us as we navigate the tumultuous yet transformative changes that will, if we invite them in, secure a healthy and prosperous future.

In all of this, your own singular insight, imagination, and service to others is not only welcome but also instrumental. It's a beautiful time to be alive. We're putting compassion into action, and we are delighted to journey with you on a focused, talented, committed, and ambitious team that knows what needs to be done. The future is looking brighter.

Ottawa, Canada
January 2022

Acknowledgements

From David

And so, we have come to the end, which is just another way of looking at a new beginning. For you, I hope it is the beginning of a new journey that seeks to shift empathy to action whenever and wherever possible. I am certain that a large part of what you have just read is, in some ways, second nature. And yet, we can always find creative and innovative paths to make the world around us better, smarter, and kinder. I hope that you find yourself inspired by something you have read here and will share it with those around you. After all, I always consider my personal corner of the world to be a happier and fuller place the more I invite people in to share it with me.

With that said, here are some of the people who have shared in this empathy journey with me over the past couple of years. And yes, I do mean years. We started this book pre-pandemic and I can honestly say that working on it with the following group of people has been a balm through the hard times. With them as collaborators to inspire this empathy journey, it has been one of joy.

First to my family and the best bubble anyone could hope for: my wife, Sharon, and our five daughters and sons-in-law and all of our grandchildren, who keep me young and looking for new ways of seeing the world. As is clear throughout this book, from them, led by Sharon, I have learned empathy. No one could be more blessed than I am.

Brian Hanington is a magician with ideas and their expansion in words, but even he does not have the words to express my gratitude to him. He has been with me through four books now and only in this fifth have I been able to persuade him to let his name stand on the cover with mine. Through this we have become dear friends, and through his skillful interrogations he has caused me to learn more about myself and discuss more of that inner self than I could have ever done on my own. He also epitomizes empathy and was thus able to take our explanation of this complicated subject beyond my own boundaries. His eloquent and crystal-clear prose is to me, well, magic.

Thank you to everyone who contributed to the various stages of writing this book, from the thinking, to the research, to the writing and revising, and everything in between. They include Stephen Wallace, Lois Claxton, Harry Rakowski, Natalia García Basilio, Jackie Riopelle, Allison MacLachlan, Maryanne Murphy, and of course Kelly-Ann Benoit, my executive assistant. Words cannot adequately describe my gratitude to Kelly-Ann. She has been an essential partner in the creation of this book, elegantly moving everything forward with gracious and professional determination. Her contribution ran the gamut from deciphering my impossible handwriting and dictated electronic passages, to fine editing and fact checking, and to orchestrating the numerous meetings and phone calls we had with collaborating partners, and all of that accomplished with a wide smile.

Thank you to the team at Signal/McClelland & Stewart and Penguin Random House Canada, among them Doug Pepper, my long-time publisher and editor; CEO Kristin Cochrane; publisher of M&S Jared Bland; managing editor Kimberlee Kemp; designer Matthew Flute; and publicist Shona Cook. And, of course, thank you to the wonderful and talented team at STIFF, led by James Hanington and Anna Jackson, a team that includes John Phillips, a wise scribe who has also collaborated on four of our books, as well as Stewart Dudley, Liam Dynes, Rafael Nuncio Lappe, and Dan Lalande. You have all helped to shape this book and give it life, and for that I cannot thank you enough.

Thank you to all of those great people I have had the honour of working with over the past decade as these empathy ideas percolated. You have been exceedingly patient with me as I have tested out new thoughts and theories, first on *The Idea of Canada*, then *Ingenious*, then *Trust*, now *Empathy*, always bringing me back to the topic at hand with the utmost kindness and tolerance: the staff at the Rideau Hall Foundation, led by the indomitable Teresa Marques, president and CEO; the RHF board of directors, where I have the good fortune of working with the incredible Huguette Labelle as vice-chair, among so many other smart and thoughtful leaders from across the country; the Leaders' Debates Commission staff, led by Michel Cormier, and its advisory board, who challenge my thinking and keep me on my toes; and finally, all of the people Sharon and I had the privilege of learning from and working with at the Office of the Governor General, I think of you all often and remember those days fondly.

A very special thank you to the Honourable Rosalie Abella, for contributing the very thoughtful foreword to this book. Rosalie is a dear friend of mine, and is known in Canada and around the world as a brilliant lawyer, a distinguished Canadian jurist, and the first Jewish woman and refugee to sit on the Canadian Supreme Court bench.

Thank you to all of you who have endeavoured to put empathy first throughout this pandemic. Sometimes it takes a little more energy and effort to meet people with kindness, and for those of you who do, I thank you. And finally, I would like to acknowledge everyone who has lost someone as a result of or during the pandemic. There are so many ways that we can lose people, and all of them weigh heavy on the heart. So my thoughts are with you; know that you are not alone.

Appendix A: For further reading and viewing

We offer here a small selection of books and films we believe expand on the themes of empathy raised in each chapter. Our recommendations are the result of an intergenerational, collective effort, beginning with the favourites of Brian and his wife Deborah, and of my wife Sharon and me, augmented by the zealous nominations of our children and their children, collectively seven children and sixteen grandchildren altogether (so far). In an earlier draft we had provided a précis of the main themes and messages of each book and film, but have been persuaded to hold back these summaries to allow you the freedom to draw your own conclusions. That said, we are confident that each book and film will spark reflection and contribute to your practical understanding of the issues at play.

1. Learn from the young.
For further reading.
What Our Children Teach Us: Lessons in Joy, Love and Awareness by Piero
    Ferrucci
*If I Get to Five: What Children Can Teach Us About Courage and
    Character* by Fred Epstein
*Hunt, Gather, Parent: What Ancient Cultures Can Teach Us About the Lost
    Art of Raising Happy Helpful Little Humans* by Michael Dougleff
For viewing.
A Mind of Her Own, 2006

For children to read.
The Secret Garden by Frances Hodgson Burnett
The Lion, the Witch and the Wardrobe by C. S. Lewis
The Bluest Eye by Toni Morrison

2. Stay curious.
For further reading.
Innovation in Real Places: Strategies for Prosperity in an Unforgiving World by Dan Breznitz
The Upswing, How America Came Together a Century Ago and How We Can Do It Again by Robert. B. Putnam
How to Fly a Horse: The Secret History of Creation, Invention, and Discovery by Kevin Ashton
Ingenious: How Canadian Innovators Made the World Smarter, Smaller, Kinder, Safer, Healthier, Wealthier and Happier by David Johnston & Tom Jenkins
For viewing.
Dead Poet's Society, 1989
The Imitation Game, 2014
Tesla, 2020

3. Be charitable.
For further reading.
Sapiens: A Brief History of Humankind by Yuval Noah Harari
Humankind: A Hopeful History by Rutger Bregman
Tribe: On Homecoming and Belonging by Sebastian Junger
For viewing.
How to Change the World, 2015
Forrest Gump, 1994
Pay It Forward, 2000

4. Donate your talent.

For further reading.

On Human Kindness: What Shakespeare Teaches Us About Empathy
   by Paula Marantz Cohen

The Second Mountain: The Quest for a Moral Life by David Brooks

Fifteen Dogs by André Alexis

For viewing.

Schindler's List, 1993

Wonder, 2017

Sweet Inspirations, 2019

5. Build a team.

For further reading.

Terry Fox: A Story of Hope by Maxine Trottier

Open Heart, Open Mind by Clara Hughes

Rick Hansen: Man in Motion by Jim Taylor and Rick Hansen

For viewing.

Ted Lasso, 2020

Invictus, 2009

Hoosiers, 1986

6. Make it smart and keep it fair.

For further reading.

Excellence: Can We be Equal and Excellent Too? by John Gardner

Bowling Alone: The Collapse and Revival of American Community
   by Robert Putnam

The Upswing: How America Came Together a Century Ago and How
   We Can Do It Again by Robert Putnam

A Matter of Equality: The Life's Work of Senator Don Oliver by
   Don Oliver

For viewing.

Hidden Figures, 2016

Moonlight, 2016
A Beautiful Day in the Neighborhood, 2019

7. Build a healthy neighbourhood.
For further reading.
The Death and Life of Great American Cities by Jane Jacobs
Community: The Structure of Belonging by Peter Block
Building the Cycling City: The Dutch Blueprint for Urban Vitality
    by Melissa Bruntlett
For viewing.
Moonlight, 2016
Charm City, 2018
Within Reach: Journey to Find Sustainable Community, 2013

8. Advance the well-being of all.
For further reading.
Pandemic: Tracking Contagions, from Cholera to Ebola and Beyond
    by Sonia Shaw
*Chronic Condition: Why Canada's Health System Needs to be Dragged into
    the 21st Century* by Jeffrey Simpson
William Osler: A Life in Medicine by Michael Bliss
For viewing.
Contagion, 2011
The Crime of the Century, 2021
The Constant Gardener, 2005
Erin Brockovich, 2000
Living in Emergency: Stories of Doctors Without Borders, 2008

9. Be in the business of trust.
For further reading.
Trust: Twenty Ways to Build a Better Country by David Johnston

The Speed of Trust: The One Thing that Changes Everything by Stephen
   M.R. Covey
*The Rural Entrepreneur John Bragg: The Force Behind Oxford Frozen Foods
   and Eastlink* by Donald J. Savoie
For viewing.
Enron: The Smartest Guys in the Room, 2005
Margin Call, 2011
Glengarry Glen Ross, 1992

10. Look ahead and act now.
For further reading.
*The Citizen's Guide to Climate Success: Overcoming Myths that Hinder
   Progress* by Mark Jaccard
Storming the Wall: Climate Change, Migration, and Homeland Security
   by Todd Miller
Losing Earth: A Recent History by Nathaniel Rich
For viewing.
Dark Waters, 2019
Honeyland, 2019
Before the Flood, 2016

11. Cherish the rule of law.
For further reading.
Team of Rivals: The Political Genius of Abraham Lincoln by Doris Kearns
   Goodwin
Truth Be Told: The Story of My Life and My Fight for Equality by
   Beverley McLachlin
*Champlain's Dream: The Visionary Adventurer Who Made a New World in
   Canada* by David Hackett Fischer
For viewing.
Beatrice Mtetwa and the Rule of Law, 2013

To Kill a Mockingbird, 1962
Judgment at Nuremburg, 1961

12. Right the wrong.
For further reading.
Returning to the Teachings: Exploring Aboriginal Justice, by Rupert Ross
Inside the Criminal Mind, by Dr. Stanton Samenow
Just Mercy: A Story of Justice and Redemption, by Bryan Stevenson
For viewing.
Just Mercy, 2016
Twelve Angry Men, 1957

13. Protect the most vulnerable.
For further reading.
Leadership in Turbulent Times by Doris Kearns Goodwin
Meditations by Marcus Aurelius
Why Nations Fail: The Origins of Power, Prosperity, and Poverty, by Daron
    Acemoglu and James Robinson
For viewing.
Same Kind of Different as Me, 2017
The Choice Is Ours, 2016
How Democracy Works Now, 2010

14. Do nothing about us without us.
For further reading.
*21 Things You May Not Know About the Indian Act: Helping Canadians
    Make Reconciliation with Indigenous Peoples a Reality* by Bob Joseph
Religious Freedom by Jack Weatherford
For viewing.
NÎPAWISTAMÂSOWIN: We Will Stand Up, 2019
The Secret Path, 2016

The Body Remembers When the World Broke Open, 2019

15. Open more doors.
For further reading.
Caste: The Origins of Our Discontents by Isabel Wilkerson
None Is Too Many: Canada and the Jews of Europe, 1933-1948 by Irving
    Abella and Harold Troper
A Promised Land by Barack Obama
Becoming by Michelle Obama
For viewing.
In America, 2002
In the Heat of the Night, 1967
Namesake, 2006

David's Bonus Recommendation:
The Story of Civilization by Will and Ariel Durant
Were I bold enough to recommend only one, single work that offers insights on all the issues addressed in our book, it would be Will and Ariel Durant's *The Story of Civilization*. Written between 1935 and 1975, this eleven-volume set created by two married scholars is one of the most profound, illuminating, and entertaining surveys of the rise and fall of societies I have ever encountered. I inhaled the set twice in my earlier days and am now embarking on a third reading, confident that I will continue to find new wisdom and fresh inspiration in each chapter. I heartily recommend this series to each of you. Canadians will be intrigued to know that Will Durant was born in North Adams, Massachusetts, to French Canadian Catholic parents who had immigrated from Quebec. Early on, he felt destined for the priesthood, but, while teaching at the Modern School in New York, he fell in love with and married a fifteen-year-old pupil named Chaya Kauffman, whom he later nicknamed Ariel. From this Catholic-Jewish union came a

magnificent literary legacy. Scholarly and engaging, this unique series of books reviews the history of civilization not just as a string of events, but as the enfolding dynamic of forces and counterforces that brought them into being. You'll understand, as I began to, why these events happened, how they influenced events that followed, and why they matter to us today.

If you'd like to whet your appetite, first pick up a copy of Will Durant's *The Lessons of History: Conversation Starters*. You'll soon be hooked.

Notes

Things we can do as individuals

1. Learn from the young.

1. Medical specialists in the United Kingdom are addressed as Mister to differentiate them from general practitioners, who are addressed as Doctor.

2. The prevalence of kindness in daily human activity is brilliantly documented by Dutch historian Rutger Bregman and colleagues in *Humankind: A Hopeful History* (2020). Using decades of meticulously documented research and hundreds of notable examples, the book will banish any cynicism a reader may have about our instinct to trust others, to share resources even when they are scarce, and to collaborate with members of our community even at great personal cost.

2. Stay curious.

1. Antonio and Robert Stickgold, *When Brains Dream: Exploring the Science of Mystery of Sleep* (New York, N.Y.: W.W. Norton & Company, 2021).

2. At the time, Ontario, with Oregon and North Carolina, was one of the three North American school systems that had a fifth year of high school called Grade 13. Designed to prepare kids for university, Grade 13 was tough, and the province-wide exams that tested students for their readiness to move on were notoriously difficult.

3. These innovations share another quality: they are all Canadian. I encountered them when Tom Jenkins and I were researching *Ingenious*, our 2017 book on the many ideas by which Canada has helped make the world a better place.

3. *Be charitable.*

1. For those who prefer the New Testament rendition of this fundamental truth, the King James translation of 1 Corinthians 13:13 reads "And now abideth faith, hope, charity, these three; but the greatest of these is love."

2. For me, one of the most poignant recent films about kindness is *A Beautiful Day in the Neighborhood*, in which Tom Hanks plays the iconic Fred Rogers, who himself began each of the 912 episodes and specials of his children's television show with the phrase "Welcome to my neighbourhood." For many little viewers, this show was the safest place they knew.

3. Much beloved by most of his subjects, Henri IV decreed that workers in his kingdom should be paid a reasonable wage for their work, saying, "If God grants me longer life, I will see to it that no peasant in my kingdom will lack the means to have a chicken in the pot every Sunday." So popular was that phrase that it was adopted three hundred years later as a slogan for members of the U.S. Republican Party as they fought for re-election in 1928 on Herbert Hoover's prosperity platform. Had Henri IV's injunction been followed, the French Revolution might never have been necessary.

4. *Donate your talent.*

1. The equivalent pejorative in English is *gypsy*, an exonym for the Roma people now widely discouraged.

2. Bethune's expertise in battlefield medicine was celebrated worldwide. For his voluntary contributions, and among other accolades, he became the only non-Chinese figure mentioned in *Quotations of Chairman Mao*, the so-called Little Red Book, itself the most widely circulated printed text in history. His life is eloquently recorded in a biography written by Canada's twenty-sixth Governor General Adrienne Clarkson, in 2011.

3. For Sharon and me, some of the most painful and saddening duties during our time at Rideau Hall were the times we stood with a devastated family at our air force base in Trenton, Ontario, as they awaited an aircraft returning from Afghanistan bearing their deceased son or daughter or spouse.

4. Stated in contemporary units, the practice of the commercialization of human blood had missed my values by 1.62 kilometres, give or take a centimetre. Years later we met up with visiting American friends; when they arrived I mentioned that I'd be heading out that evening to give blood at our local church blood clinic. They were confused and asked, "Why would you do that? Surely you don't need the money!" I replied that in our country we are never paid to donate blood and never charged to receive it, an explanation that earned a quizzical look and a bemused, "You Canadians are odd folks." Yup.

5. Build a team.

1. Eventually, the two became fast friends, exploring in frequent conversation the role of fiction in the development of human society.

2. To experience this phenomenon of presumed kinship, pop into any sports bar on the night of a Stanley Cup final. The jerseys on the TV–watching patrons unambiguously declare their kinship with others in the same outfits. Those wearing them will be instinctively friendly to each other and, on less admirable occasions, immediately hostile to those wearing jerseys of the opposing colour. The fiction they all embrace is that the story of one team is inherently more valid than that of the other.

3. It's impossible to estimate how many people have seen, read, or listened to the space-opera franchise, but a worldwide box office tally of over US$10 billion (so far) suggests that *Star Wars* has taken its place among the world's great myths, just as Lucas had hoped and intended.

4. The song appeared on Stan's 1984 album "From Fresh Water," which had to be released posthumously as Stan Rogers had recently died in a flash fire aboard an aircraft in Kentucky.

5. Growing up in this cultural mosaic was fascinating, so much so that my wife, Sharon, wrote her historical novel *Patchwork Society* to explore it further.

6. In football we wore helmets but not in hockey. Until Montreal Canadiens goalie Jacques Plante took (yet another) shot to the face in 1959 that broke his nose and cut a seven-stitch slash in his face, playing

without masks for goaltenders and without helmets for other players was still the custom.

7. Ralph "Cooney" Weiland (1904–1985) enjoyed an illustrious career in hockey, both on the ice and behind the bench. A native of Seaforth, Ontario, he was a member of the Owen Sound Greys team that won the Memorial Cup in 1924 as the top junior squad in Canada. He went on to play twelve seasons in the National Hockey League, capturing the scoring title in 1930 and winning the Stanley Cup with the Boston Bruins in 1928–29 and 1938–39, the second time as the team's captain. Following his playing days, he coached the Bruins to a Cup victory in 1940–41, piloted teams in the American Hockey League for six seasons, and led Harvard University's men's varsity hockey team from 1950 to 1971. Upon his retirement from the game, Cooney Weiland received two of hockey's highest honours: he was inducted into the Hockey Hall of Fame in 1971 and was given the Lester Patrick Award the following year to recognize his contribution to the game in the United States.

8. Almost 30 million viewers saw that philosophy in action during the final game between Canada and the United States at the 2010 Olympic Games in Vancouver. One of the most popular contests in hockey history, the game saw both teams playing the whole bench, not just the stars. Canada's winning goal by Sydney Crosby in the seventh minute of overtime was itself possible because of a brilliant set-up by Jerome Iginla.

9. The fraternity in question, as I learned in the first few weeks, did not have Black students as members, and at the time there were still very few Black students at Harvard, with only nine in the 1960 class. When opening the membership was proposed, it was seen as risky; many felt that such a progressive step would cause some alumni to withdraw their funding. (There's always a reason.) It didn't occur to me then, as it would now, to challenge that stance outright, but I knew right away that I had no interest in joining a society that held such values, and I quietly withdrew. The aftermath would not be so quiet.

10. Segal had been a sprinter in high school, choosing later to concentrate on the two-mile run and marathon in college. When we ran, he talked (effortlessly) about writing and I talked (wheezingly) about hockey. He

later wrote a number of bestselling novels and a screenplay or two, and his character Davey Johnston—the hockey player and team captain in his 1970 book *Love Story*—was, as he did not confide to me during our runs—based on me. My one brush with literary celebrity was fiction indeed. I never made captain.

11. *Varsity* is a funny term. It came into vogue in the late 1600s when students each began referring to their particular university with the short form 'versity, which became *varsity* over time. The word is now used almost exclusively to describe contests between universities, such as those celebrated rivalries between Harvard and Yale in the United States and Oxford and Cambridge in the United Kingdom.

12. The owners of most successful companies know that their success is entirely dependent upon the performance of their employees. Nothing happens without human attention, and it looks like that reliance will last right through the age of artificial intelligence; even robots need to be oiled and reprogrammed from time to time.

13. Indeed, Roosevelt at first had been asked to command the regiment himself but, a seasoned sportsman, he could name his weaknesses as well as his talents and admitted that he had no experience in organizing, provisioning, and deploying a large force. It was Roosevelt who recommended Colonel Wood for the position and then helped the new co make the regiment a success and, in time, a military legend.

14. Conducted by sociologists Robert and Helen Lynd, the Middletown studies were a body of field research made in a small American urban centre to understand the causes and effects of social change.

15. Apt that our word *athlete* comes directly from αθλον (athlon), the Greek term for prize.

16. Fatigue was the great challenge. As she swam, Bell maintained her strength by eating Pablum, a Canadian innovation. Designed in the early 1930s at the Hospital For Sick Children in Toronto by Doctors Alan Brown, Theodore Drake, and Frederick Tisdall, the vitamin-D rich cereal offered a vast range of benefits, including the prevention of rickets, a crippling childhood disease caused by infant malnutrition.

Things we can do as communities

7. Build a healthy neighbourhood.
1. A striking example of this comes from a comparison of the effects of the COVID pandemic. Denmark and Canada stand well up in the top quintile of deaths per capita; the United States is in the bottom quintile. Denmark and Canada are also well up in the top quintile in affirmative answer to two questions:
   1. Do you trust your government?
   2. Do you trust your neighbours?
   The United States is in the bottom quintile of the first and well below the halfway point on the second.

8. Advance the well-being of all.
1. Nature, December 2020. "The lightning-fast quest for COVID vaccines—and what it means for other diseases."
2. It's an unfortunate yet persistent habit to nickname a disease by the location in which it may have first been noticed. Spanish influenza did not originate in Spain any more than German measles began in Germany, Ebola bubbled up from the Ebola River in Democratic Republic of the Congo, the West Nile virus hatched in the Nile, and Zika was engineered in Uganda's Zika forest. They all began somewhere else. Naming infectious diseases after a geographic location is a lazy, inappropriate convention inviting racism and fear mongering, which is why the World Health Organization in 2015 set out guidelines for naming new infectious diseases, advice that includes avoiding names of places, people, and animals. And while epidemiologists were quick to call the 2019 virus COVID-19, an abbreviation for corona virus disease of 2019, the choice of some to weaponize the disease politically by calling it Wuhan Virus, Wuhan Pneumonia, or China Virus might leave some wondering if we read the WHO guidelines at all.
3. Although I bet Scottish soldiers had a tough time getting dates for a while.
4. Vincent Lam, *Extraordinary Canadians: Tommy Douglas* (Toronto: Penguin Canada, 2011).

5. Anne Case and Angus Deaton, *Deaths of Despair and the Future of Capitalism* (Princeton, New Jersey: Princeton University Press, 2020).

6. Daron Acemoglu and James Robinson, *Why Nations Fail: The Origins of Power, Prosperity, and Poverty* (New York: Crown Publishing, 2012). Their thesis is that societies that are inclusive in both politics and economics exist in a virtuous, upward cycle, while those that are extractive are doomed to spiral downward.

9. Be in the business of trust.

1. In hindsight, there was nothing environmentally wrong with the service manager. He was a superb technician with an almost supernatural ability to sense what was wrong under the hood and a laudable knack for fixing those issues. His sole mistake was assuming that by doing that at which he excelled, he would create a successful business. In the 1980s, business writer Michael E. Gerber identified that fallacy as the E-Myth, where E stands for the entrepreneur that skilled, dedicated, and passionate technicians naively presume they can be. In fact, those who are great at automotive mechanics make great mechanics, while those who are great at business build great businesses by hiring them.

2. By 2018, I had been impressed with enough thoughtful ways to rebuild trust that I was compelled to set them down in a book, which I called *Trust* so there could be no confusion about its contents.

3. It strikes me that the eighth commandment, "Thou shalt not bear false witness against thy neighbour" could usefully be amended to read, "and neither shalt thou make false claims to land thy neighbour a high-paying job."

4. Occasionally I joke that I am forming a new Canadian "T" Party based on three qualities: truth, transparency, and trust.

5. Only in understated Canada would one give the most senior of public servants the title "clerk."

6. E.S.G. has become central in financial regulation and investment practices worldwide. Mark Carney's 2021 book *Value(s)* is especially instructive. Mark is the former governor of the Bank of Canada and

more recently the governor of the Bank of England. Currently, having
returned to Canada, Mark serves pro bono as the United Nations'
special representative on financial regulation and climate change and,
to my delight, as a director at the Rideau Hall Foundation.

7. The picture in the United States is evolving, and the shareholder versus
stakeholder debate is alive and vibrant. Delaware is the state in which
the majority of the larger U.S. corporations are chartered given its
business-friendly laws. These laws and their state court decisions
maintain the shareholder primacy, but other major voices in the United
States, such as the United States Chamber of Commerce and the U.S.
Business Council, have endorsed the principles of stakeholder capitalism. If one were to summarize the evolution of the stakeholder
approach it would be to restate that the business of business is trust.

10. Look ahead and act now.

1. Fortunately, the board chair and the chancellor at McGill were wise,
insightful Canadians who had been put into their leadership positions
for good reason, and trust among the three of us was strong. Even as I
blurted my acceptance, I was confident I had their support. I did not
know at the time that the prime minister had also taken up this
initiative without consultation. He hadn't yet spoken with his cabinet,
nor in particular with the minister of environment, though that did
happen shortly afterward.

Things we can do as nations

11. Cherish the rule of law.

1. Duplessis was comfortable being unpopular with many, maintaining his
habit of acting as a strong man in the expectation that a majority of
voters would back him. Five consecutive terms as premier of Quebec
did little to dim that confidence, and his behaviour on many issues
rankled. The intentional and wrongful certification by his provincial
government of twenty thousand Canadian children as mentally ill, all
part of a plan to misappropriate additional subsidies from the

Government of Canada, was believed by many to have been at his direction. While his culpability as premier was never established, the victims were widely known as Duplessis Orphans.

2. Before the 1995 referendum, the PQ had tabled in the Quebec National Assembly Bill 1, An Act Respecting the Future of Quebec. In the event of a favourable referendum outcome, it would have empowered the National Assembly to unilaterally declare independence one year after the referendum

3. Reference questions are a tool, under s.53 of the Supreme Court of Canada Act, that the federal government can use to ask the SCC for legal opinions on the Constitution and government powers. *The Reference Re Secession of Quebec*, [1998] 2 SCR 217 was a landmark judgment of the Supreme Court of Canada.

12. Right the wrong.

1. While Canada's criminal justice system is regarded as of good standard overall by many respected international experts, there are clearly elements that require change to improve the administration of justice, the treatment of Canada's Indigenous peoples being an alarming example. This brief chapter explores only a handful of issues to illustrate how positive empathy can be channelled to ensure fairness, fairness being the foundational value of justice. Perhaps our thoughts will inspire others to address the many elements of our system that do need correction.

2. I've seen those qualities in court often, and up close. Our eldest daughter, Debbie, has spent her entire career in the Department of Justice and the Public Prosecution Service of Canada as a prosecutor and also working in human rights law. She is currently the executive director of the Competition Bureau's Legal Services.

3. A cheeky Australian quip appeared on a bumper sticker issued on the occasion of that nation's bicentenary, stating, "The reason the Australian people are so superb is because they were chosen by the finest judges in Europe."

4. Yukon will soon join.

5. The same Justice Rand who had written the judgment in *Roncarelli vs Duplessis.*

13. *Protect the most vulnerable.*

1. Champlain was Canada's first governor general in all but name.
2. Not to mention his suspense novel, *The Thirty-Nine Steps,* the 1935 Alfred Hitchcock adaptation of which was hailed as one of the top twenty-one British films of all time. The prodigious Buchan authored over a hundred books, even though writing was never his full-time job.
3. At the time, the committee was informal; two years later it was formally established as the Advisory Committee on Vice-Regal Appointments, created specifically to ensure the true suitability of candidates considered for the post. It later slipped into hibernation.
4. The title of that address was "A Smart and Caring Nation—A Call to Service." In it, I said that if listeners remember only three words from what I said, "I hope they are 'cherish our teachers'. Teachers, after parents, are among our greatest influences, and, if you are lucky as I have been, you will have had great ones."
5. Within Canada's honours system, each governor general is granted a heraldic achievement, a graphic device made of such elements as crest, shield, coat of arms, and motto. Together these symbolize the achievements (thus the name) and aspirations of a person or family. I was delighted to work with Stephen Wallace, herald chancellor of Canada (and the secretary of the office of the governor general) and Canada's chief herald, Claire Boudreau, to build a coat of arms that echoed the values of a smart and caring nation.
6. . . . and housing, as many of those visitors are invited to stay at Rideau Hall.
7. If you think that sounds suspiciously close to the motto beneath my own coat of arms, you're right. You've caught me stealing.
8. As with so many Anglophone Canadians, I had studied French all though high school but was not yet fluent upon graduation. I addressed the gap, first with a three-week summer immersion course and then with intensive tutorials over a two-year period. One of the many reasons I am

grateful to McGill was giving me the opportunity as principal to function in both of Canada's official languages. Later, at Rideau Hall, I generally communicated with my executive assistant in French. In hindsight, I believe that best way to learn is simply to use the language every day.

9. My mother often advised that God gave me two ears and two eyes but only one mouth for a good reason.

14. Do nothing about us without us.

1. The phrase originated in Poland in the mid-1600s and has since been employed in many eras and parts of the world to remind authorities that no initiative will succeed if the intended beneficiaries cannot participate in its design.

2. *Allyship* is a term referring to a situation or time when a person in a position of privilege supports, is present to, amplifies the voices of, and works in solidarity with marginalized and oppressed groups. Allyship adds co-creation to the former, less collaborative concept of advocacy.

15. Open more doors.

1. Data from the National Oceanic and Atmospheric Administration, U.S., Department of Commerce. Updated April 2022.

2. Written by Scott A. Kulp and Benjamin H. Strauss, the report is called "New Elevation Data Triple Estimates of Global Vulnerability to Sea-Level Rise and Coastal Flooding," and was published in *Nature Communications* on October 29, 2019.

3. Desmond Dillon Paul Morton OC CD FRSC (1937–2019) was a crisply analytic military historian, much recalled for his original observation that Canadian unconventional leadership during the Battle of Vimy Ridge in 1917 set Canada apart from the United Kingdom and was thus the defining moment in our sense of distinct nationhood. Desmond became a close and admired friend when he became founding director of the Institute for the Study of Canada at McGill, thanks to an extraordinarily generous gift from Charles Bronfman.

4. It was the largest peacetime exodus the world had seen to that point. Many of the Boat People drowned. Many others reached foreign shores

only to be warehoused in camps. Would Canada do the right thing? Two Canadian historians intended to make sure Canada did. Irving Abella and Harold Troper had just finished documenting Canada's woeful record of turning away European Jews before, during, and after the Second World War. They sent their as-yet-unpublished manuscript to Ron Atkey, Canada's immigration minister, imploring him to learn from our previous mistakes. Rumour has it that he placed a copy of the manuscript on the desk of every cabinet minister as they sat down to deliberate on immigration reform. Canada responded. In the end, Canada took in fifty thousand refugees from Vietnam, Laos, and Cambodia in 1979, and another ten thousand in 1980. Some thirty-nine thousand of the Southeast Asian refugees arrived under private sponsorship. Combining government with private sponsorship on that scale was unprecedented. Atkey later stated that he had wanted Canadians to show the world that "we are a compassionate nation," and he gave Canadians full credit, saying, "What permitted this to go ahead was a genuine change of heart by the Canadian community." Worth adding that the title of Abella and Troper's book was *None Is Too Many*, the reply made by a scoffing immigration official when asked how many Jews should be allowed into Canada after the war.

The Right Honourable David Johnston, C.C.
Governor General of Canada, 2010–2017
Chair of the Rideau Hall Foundation

The Right Honourable David Johnston was Canada's twenty-eighth governor general. During his mandate, he established the Rideau Hall Foundation (RHF), a registered charity that supports and amplifies the Office of the Governor General in its work to connect, honour, and inspire Canadians. Today, he is actively involved as chair of the RHF board of directors. In 2018, he was appointed colonel to the Royal Canadian Regiment. Prior to his installation as governor general, Mr. Johnston was a professor of law for forty-five years, and served as president of the University of Waterloo for two terms and as principal of McGill University for three terms. He was president of the Association of Universities and Colleges of Canada and of the Conférence des recteurs et des principaux des universités du Québec. He was the first non-U.S. citizen to be elected chair of the board of overseers at Harvard University, from which he graduated in 1963 magna cum laude and where he was twice named all-American in hockey and was named to Harvard's Athletic Hall of Fame. He holds degrees from Harvard, Cambridge, and Queen's and has received more than three dozen honorary degrees or fellowships. He has authored or co-authored more than thirty books. He was named Companion of the Order of Canada in 1997. He has chaired or served on many provincial and federal task forces and committees, and has served on the boards of more than a dozen public companies. He has been married for fifty-seven years to Sharon and they have five daughters and fourteen grandchildren.

Brian Hanington

Brian Hanington has spent his life writing stories about Canada. He has collaborated on many books with David Johnston, including *The Idea of Canada* and *Trust*. His most recent book is *Operation Medusa: The Furious Battle That Saved Afghanistan from the Taliban*, written with Canadian general David Fraser. He has published a dozen or so books, lectured in twenty countries, and crafted speeches for heads of state, admirals, generals, a knight or two, and the Pope.